F O R

FREEZING

Juliet Brigstocke
Consultant: Ann Nicol

HarperCollins*Publishers*

HarperCollins Publishers
P.O. Box, Glasgow G4 0NB

First published 1992

Reprint 10 9 8 7 6 5 4 3 2 1 0

ISBN 0 00 458989 0

Printed in Great Britain by
HarperCollins Manufacturing, Glasgow

Introduction

The Collins Gem Food for Freezing is a concise and easy-to-use pocket reference book. It is a practical guide to freezing the large variety of foods that are now available to the British consumer, and can be easily referred to in either the kitchen or the supermarket.

The guide lists in alphabetical order common foodstuffs, freezing equipment and technical terms, providing freezing information and advice. Each food entry explains how to freeze that particular item, the length of time it may be stored satisfactorily in the freezer and the way it should be thawed prior to cooking. The freezer life of made-up dishes should be calculated by referring to the individual ingredients in the guide, and it is also then possible to gauge how successfully they may be frozen.

Entries concerning equipment and technical terms explain their functions during the freezing process and their effectiveness.

The introduction explains how freezing preserves food and how to ensure that this is achieved. The appendices advise on buying, using and maintaining a freezer and also explain the various freezing, packaging and thawing techniques.

The Collins Gem Food for Freezing is thoroughly cross-referenced to give easy access to information, and cross-references appear in **bold lettering**.

Food preservation by freezing

A deep freeze is a cold chamber normally operating at −18°C (0°F) and is designed to hold frozen food in perfect condition, or at least maintain the condition it is in when placed in the freezer. It is also capable of fast-freezing fresh food when operated at temperatures lower than 0°F.

The freezer can only preserve food in its present state. Poor quality food can never be improved by freezing, although some fresh foods are believed to improve during storage, e.g. shortcrust pastry. The freezing of fresh food stops the natural process of ageing, which would ultimately end in decomposition, but once removed and thawed, previously frozen food will again be subject to deterioration in the normal way.

Food spoilage under normal conditions is caused by microorganisms and enzymes. These are naturally present in foods and in the surrounding air, and cause rapid deterioration and decay of food. Under certain conditions, in which temperatures are high and ventilation poor, bacteria multiply rapidly, increasing the danger of food poisoning. Under normal refrigeration, bacterial growth and food deterioration is slowed down, and although food poisoning bacteria are dormant below 4°C, some of the food spoilage bacteria, such as moulds, are more resilient and will grow very slowly even at −12°C. However, all bacteria are completely dormant at −18°C, the temperature of the home freezer. A small amount of enzyme activity can still occur and it is this which causes loss of quality in the long term. It is important to realize that different foods have different storage limits after which time the food will begin to deteriorate. It is also important to remember that once the food is thawed, bacterial action begins again, and so the food should be used as soon as possible.

How freezing works

Most foods are made up largely of water, and freezing works by converting this water to ice crystals. Quick freezing by means of a fast-freeze switch results in tiny ice crystals being retained within the cell structure, so that on thawing, the structure is relatively undamaged and the food value unchanged. But care must be taken, because slow freezing results in the formation of large ice crystals which damage the cell structure and cause loss of nutrients, texture, colour and flavour.

Why Freeze?

Traditional methods of food preservation have always been limited to a certain extent, but freezing has evolved as one of the most successful and far-ranging methods, preserving the colour and flavour of food much more efficiently. It is also quick and simple, providing that a few basic rules are followed. Freezing has the most obvious advantages for the keen market gardener. All the surplus fruit and vegetables produced throughout the year can be preserved and be consumed later when prices are high and variety is limited. Meat, poultry, game and fish can all be frozen and this enables the freezer owner to take advantage of lower prices, bulk offers and seasonal produce.

Apart from the economic advantages of owning a freezer, many people find it indispensable for the amount of time it saves. A freezer owner with a young family can bake and freeze in advance of the school holidays, and prepare cooked meals to save time later on. Someone who entertains a great deal may use the freezer in the same way, to make maximum use of the time available. For those who go out to work every day, owning a freezer can mean that there is always a nourishing meal available to come home to – whether it has been commercially prepared or home-made in spare time and holidays. Consequently there is no doubt that freezing has numerous advantages to all kinds of people.

Freezing and other food preservation techniques

Freezing is one of the easiest and quickest methods of preserving food and as long as simple basic rules are followed, little cell damage occurs. For example, food must be as fresh as possible and all equipment scrupulously clean; food must be cooked rapidly, cooled as quickly as possible and then frozen as soon as possible to prevent contamination by germs; the food must be wrapped correctly and sealed securely, and, once thawed, frozen food should be reheated or cooked immediately and thoroughly.

As a method of food preservation, freezing extends to a far wider range of food than older, more traditional methods, such as drying, smoking, canning and bottling, and although it is initially a more expensive method it is generally more efficient in the long-run.

The deep freeze can be used for three categories of food preservation: long-term preservation for fruit and vegetables; medium-term preservation of meat, poultry, game or fish; and short-term storage of ready meals to provide nutritious meals, quickly and easily.

Meat, poultry, game and fish are items that cannot be preserved by some of the more traditional methods, but they can all be deep frozen successfully. Consequently, many of these foods can be bought in bulk when they are cheap, which will result in saving considerable amounts of money and time spent on shopping.

Overall, freezing retains more of the nutritional value, colour, texture and taste of most foods than other preserving methods and will only take a fraction of the time needed to preserve food by curing, smoking or pickling.

The Basic Rules for Successful Freezing

1) Freeze only good quality foods. Freezing cannot improve food and freezer space is valuable.

2) Freeze food when it is at the peak of its quality. For example, fruit and vegetables must be frozen when they are ripe and ready for eating in the usual way. Overripe fruit and vegetables are too starchy or soft and do not freeze satisfactorily. Frozen, unripe fruit may become bitter. It is best to choose fruit and vegetables early in their season.

3) Always handle food that is to be frozen quickly, because it begins to deteriorate rapidly. Fruit and vegetables should be frozen within six hours of picking if possible. All fresh fish should be frozen within 24 hours of being caught, and preferably within 12 hours. Freeze in small quantities.

4) Ensure that everything used for freezing is scrupulously clean and keep the handling of the food to a minimum. Freezing does not kill bacteria and germs, so be as hygienic as possible.

5) Use packaging materials that are moisture- and vapour-proof and also resistant to cross contamination with other foods. Exposure to

air and moisture will damage frozen foods causing them to lose quality.

6) Freeze food only in small, usable quantities. It is not recommended that leftover, thawed food is refrozen.

7) Make sure that as much air as possible is extracted from each package before sealing. Exposure to air can lead to dehydration and cross-contamination.

8) If food that is to be frozen has been cooked or blanched, make sure that it is cooled rapidly and thoroughly. Never put anything warm or hot into the freezer.

9) Freeze food in the coldest part of the freezer, and make sure it is spread out and not packed too closely together until it is firm.

10) Once food has been frozen, remember to transfer it from the fast-freeze section to the main cabinet if necessary.

11) Remember to turn the super-freeze switch off after newly frozen foods have been in the freezer for about 24 hours.

12) Always label and date packets of frozen food clearly, and with either a Chinagraph pencil or permanent felt-tip ink pen, so that a good

ensured. It is helpful to keep a list of all the items in the freezer and to tick them off as they [illegible]

13) Always maintain a steady temperature of -18°C (0°F). Do not [illegible] frequently and do not add too many fresh [illegible] super-freeze switch correctly.

14) Defrost the freezer regularly, especially around the door seal. Try and defrost when stocks are low, and on a cold day if possible.

15) Be prepared for emergencies, such as power cuts and breakdowns.

Equipment needed for successful freezing

There is very little supplementary equipment needed for freezing, apart from packaging materials and containers, but it is useful to have some accessories.

1) A fine-mesh wire basket with a handle for blanching vegetables.

2) A large saucepan or steamer with a lid that is big enough to hold the wire basket.

alfalfa The seeds of a Eurasian plant, which are generally soaked for a few days to form sprouts before being sold for human consumption. Alfalfa tends to lose its crispness in the freezer, but it is still perfectly acceptable for use in cooked dishes.

FREEZING: pack straight into **polythene bags**, expelling as much air as possible before **sealing**.

FREEZER LIFE: 2 months.

THAWING: leave to thaw in the refrigerator for 3–4 hours before using.

almond The oval-shaped kernel of a tree of the peach family from West Asia. Almonds can be bought whole (in its shell) or blanched, flaked, shredded, diced or ground. They may be frozen whole, chopped, flaked or toasted.

FREEZING: wrap tightly in small **foil** packages.

FREEZER LIFE: toasted, 4 months; untoasted, 1 year.

THAWING: allow to thaw at room temperature for 3 hours.

almond paste A smooth, yellow paste made of ground **almonds**, **eggs** and icing sugar. Almond paste can be frozen for a short period, but after a while the oil within it begins to separate out, which makes it hard and difficult to handle. Alternatively, it can be stored successfully in the refrigerator for up to 3 months.

FREEZING: wrap in **foil**, then **overwrap** in a **polythene bag**.

FREEZER LIFE: 3 months.

THAWING: allow to thaw in its wrapping for 8–10 hours, or overnight at room temperature

aluminium foil See **foil**.

ambient atmosphere A term used in relation to the air in the immediate area around the freezer. It is important when locating a freezer to ensure that there is sufficient space around it. The freezer generates heat and without adequate ventilation it must work harder to maintain the correct temperature inside the cabinet. If the ambient atmosphere is too humid, condensation may form on the cabinet and cause rust to develop.

anchovy A tiny fish belonging to the **herring** family, similar to a sardine. Anchovies are commonly sold canned in vegetable oil, but fresh anchovies are also available which can be frozen. Canned anchovies should not be frozen because the salt within them oxidizes (see **oxidation**) and makes them go **rancid**.

FREEZING: fresh anchovies should be cleaned and their backbones removed. Wrap them in **clingfilm** and then place in a **polythene bag**.

FREEZER LIFE: 3 months.

THAWING: cook from frozen.

antioxidant A substance used in foods to delay, retard or prevent the development of rancidity or other flavour deterioration due to **oxidation**. Fats and oils are oxidized when they come into contact with oxygen in the air and this causes them to go **rancid**. This produces an 'off' flavour, which may cause sickness if eaten. Antioxidants are used in a wide range of food products, such as butter, margerine, meat products, cakes, biscuits, and pastry. **Ascorbic acid** may be used as an antioxidant when added with sugar or syrup to help prevent cut **fruit** and **vegetables** from discolouring.

apple Any of a variety of firm-fleshed fruit, which is best frozen either sliced or as a purée. Choose firm, crisp apples.

FREEZING: wash, peel and core the apples. Then either (a), cut up into small pieces and stew, sweetened or unsweetened, with a minimum amount of water until soft. Then sieve or liquidize and allow to cool. Pack the purée into **rigid containers** or **polythene bags**; or (b), slice the fruit into a bowl of salted water. Then rinse and pack with sugar in alternate layers into rigid containers. Allow 500 g (1lb) of sugar for every 1.5 kg (3lbs) of fruit, and leave a 1 cm ($\frac{1}{2}$ inch) **headspace**.

Baked apples may also be frozen. Cook them as usual, then allow to cool completely and freeze unwrapped until firm. Pack the apples into a rigid container and divide them with a sheet of **greaseproof paper**.

FREEZER LIFE: apple slices, 12 months; purée, 6 months; baked apples, 3 months.

THAWING: leave the apple slices or purée to thaw in an unopened container at room temperature for 2–3 hours. If they are to be heated no **thawing** is necessary. Heat baked apples through from frozen at 190°C/375°F/Gas 5 for 20 minutes.

apple juice A **fruit juice** that can be made from windfalls and bruised apples at the end of the season. Apple juices freeze well for at least 6 months.

FREEZING: wash the apples thoroughly and cut out any bruised and damaged parts. Cut into thick slices, unpeeled and uncored. Place in a large pan with a little water and simmer until the apples are soft. Strain the apples through a muslin cloth or jelly bag into a bowl and leave to cool completely. Add more water and sweeten if desired. When the juice is completely cold, pour into **rigid containers** leaving a 1–2 cm (½–1 inch) **headspace** before **sealing**.

FREEZER LIFE: 6 months.

THAWING: allow the apple juice to thaw in the fridge overnight.

apricot The small, smooth skinned fruit of the apricot tree. Apricots are best frozen either whole (with the stone removed) or sliced in a syrup. An unstoned fruit may develop an almond flavour around the stone if kept frozen for a long time. Alternatively, freeze as a purée. Choose apricots that are firm and unwrinkled, with velvety, pale orange skins.

FREEZING: wash and dry the fruit, plunge into boiling water for 30 seconds and then peel. Then either (a), remove the stones and slice into a syrup made with 500 g (1lb) of sugar to 1.2 litres (2 pints) of water with 1–2 tbsp **lemon juice** (to prevent **discoloration**). Immerse the fruit in a **rigid container**, by placing crumpled **foil** over the top before **sealing**. Or (b), keep the fruit whole and immerse in cold syrup as before; or (c), purée cooked fruit, either sweetened or unsweetened, then pack into rigid containers.

FREEZER LIFE: in syrup, 9–12 months; purée, 6–8 months.

THAWING: leave to thaw in an unopened container either in the refrigerator for 6–8 hours per 250 g (8 oz), or at room temperature for 2–4 hours.

artichoke See **globe artichoke**; **Jerusalem artichoke**.

ascorbic acid The chemical name for vitamin C, which is often used to prevent **fruit** from discolouring. It is available from chemists in powder or tablet form and can be added to syrup or sprinkled directly onto fruit. It is virtually tasteless and is therefore preferable to lemon juice, which also prevents **discoloration** if added in approximate quantities of 4 tbsp to 500 g (1lb) of fruit, but it taints the fruit.

asparagus The stem and leaves of the young asparagus plant, which can be frozen successfully. Choose young stems with firm, compact heads.

FREEZER LIFE: meat in cooked dishes, 1–2 months; fruit or vegetables, 3–6 months.

THAWING: thaw in the refrigerator for 3–4 hours, then reheat thoroughly and allow to cool before serving; use immediately. See **food poisoning**.

bacon Meat from the back and sides of a pig, which may be dried, salted or smoked. Bacon must be frozen when it is very fresh. Do not freeze previously cooked bacon.

FREEZING: vacuum-packed bacon freezes best. For other types of bacon, wrap the meat closely in small parcels of **freezer wrap** or **foil** and then overwrap in **polythene bags**. Bacon chops, gammon steaks and joints should be wrapped individually in foil and polythene bags.

FREEZER LIFE: vacuum-packed bacon, 3 months; smoked rashers, chops, gammon steaks and joints, 2 months; unsmoked rashers, chops, steaks and joints, 1 month.

THAWING: leave overnight in the refrigerator and cook as soon as possible; do not **refreeze**.

bacteria Microscopic organisms present in the body and in almost every form of food. If the bacteria in foods are not destroyed by heat treatment, chemical preservatives or inhibited by drying, refrigeration or freezing, they cause damage to food and may cause **food poisoning**. Refrigeration will slow down bacterial growth and food deterioration, but freezing renders all bacteria completely dormant at –18°, the temperature of the home freezer. It is important to remember that once frozen food is thawed it should be used as soon as possible because bacterial action will begin again.

bagel A hard, ring-shaped **bread** roll, which is a Jewish speciality. Due to their texture, bagels do not freeze particularly well, because they become tough and leathery.

bamboo shoot The young stems of bamboo grass, which are normally available in tins. Partially used tins of bamboo shoots can be transferred to small cartons and frozen successfully.

FREEZING: transfer the contents with their liquid into small containers, leaving a 2.5cm (1 inch) **headspace**.

FREEZER LIFE: 6 months.

THAWING: leave to thaw overnight in the refrigerator or for 3–4 hours at room temperature.

banana The crescent-shaped fruit of any of a variety of tropical palm-like trees. Bananas do not freeze well because they turn a nasty black colour. However, bananas can be mashed with **lemon juice** and frozen in small containers or used in desserts, such as banana whip, which freeze well provided they contain sufficient lemon juice to prevent **discoloration**.

FREEZER LIFE: 6 months.

THAWING: leave overnight in the refrigerator or allow to thaw for 4 hours at room temperature.

basil The aromatic leaves of a Eurasian plant used as a **herb**. Basil freezes very well, but it must be packed carefully because it has a very strong smell that could taint other foods in the freezer.

FREEZING: wash and dry the basil thoroughly. Then either (a), pack leaves into **polythene bags**, expelling as much air as possible before **sealing**; or (b), chop the basil and freeze with a little water in ice cube trays.

FREEZER LIFE: 6 months.

THAWING: either use the basil cubes straight from the freezer or allow the leaves to thaw a little before chopping and using.

bass Any of a variety of sea perch with firm white flesh. Bass can be frozen successfully, although the flesh may become a little soft with the freezing and **thawing** processes. It is best to keep frozen for as short a time as possible.

FREEZING: wash the fish, remove the scales and gut. Then **ice glaze**, wrap in **clingfilm** and **overwrap** in a **polythene bag**. Fillets and steaks should be wrapped in clingfilm and overwrapped with **foil**.

FREEZER LIFE: 3 months.

THAWING: allow a whole fish to thaw for 24 hours in a cool place. Fillets and steaks may be cooked from frozen or allowed to thaw in the refrigerator.

batch cooking A method of cooking food in large quantities in order to save time and energy. Meals prepared in this way can be divided into individual portions for freezing. This is very useful for those who lead busy lives and need to provide nutritious meals quickly and easily.

batter A mixture of flour, eggs and milk, such as batter used to make **pancakes** and **Yorkshire pudding**. The mixture may be frozen in **rigid containers**.

FREEZING: prepare the batter in the usual way, then pour 250 ml or 500 ml ($\frac{1}{2}$ or 1 pint) quantities into rigid containers, leaving a 2.5 cm (1 inch) **headspace**. Seal well, and place upright in the freezer until frozen solid.

FREEZER LIFE: 3 months.

THAWING: leave to thaw in the container for 2–4 hours at room temperature, then whisk again thoroughly before using.

beansprout The sprout of a mung bean. Beansprouts do not freeze successfully because they lose their crispness and become soggy, but they can be used in cooked dishes.

FREEZING: **blanch** for 1 minute, then drain and cool. Dry as much as possible, then pack into **rigid containers** or **polythene bags**.

FREEZER LIFE: 2 months.

THAWING: leave to thaw in a refrigerator for 3–4 hours before using.

beef The **meat** of various bovine animals, particularly the cow. Beef can be frozen in joints, on or off the bone, in steaks, chunks or **chops** or minced. It can be frozen successfully raw or cooked in **stews** or **casseroles** and then reheated. Sliced cooked beef, however, tends to dry out if frozen and then reheated, but it can be frozen to serve cold. Choose fresh meat with as little **fat** as possible, because fat has a shorter storage life than lean meat. Raw beef should be cut into manageable portions and, if possible, de-boned to save space.

FREEZING: trim surplus fat off joints, steaks and chops. Wrap any bones in **foil** to prevent damage in the freezer. Wrap joints (on the bone or boneless) in **freezer wrap** and tie up securely, then **overwrap** in foil and place in a **polythene bag**. Withdraw as much air as possible and fasten securely, because if any air comes into contact with the meat it will become damaged. Pack steaks and chops in **clingfilm**, dividing them up with small sheets of foil. Overwrap with freezer wrap and seal. Freeze mince and chunks of beef in small portions, wrapped in clingfilm and overwrapped in freezer wrap. It is possible to cook mince before freezing if desired.

Always label packages of meat clearly because frosting makes the meat unidentifiable. Use a **Chinagraph pencil** or felt-tipped pen and record the date that the meat was frozen.

FREEZER LIFE: joints on or off the bone, 8 months; steaks and chops, 6 months; diced and minced beef, 3 months.

THAWING: joints on or off the bone, 8–10 hours per 500 g (1lb) in the refrigerator, or 2 hours at room temperature. Steaks or chops, 8–10 hours per 500 g (1lb) in the refrigerator or 2–4 hours at room temperature (depending on the thickness of the meat). Diced or minced meat, 8–10 hours per 500 g (1lb) in the refrigerator. See also **beefburger**.

beefburger (also called **hamburger**) A flat cake made of minced **beef** and seasonings, which must be frozen as fresh as possible.

FREEZING: shape the mince mixture into small, flat cakes and layer the burgers with small sheets of **foil**, so that they can be separated easily. Wrap several in **clingfilm** and **overwrap** with **freezer wrap**, and label clearly.

FREEZER LIFE: 3 months.

THAWING: leave to thaw in the refrigerator for six hours per 500 g (1lb). Beefburgers may be cooked from frozen if desired.

beetroot The dark purple root of a variety of beet plant, which can be frozen whole or sliced. Choose small, firm beets.

FREEZING: wash well, then cook in boiling water until tender; 5–10 minutes for small beets and up to 45–50 minutes for larger beets. Drain and allow to cool, then rub the skins off. Pack small beets into **polythene bags** and slice large ones into **rigid containers**.

FREEZER LIFE: 6 months.

THAWING: leave to thaw in unopened containers in the refrigerator for 6–8 hours or at room temperature for 2–4 hours.

THAWING: allow to thaw overnight in the refrigerator, or for 3–4 hours at room temperature.

blackcurrant juice The juice of the **blackcurrant**. Blackcurrant juice can be easily made from any surplus blackcurrants and frozen successfully. It is a very good source of vitamin C.

FREEZING: wash the fruit, and place in a pan with 300 ml (½ pint) of water to each 500 g (1lb) of fruit. Boil for 1 minute only, then tip into a fine sieve or muslin covered container and allow the fruit juice to drip through. Measure the juice and add 300 g (12 oz) of sugar to each 500 ml (1 pint) of juice. Stir until dissolved and pour into **rigid containers**, allowing a 2.5 cm (1 inch) **headspace**. Alternatively, freeze the juice in ice cube trays until firm, then wrap them individually in **foil** and place them into a **polythene bag**.

FREEZER LIFE: 1 year.

THAWING: allow to thaw in containers for 2–3 hours at room temperature.

black pudding A mixture of pigs' blood, pork, fat and cereals, stuffed into a pig's intestine. Black pudding can be frozen for up to 3 months, although if it is a particularly highly seasoned pudding the flavour may deteriorate with storage.

FREEZING: pack the puddings into **polythene bags** and expel as much air as possible before **sealing**.

FREEZER LIFE: 2–3 months.

THAWING: allow the black pudding to thaw in the

refrigerator overnight before frying or grilling in slices.

blanching A method of preparing food for freezing by placing it into boiling water or steam for a short time, then plunging into cold water. Blanching inhibits the action of **enzymes**, which would otherwise cause food to lose its flavour, colour and nutritional content in storage. It is also often used to help peel fruit and nuts and to tenderize vegetables.

bloater (also called **buckling**) A lightly salted, smoked inshore herring. Bloaters can be frozen, but it is important to wrap them well because of their strong smell, and they should only be stored for a short period because their flavour changes.

FREEZING: wrap carefully in **clingfilm**, then **overwrap** in **polythene bags** or **foil**. Seal securely because their strong smell may taint other foods in the freezer.

FREEZER LIFE: 2 months.

THAWING: allow to thaw in wrappings overnight in a refrigerator or for 3 hours at room temperature.

blueberry (also called **bilberry** or **whortleberry**) A small blue-black berry of a North American shrub. Blueberries are usually used in pies and cheesecakes, which can be successfully frozen. Choose firm, ripe berries.

FREEZING: wash, dry and steam **blanch** for 1 minute, by placing fruit in a steamer or colander over a pan of boiling water. Cool and pack in **polythene bags** or **rigid containers**. Blueberries can also be packed with sugar, allowing 125 g (4 oz) of sugar per 500 g (1lb) of fruit, or in a syrup using 300 g (12 oz) to 500 ml (1 pint) of water. Allow a 2.5 cm (1 inch) **headspace**.

FREEZER LIFE: 1 year.

THAWING: allow to thaw overnight in the refrigerator or for 4 hours at room temperature, in containers.

bouquet garni A small bunch of fresh, mixed **herbs**, usually parsley, sage, rosemary, thyme and a bay, leaf tied together. Bouquet garni is used to flavour dishes such as stews and casseroles. A bouquet garni can be frozen although the texture of the herbs will alter.

FREEZING: place herbs in a **polythene bag** and secure.

FREEZER LIFE: 1 year.

THAWING: bouquet garnis may be used straight from the freezer.

boysenberry The large red **fruit** of a type of bramble, which is a cross between a loganberry and a raspberry. A boysenberry is a very large berry, but it can be used in recipes in the same way as a raspberry. It can be satisfactorily frozen alone or packed with sugar.

FREEZING: **open freeze** whole boysenberries on trays until firm, then transfer into **polythene bags** to store. Alternatively, they may be packed with sugar, adding 125 g (4 oz) of sugar to every 500 g (1 lb) of fruit and packed into polythene bags. If preferred the berries could also be puréed and frozen in **rigid containers**, leaving a 2.5 cm (1 inch) **headspace** before **sealing**.

FREEZER LIFE: 1 year.

THAWING: allow whole berries and purée to thaw at room temperature for about 3 hours. Fruit that has been open frozen may be used straight from the freezer for decoration.

brain The brain of a calf or lamb eaten as **offal**, which may be frozen.

FREEZING: wash the brains and pat dry. Remove as much skin and membrane as possible and pack in **polythene bags**.

FREEZER LIFE: 3 months.

THAWING: allow to thaw overnight in a refrigerator.

brandy butter A flavoured **butter** traditionally used to accompany Christmas pudding and mince pies, although it may be used with a variety of pastries and desserts.

FREEZING: use freshly made brandy butter, place in **rigid containers** and seal well because the brandy could taint other foods in the freezer.

FREEZER LIFE: 2 months.

THAWING: allow to thaw at room temperature for 2–3 hours, then store in a refrigerator or cool place until required. Beat until fluffy if the butter has become grainy.

brazil nut The crescent-shaped nut of a tropical South American tree with a woody, brown shell and off-white kernel. Brazil nuts can be frozen whole, chopped, flaked or toasted, but salted nuts should not be frozen because they turn **rancid**.

FREEZING: pack in small cartons or **polythene bags**.

FREEZER LIFE: toasted, 4 months; whole, chopped or flaked, up to 1 year.

THAWING: allow to thaw at room temperature for 3 hours.

bread A food made from flour **dough**, which can be frozen cooked or uncooked. It is possible to freeze commercially baked, wrapped and home-baked bread – provided it has been baked on the same day.

FREEZING: **overwrap** commercially baked bread with **freezer wrap** if it is already in a plastic bag. If not then wrap in clingfilm, then overwrap in freezer paper. Home-baked bread should be cooled then wrapped well in clingfilm and a **polythene bag**.

FREEZER LIFE: home-baked and commercially baked (unwrapped), 6 weeks; commercially baked (wrapped), 6 months. It is important to remember that certain breads, such as French or Vienna, lose their crispness and texture very rapidly, so keep frozen for a maximum of three days.

THAWING: remove overwrapping if used, and thaw inside wrapper for about 4 hours. Sliced bread can be toasted from frozen.

breadcrumbs These can be useful to freeze for future use in **stuffings**, **puddings** and **sauces**. They can also be fried and frozen and then used as a topping for gratin dishes or desserts.

FREEZING: pack into **polythene bags** the required quantities.

FREEZER LIFE: fried, 1 month; fresh, 3 months.

THAWING: breadcrumbs can be used from frozen or allowed to thaw at room temperature for 30 minutes.

bread sauce A milk sauce thickened with breadcrumbs. Bread sauce can be frozen ready-made and so save time when cooking roast chicken or turkey.

FREEZING: cook and season well. Allow to cool completely, then pack in **rigid containers**, leaving a little **headspace**.

FREEZER LIFE: 1 month.

THAWING: allow to thaw for 1–2 hours at room temperature or cook slowly from frozen. Beat the sauce thoroughly to ensure there are no lumps and add a little more milk if required.

breakdowns If the freezer is not operating correctly or not at all, before calling out the engineer check that the plug has not been pulled out of its socket or switched off. Check that a fuse has not blown or that there is no power cut. Also check that the thermostat has not been tampered with. For guidelines about refreezing food and tips for keeping food frozen, see **power cut** and **refreezing**.

bream A round red and silver **fish** with white, mild-tasting flesh. Bream is normally sold whole and should only be frozen when very fresh.

FREEZING: wash, remove the scales and gut. **Ice glaze** the fish then wrap it in **clingfilm** and **overwrap** with **freezer wrap**.

FREEZER LIFE: 3 months.

THAWING: allow the whole fish to thaw in a cool place for 24 hours. Once the fish is thawed it should be cooked immediately.

brick freezing A method of freezing food in same-sized rectangular blocks for easy and efficient storage. The food is placed into a **polythene bag** that is put inside a rectangular container and then sealed and frozen. When it is firm, the polythene bag is removed from the container and the block of frozen food can then be neatly stored in the freezer. It is also possible to freeze purées, **soups** and **sauces** in this way, although it is important to remember that the block should be replaced into a container when **thawing**. It is also important to remember to spread out fresh food in the freezer, to allow air to circulate around it. Do not stack the freezer so completely or neatly that there is no room for any air.

brill A flatfish with a firm texture, similar to turbot. Choose **fish** with white-yellow flesh and avoid any with a blue tinge. Brill is normally sold whole or in fillets.

FREEZING: for a whole fish, wash, remove the scales and gut. **Ice glaze**, pack in **clingfilm** and

overwrap with **freezer wrap**. Wash and wipe dry fillets and separate them with a double layer of clingfilm, then overwrap in **foil** or freezer wrap.

FREEZER LIFE: 3 months.

THAWING: allow a whole fish to thaw in a cool place for 24 hours. Fillets may be cooked from frozen or allowed to thaw in the refrigerator.

brine packing The packing of vegetables in a cold brine solution (1 tbsp of salt per 1 pint of water) prior to freezing. The vegetables are first **blanched** then put into **rigid containers** with the cold brine solution and frozen immediately. It has been suggested that vegetables wet-packed in brine are less likely to toughen during storage, but it is a controversial point and thought to be rather an old-fashioned process. Most of the non-leafy vegetables, such as asparagus, runner beans and broccoli, may be packed in brine.

brioche An enriched bread that can be frozen.

FREEZING: wrap in **foil** or **polythene bags**, expelling as much air as possible before sealing.

FREEZER LIFE: 2 months.

THAWING: allow to thaw in its wrappings for 2–3 hours at room temperature.

broad bean The pale green seed of a Eurasian bean plant. Although a broad bean is a **pulse** it is eaten as a **vegetable** and can be frozen successfully. Choose small, young and tender pods and unblemished beans.

FREEZING: **blanch** podded beans for 3 minutes, then cool and drain. Pack in **rigid containers** or **polythene bags**. Alternatively, **dry freeze** on trays, then tip into polythene bags and seal.
FREEZER LIFE: 12 months.
THAWING: cook from frozen in boiling water.

broccoli (also called **calabrese**) The flower-head of a variety of cabbage. Broccoli is a vegetable that freezes successfully, retaining both its flavour and colour. Sprouting broccoli produces many purple, white or green shoots, whereas other types have one firm green compact head. Choose tender stalks that are not too thick and trim off any large leaves.
FREEZING: **blanch** trimmed spears for 3 minutes, then plunge into cold water, drain and pack into **polythene bags** or **rigid containers**.
FREEZER LIFE: 1 year.
THAWING: cook from frozen in boiling water.

Brussels sprout The small bud of a variety of cabbage. Choose small round sprouts for freezing, and trim off any discoloured or wilted leaves.
FREEZING: wash and **blanch** for 3 minutes, then plunge into ice-cold water. Drain and place on flat trays and **open freeze**. When frozen, tip the sprouts into **polythene bags** and **seal**.
FREEZER LIFE: 1 year.
THAWING: cook from frozen in boiling water for 4–8 minutes until tender.

buckling See **bloater**.

bulgar A form of wheat that has been hulled and parboiled to make the grains easier to cook and the texture lighter. Bulgar is normally cooked and eaten in place of **rice** in salads and composite dishes. It can be successfully frozen once it has been cooked.

FREEZING: cook the bulgar as usual and pat as dry as possible. Pack it loosely into **polythene bags**, seal it and place in the freezer. When it has half frozen, squeeze the bag to separate out the grains and return it to the freezer to store.

FREEZER LIFE: 6 months.

THAWING: bulgar should be allowed to thaw in a cool place for about 1–2 hours before using.

bulk buying The buying of food in large quantities and therefore generally at lower or discounted prices in order to save time and money. Freezer owners can be economical by buying large, family-size packs of popular frozen foods, such as peas and fish fingers. It is also possible to bulk buy meat and poultry, which can then be divided up as required and frozen in small quantities. Freezer owners can also save by buying food, such as seasonal fruit and vegetables, in its cheapest season. Many butchers sell specially-prepared freezer packs for bulk purchase.

buns Small rolls similar to bread, but often containing extra ingredients such as sweetening, currants and spices.

FREEZING: freeze only buns that are very fresh and have been baked on the same day. Pack in **polythene bags** and exclude as much air as possible before sealing.

FREEZER LIFE: 1 month.

THAWING: either allow to thaw at room temperature for about 1 hour or split and toast them from frozen.

butcher's muslin A type of stockinette material that is used, particularly by butchers, for wrapping **meat** when chilling or freezing it.

butcher wrap A method of wrapping **meat**, baked goods and irregularly shaped foods in order to take up as little space as possible in the freezer. The food is placed near the corner of the wrapping paper and the corner is folded over the food. The two sides are then folded across the top and the package then rolled over to complete the wrap. It should then be fastened with **freezer tape** and **labelled** clearly.

butter A fatty whitish-yellow paste made from churning the cream of cows' milk. Butter that has never been softened freezes well, although if it is stored for too long its texture may become granular. Unsalted butter freezes more successfully than salted. Do not freeze butter that has been made from unpasteurized milk.

FREEZING: only freeze butter that has not softened at any time. Leave in original wrapping, but **overwrap** with **foil** or **freezer wrap**. Alternatively, make into butter balls or curls (or any other shape required) and freeze in **polythene bags**.

FREEZER LIFE: salted, 6 months; unsalted, 9–12 months.

THAWING: either in a refrigerator for 2 hours per 500g (1lb) or at room temperature for 1 hour per 500g (1lb). See also **flavoured butters**.

buttercream A type of **cake icing** or filling, made of **butter** and icing sugar, which freezes extremely well. Flavoured buttercreams do not lose their taste by freezing.

FREEZING: place in small cartons or containers, leaving a little **headspace**.

FREEZER LIFE: up to 3 months.

THAWING: thaw at room temperature for 3–4 hours.

buttermilk The liquid left after churning cream to make butter. Manufactured buttermilk is made from skimmed **milk** with a culture added to make it thicker and a little acidic. It can be frozen, although it tends to separate on **thawing**, but this can be rectified by stirring it thoroughly.

FREEZING: freeze in **rigid containers**, leaving a 2.5 cm (1 inch) **headspace**, or if freezing manufactured buttermilk, freeze in the **waxed cartons** it is sold in.

FREEZER LIFE: 6 weeks.

THAWING: allow to thaw overnight in a refrigerator, in its container. Whisk before using.

cabbage The large leafy bud of a variety of European plant. Most cabbage may be frozen, but it is not necessary to do so because it is available all year round and is not particularly expensive. However, **red cabbage** is not always available, and it may be sensible to make the most of its short season. Choose cabbages that are crisp and have a firm heart.

FREEZING: wash the cabbage thoroughly, and **blanch** it in boiling water for 1–2 minutes. Plunge into ice-cold water, drain and pack into **polythene bags**. It can be diced or shredded before freezing if desired.

FREEZER LIFE: blanched, 6 months.

THAWING: cook from frozen for 5–8 minutes.

cake Cooked cakes and uncooked cake mixtures (that do not contain raising agents) can be frozen. When baking, it is useful to double the quantity of ingredients and freeze the cake mixture for another occasion. Whisked sponge mixture does not freeze well. Cakes may be filled and iced, although they store better if undecorated. **Buttercream** freezes very well, but other **icings** such as boiled American frosting do not. Do not fill with **fruit** or **jam** before freezing because this makes the cake soggy. Fruit cakes may be frozen, but they keep just as well in a tin in a cool place. Avoid synthetic flavouring or too many spices within the cakes because the flavours tend to deteriorate with freezing.

FREEZING: plain sponge cakes should be cooled thoroughly, then wrapped individually in **clingfilm**. Small cakes and slices of cake may be packed in **polythene bags** or containers, placing pieces of **freezer wrap** between the layers or slices. Iced cakes should be frozen unwrapped until the icing has frozen and then covered in clingfilm and placed in a tin or box. Swiss rolls are best frozen rolled up in cornflour rather than sugar, which becomes sticky on thawing. Uncooked cake mixtures should be placed in **rigid containers**.

FREEZER LIFE: plain cakes, 4–6 months; iced or filled cakes, 2 months; uncooked mixtures, 2 months.

THAWING: allow plain cakes to thaw in their wrappings, but unwrap iced cakes to prevent the icing from sticking to the paper. Thaw large cakes for about 2–3 hours and small cakes for about 1 hour at room temperature. Allow uncooked cake mixture to thaw for 2–3 hours at room temperature, before placing in tins and baking.

calabrese A variety of **broccoli**.

candied peel Candied citrus peel can be satisfactorily stored in a cool, dry place for several months, although it tends to dry out and lose its flavour over time. It does, however, freeze successfully keeping moist and fresh for up to a year. It can be frozen either in large pieces or chopped up.

FREEZING: pack tightly in **polythene bags** or **foil**, excluding as much air as possible.

FREEZER LIFE: 1 year.

THAWING: allow to thaw at room temperature for 3–4 hours.

canned food Food that is cooked and preserved in cans. Although food is preserved effectively by the canning method, once the can has been opened the food should be removed and consumed within a short period of time. However, if a large can is opened and only half the contents are required, it is possible to transfer the remainder into small containers and freeze them for later use.

FREEZING: transfer canned food into **rigid containers**. Never use the cans for freezing purposes.

FREEZER LIFE: **meat**, 2 months; **fruit**, **vegetables**, 6 months.

THAWING: allow to thaw in a refrigerator for 3–4 hours.

cape gooseberry A small, golden fruit from South Africa. Cape gooseberries are commonly used to make **jams** and **jellies**, but they may be eaten raw, when very ripe or encased in fondant as petit fours. They can be frozen if necessary.

FREEZING: remove the berries from their papery shells, wash and **dry freeze**. Tranfer to **polythene bags**, expelling as much air as possible before sealing.

FREEZER LIFE: 6–8 months.

THAWING: thaw in the unopened bag for 1–2 hours at room temperature.

capon A castrated young cockerel.

FREEZING: truss and tie the legs to the body and clean the bird thoroughly inside and out. Remove the **giblets** and freeze them separately if required. Do not stuff the capons before freezing. Pad any exposed bones with **foil**, then pack into **polythene bags** and extract as much air as possible before **sealing**.

FREEZER LIFE: 10 months.

THAWING: allow the capons to thaw in a cool place or refrigerator for up to 24 hours. Use immediately when completely thawed. It is important to thaw all poultry and game thoroughly to minimize the risk of **food poisoning**.

capsicum Any of several varieties of tropical American plants with seeds used to make pepper. See **chilli**; **peppers**.

caramel A chewy sweet made by combining and heating sugar, butter, milk etc. and pouring onto a tray to set. When hard, it may be crushed and frozen to use as decoration for **puddings** and **cakes**.

FREEZING: make the caramel as usual. Allow to cool completely, then crush into small pieces and pack into small **polythene bags** and freeze.

FREEZER LIFE: 1 year.

THAWING: allow the caramel to thaw at room temperature for 2–3 hours before using.

carp A large freshwater **fish**, which has a muddy flavour so it is best soaked in salted water overnight and rinsed well before freezing.

FREEZING: wash thoroughly, remove the scales, gut and then **ice glaze**.

FREEZER LIFE: 3 months.

THAWING: allow to thaw for up to 24 hours in a cool place, then cook as soon as possible.

carrot A root **vegetable** available all year, but it is a good idea to freeze a supply of young baby carrots for later use. Choose small, young, unblemished carrots.

FREEZING: carrots can be frozen whole or sliced. If freezing whole, remove tops, wash and scrape them, then **blanch** for 3 minutes. Sliced carrots should only be blanched for 2 minutes. Cool in ice, cold water, drain and pack into **polythene bags**, expelling as much air as possible before sealing.

FREEZER LIFE: 1 year.

THAWING: cook from frozen in boiling water or in a little **butter** and **stock**.

cashew nut The kidney-shaped nut of a tropical South American tree, which will keep moist and fresh in the freezer for up to a year. Cashew nuts can be frozen whole, chopped, or roasted, but it is best not to freeze salted cashews because they become **rancid**. Cashews may also be blended with **butter** to make a nut butter, which can then be stored in the freezer.

FREEZING: pack in **foil** or small containers and seal well.

FREEZER LIFE: up to 1 year.

THAWING: allow to thaw at room temperature for 3 hours.

casserole Any food cooked and served in a covered dish. Cooked casseroles and **stews** may be successfully stored in the freezer, but it is important to have enough liquid in the **gravy** to ensure that the food does not dry out when **reheated**. Remove any surplus **fat** that rises to the surface after cooling the casserole, because it does not store well in the freezer. It is advisable not to include **garlic** prior to freezing as the flavour changes and may taste unpleasant.

FREEZING: only cook the casserole for three quarters of the time stated on the recipe, because the reheating process will finish off the cooking, and if overcooked the meat disintegrates and becomes mushy. Allow to cool completely, remove the excess fat, then pack in **rigid containers**, leaving a 2.5 cm (1 inch) **headspace**.

FREEZER LIFE: casseroles containing **bacon**, **ham** or **pork**, 6 weeks; for any other meats, 4 months.

THAWING: reheat slowly from frozen, then allow to simmer gently for 20 minutes to heat through thoroughly.

catfish A strange looking freshwater fish with long barbs hanging from its mouth. Catfish is normally skinned and filleted and deep fried. It can be succesfully frozen as long as it is absolutely fresh.

FREEZING: remove the skin and gut, then cut into fillets. **Interleave** the fillets with **freezer wrap** and pack several into a **polythene bag**, extracting as much air as posssible before **sealing**.

FREEZER LIFE: 2 months.

THAWING: allow the fillets to thaw for 2–3 hours, then dip in **batter** or **breadcrumbs** and deep fry.

cauliflower The tightly packed, white flower of a variety of cabbage, which can be frozen either **blanched** or cooked, for example in **cauliflower cheese**. Choose white heads that are firm and unblemished.

FREEZING: remove leaves, wash and divide into small florets – about 5 cm (2 inches) in size. Blanch in boiling water with the juice of one **lemon** for 3 minutes. Plunge into cold water, drain and allow to cool. Put the florets into **polythene bags**, seal and leave a 2.5 cm (1 inch) **headspace** and freeze. Or **open freeze** on trays before storing in polythene bags.

FREEZER LIFE: 6–8 months.

THAWING: cook from frozen in boiling water, and simmer for 4 minutes until tender.

cauliflower cheese A cooked dish made with **cauliflower** and **cheese sauce**, which can be successfully frozen and reheated.

FREEZING: cook the cauliflower until tender, then cover in cheese sauce. Place in a **rigid container** and leave to cool completely, then seal, leaving a 2.5 cm (1 inch) **headspace** and freeze.

FREEZER LIFE: 6 months.

THAWING: thaw in a refrigerator for 2–3 hours, then continue to cook in a moderate oven until heated through and golden brown.

caviar The salted **roe** of the sturgeon, which can be frozen for a short period only.

FREEZING: pack tightly into **polythene bags** and exclude as much air as possible before sealing.

FREEZER LIFE: 2–3 months.

THAWING: allow to thaw at room temperature for 2–3 hours, then consume as soon as possible.

celeriac The large bulbous white root of a variety of celery. Celeriac stores very well in a cool place, but it can be successfully frozen either **blanched** or puréed.

FREEZING: peel all the knobbly skin off, then wash and cut into chunks. Blanch the celeriac in boiling water for 4 minutes, then allow it to cool, drain and pack into **polythene bags**. Alternatively, it may be peeled and chopped, then cooked until tender and puréed. Allow the purée to cool and then pack into **rigid containers**.

FREEZER LIFE: blanched and puréed, 1 year.

THAWING: cook blanched celeriac from frozen in boiling water until tender. Allow the purée to thaw at room temperature for 3–4 hours, before reheating with butter and seasoning.

celery The crisp white or green stalks of a Eurasian plant, which freezes moderately well, but afterwards it is only suitable for cooking because it loses its crunchy texture. Choose celery with crisp, unblemished stalks and fresh leafy tops.

FREEZING: wash thoroughly and trim, removing any tough fibres, then cut into small lengths – about 5 cm (2 inches) long – and **blanch** for 2 minutes. Allow it to cool, then drain and pack into **polythene bags**.

FREEZER LIFE: 1 year.

THAWING: cook from frozen, either boiled or braised or add to **soups** and **casseroles**.

chain cooking A method of saving time and money by buying or preparing a basic ingredient in bulk and using it to provide a wide varity of dishes. For example, basic bread dough that could be used to make a variety of foods, such as pizzas, bread rolls, and loaves, for the freezer. Or mince that could be made into shepherd's pie, lasagne, or meat loaf.

chapati or **chapatti** A flat, coarse unleavened Indian **bread** made from finely ground wholewheat flour. Chapatis may be frozen satisfactorily provided that they are very fresh, otherwise they toughen in the freezer.

FREEZING: leave commercially produced chapatis in their packaging and **overwrap** in a **polythene bag**, expelling as much air as possible before **sealing**. If home-made, cool thoroughly and pack tightly into polythene bags.

FREEZER LIFE: 6 months.

THAWING: allow the chapatis to thaw at room temperature for 2–3 hours in their wrappings. Then warm them in an oven that has been preheated to 150°C/300°F/Gas 2.

cheese A dairy product made from the curd of milk separated from the whey. Hard cheeses such as Cheddar, Cheshire and Edam freeze well, although they tend to become crumbly. Blue cheese does not freeze well, it becomes extremely crumbly and is therefore only suitable for cooking purposes once it has been frozen. Hard cheeses can be frozen grated and stored in **polythene bags**. Mature soft cheeses, such as Brie and Camembert, can be frozen successfully and freezing can also be used to arrest ripening if necessary, but the cheese must be given ample time to return to the correct temperature. A full-fat soft cheese can be frozen if it contains more than 40% butterfat, but low-fat soft cheeses do not freeze well except in cooked dishes.

FREEZING: grate hard and soft cheeses or divide them into small portions. Wrap carefully to prevent drying out and **cross-flavouring** with other foods. Wrap in **clingfilm** then **overwrap** with **foil** or polythene bags. Freeze full-fat soft cheese in **rigid containers**.

FREEZER LIFE: 3–6 months.

THAWING: allow to thaw in a refrigerator for 24 hours in its packaging, unopened, then remove from the packaging and allow to come to room temperature before serving. Grated cheese can be used straight from the freezer for cooking purposes.

cheesecake Any of a variety of rich tarts on a biscuit base and made of cream cheese, **cream**, **eggs** and sugar. Cheesecakes can be frozen either baked or unbaked. It is advisable to freeze them without any **fruit** or cream toppings and to add these after thawing.

FREEZING: line the tin with **foil** before placing the biscuit crust inside. Make the cheesecake according to the recipe used, allow to cool if baked, then place uncovered in the freezer until firm. Remove the cheesecake from the tin, wrap it in foil and then **overwrap** in a **polythene bag**.

FREEZER LIFE: 1 month.

THAWING: allow to thaw at room temperature for 4–6 hours.

cheese sauce A plain cheese sauce is very versatile so it can be very useful to keep a stock frozen. Prepare a roux-based white sauce and simply stir in cheese to taste. Freeze in quantities suitable for use in dishes, such as **cauliflower cheese** and lasagne.

FREEZING: prepare a cheese sauce in the usual way, cool quickly to prevent a skin from forming and freeze in **rigid containers**, leaving a little **headspace**.

FREEZER LIFE: 3 months.

THAWING: heat gently from frozen, beat thoroughly and heat through before serving.

cherry The small, round red, purple or black **fruit** of the cherry tree. Cherries freeze well, the red and black varieties keeping their colour once thawed. Choose firm, ripe fruit that is not bruised. It is advisable to remove the stones before freezing because the cherries may develop an almond flavour around the stone.

FREEZING: remove stalks, then wash and dry fruit. Cherries can be frozen in three different ways. Either (a), by open freezing on trays until firm, then transferring them to **polythene bags**; or (b), the **dry sugar pack** method, allowing 250 g (8 oz) of sugar to every 900 g (2lb) of fruit, and freezing in **rigid containers**; or (c), the **syrup pack** method, using a syrup made with 500 g (1lb) of sugar to every 1 litre (2 pints) of water.

FREEZER LIFE: dry sugar or syrup pack, 9–12 months; open freeze, 1 year.

THAWING: allow to thaw very gently in an unopened container at room temperature for about 3 hours. Use immediately, otherwise the fruit becomes discoloured. Cherries in syrup can be gently heated from frozen.

chervil The leaves of a small Eurasian shrub, which have a pleasant aniseed flavour and are used as a **herb**. It is useful to freeze chervil because it is not always available and it does not dry very well.

FREEZING: wash and dry the chervil and pack sprigs in to **polythene bags**. Alternatively, chop up the leaves and freeze in small plastic containers or bags.

FREEZER LIFE: 6 months.

THAWING: chervil can be added to fish and chicken dishes straight from the freezer.

chest freezer A large capacity freezer with a lid that hinges from the top. Chest freezers are slightly cheaper to run than the upright types, but they can be less convenient to use as the lid cannot normally be used as a useful worktop or storage space (heavy items should not be kept on top of the freezer) and the contents are not so readily accessible. They are, however, very spacious and useful for storing large, bulky parcels of frozen food.

chestnut The **nut** of the sweet chestnut tree, which is well worth freezing especially for use in **stuffings**. However, the preparation of chestnuts for the freezer is tedious and time-consuming. The shell and skin must be removed from the chestnut, which can then be frozen whole, raw, or cooked, or cooked and puréed (see **chestnut purée**).

FREEZING: make a small slit with a knife in each chestnut, then place in a pan of boiling water for 2–3 minutes. Drain, shell and skin with a knife. Allow to cool, then place in **polythene bags**. Or alternatively, continue cooking them for a futher 40–45 minutes until tender, when they can either be cooled and frozen in bags or puréed and frozen in **rigid containers**.

FREEZER LIFE: 6 months.

THAWING: allow to thaw in the refrigerator for 12 hours.

chestnut purée Cooked and puréed fresh **chestnuts** can be successfully frozen for use in **stuffings** and **puddings**.

FREEZING: cook and purée fresh chestnuts and pack in **rigid containers**, leaving a 2.5 cm (1 inch) **headspace**.

FREEZER LIFE: 6 months.

THAWING: allow to thaw in the refrigerator overnight, then mix well before using.

chicken A domestic fowl, which should be frozen as fresh as possible. Choose plump, young tender birds. Do not stuff chickens before freezing as the **stuffing** inhibits the thawing process and could lead to **food poisoning**. Likewise, if thawing ready-trussed chickens, remove the bag of **giblets** because they have a far shorter freezer life.

FREEZING: wipe and clean whole chickens and cover any bones with **foil**. Place in **polythene bags**, leaving a little **headspace** and freeze. Wrap chicken joints and drumsticks in **freezer wrap** and **overwrap** in polythene bags. Cooked chicken must be cooled as quickly as possible, then packed in **clingfilm** and overwrapped in polythene bags. Freeze stuffings separately.

FREEZER LIFE: whole chickens, 1 year; giblets, 3 months; chicken portions, 1 year; cooked chicken, 2–3 months.

THAWING: it is important to always thaw chickens thoroughly. They are a fruitful source of **salmonella** and freezing does not destroy **bacteria**. It is now believed that **poultry** and **game** should be thawed at a cool room temperature rather than in the refrigerator, so leave whole birds up to 3.5 lbs to thaw at room temperature for 24 hours in their wrappings. Allow chicken joints to thaw in their wrapping for 4–6 hours at room temperature.

chicory The green-white, tightly wrapped leaves of a blue-flowered plant, eaten as a **vegetable**. After it has been frozen it can only be used in cooking because it loses its crispness and texture. Choose firm, compact heads and trim off the base and any discoloured outer leaves.

FREEZING: **blanch** in boiling water for 2 mintues. Cool and drain thoroughly then pack in **polythene bags** to freeze.

FREEZER LIFE: 6 months.

THAWING: allow to thaw in bags at room temperature for about 2 hours. The chicory tends to lose a great deal of water, so gently squeeze out any excess moisture before using.

chilli The red, or green and red, tapering pod of a variety of tropical **capsicum**. Chillis are very pungent and are added to spicy foods and bland dishes to add a fiery flavour. The seeds can burn the skin, so care is needed when preparing them.

FREEZING: trim off stalks and remove seeds and pith. **Blanch** for 2 minutes, then pack into **polythene bags** or **rigid containers**.

FREEZER LIFE: 9–12 months.

THAWING: chillis can be used from frozen, or allow them to thaw for 1–2 hours at room temperature before using.

china Ceramic ware. Solid china plates and dishes are not damaged by short-term use in the freezer, for example, for the purposes of **open freezing**, but it is preferable not to store them for too long because they may crack. Pyrosil is a toughened type of ceramic that can be used in the freezer, and can go straight from the freezer into the oven without having to be brought up to room temperature first.

Chinagraph pencil A type of pencil that writes easily on polythene bags and foil, and does not smudge or wear off in the freezer. It writes most easily if warmed first.

Chinese cabbage See **Chinese leaf**.

Chinese food There is no reason why home-cooked Chinese food cannot be frozen, but allow it to cool first for later use. Obviously it depends on the ingredients used as to whether it will retain its original colour and flavour and texture, but most cooked casserole-type dishes may be successfully frozen. Stir-fries and crispy vegetables lose their crisp texture and are not very satisfactory. If necessary, food that has been bought from a Chinese takeaway restaurant may be frozen. Again, many dishes may well lose their original flavour and texture, and the beauty of Chinese food is that it is so quick and easy to prepare that there is not really much point in freezing it.

Chinese gooseberry See **kiwi fruit**.

Chinese leaf (also called **Chinese cabbage**) A variety of cabbage with a tall, tightly packed bud of wrinkled green leaves on crisp, white stems. Chinese leaf loses its crisp texture if frozen, although it can be used in cooked dishes.

FREEZING: shred or cut into chunks and **blanch** in boiling water for 1 mintue. Cool, drain and dry thoroughly. Pack into **polythene bags** and expel as much air as possible.

FREEZER LIFE: 1 year.

THAWING: remove from polythene bags and allow to thaw at room temperature for 15 minutes before using.

chorizo A type of spicy **garlic sausage** originating in Spain. Because of the high garlic content, it is not advisable to freeze chorizos because garlic tends to develop an unusual and unpleasant flavour in the freezer. It is also likely to cause other foods to take on a highly spiced and strong flavour through **cross-flavouring**. Because chorizos are made with cured meat they store quite satisfactorily in a cool, dry place.

chip A thin strip of deep-fried **potato**. Home-made or commercially produced chips freeze very well. They can be bought in bulk and are therefore very cost-effective and are also a cheap, easy vegetable to have to hand.

FREEZING: to freeze home-made chips, peel and slicc potatoes into small chips. Fry gently in oil until soft, but not browned. Remove and drain on kitchen paper and allow to cool completely before **open freezing** and storing in **polythene bags**.

FREEZER LIFE: 6 months.

THAWING: cook from frozen, but care must be taken because the chips may spit in hot oil.

chive The thin tubular leaves of a Eurasian plant, used as a **herb**. Chives can be easily frozen and used either raw in salads and dressings or added to sauces.

FREEZING: snip small quantities of fresh chives into small **polythene bags**, containers or ice cube trays.

FREEZER LIFE: 6 months.

THAWING: because chives retain their former texture and quickly soften use them straight from the freezer.

chocolate A hard dark-brown paste made from ground, roasted cocoa seeds, and usually sweetened and flavoured. Chocolate can be successfully frozen for a short period, and it may be very useful to freeze in the summer for use in puddings and desserts. It is worth storing home-made chocolate decorations for garnishing cakes and desserts at the last minute. Frozen chocolate is excellent for grating.

FREEZING: prepare chocolate decorations in the usual way, then pack carefully in **rigid containers**, placing small sheets of **freezer wrap** between layers to protect them.

FREEZER LIFE: 2 months.

THAWING: unwrap and place on a flat tray and allow to thaw at room temperature for 1 hour.

chop A cut of **meat** from the loin of mutton, **lamb**, **pork** or **veal**, which can be cooked from frozen without much loss of texture or flavour. Chops can be cooked quickly and therefore are a very useful item to have in the freezer.

FREEZING: wipe the chops and pack into **polythene bags**, **interleaved** with small pieces of **freezer wrap** so that they can be easily separated when frozen. Remember to **label** them clearly.

FREEZER LIFE: pork chops, 3 months; lamb chops, 6 months; veal chops, 6 months.

THAWING: it is unnecessary to thaw chops before cooking, although they may be allowed to thaw overnight in the refrigerator in their wrappings. If cooking frozen chops, cook slowly and gently before increasing the heat to brown them.

choux pastry A very light **pastry** made with eggs. It can be frozen prepared and unbaked or cooked and made into the basis for desserts and cakes, such as **profiteroles** and **eclairs**.

FREEZING: prepare choux pastry as stated in any standard recipe. When smooth and glossy, pipe into desired shapes and **open freeze** on non-stick baking trays, before packing in **polythene bags**. If the pastry is to be baked, pipe the mixture onto trays as desired and cook until firm and golden brown. Allow to cool, then open freeze and pack into **rigid containers** placing small sheets of **freezer wrap** between the layers.

FREEZER LIFE: unbaked, 3 months; baked, 6 months.

THAWING: it is best not to thaw choux pastry before baking. Place frozen raw shapes on to baking trays and cook allowing 5 minutes longer than the recommended cooking time. Place frozen and baked shapes on to a baking sheet and cook for 10 minutes to become fresh and crisp once more.

Christmas pudding A rich, steamed pudding containing suet, dried fruit, spices and brandy. The traditional rich Christmas pudding need never be frozen, because it is generally thought to mature and improve in flavour the longer it is stored in a cool, dry place. The old-fashioned recipes for Christmas pudding state that it can be stored quite successfully for up to 2 years, although it does depend on the recipe. The lighter versions of Christmas pudding, which are becoming more popular today, may be frozen as they do not store as well.

FREEZING: boil as stated in the recipe, and allow to cool completely. Remove it from the basin it was cooked in and wrap tightly in **greaseproof paper** and **foil** then freeze.

FREEZER LIFE: 4 months.

THAWING: allow to thaw overnight at room temperature. Replace the pudding in a basin and continue to cook according to the recipe.

chutney A type of pickle normally made from preserving **fruits** and **vegetables** in a solution of vinegar, sugar and **salt**. Providing that there is only a low proportion of sugar included it is possible to freeze chutney, and some recipes specify that it is to be stored in the freezer. Most commercially prepared chutneys have a long storage life providing that they are kept in a cool, dry cupboard and it is unnecessary to freeze them.

FREEZING: pack home-made and low-sugar chutneys in small cartons and seal with **freezer tape**. Do not use **glass** jars because they may shatter.

FREEZER LIFE: 3 months.

THAWING: allow to thaw in the container overnight in a cool place. Once thawed, store in the refrigerator.

clam A **shellfish** that is normally sold live in its shell. Clams can be frozen only if very fresh (within 12 hours of being caught) because there is always a risk of **food poisoning** with shellfish.

FREEZING: wash thoroughly, open shells and remove clams. Drain any liquid and reserve it.

Wash the clams in salted water, then drain and place in **rigid containers**. Cover with the reserved clam juice, **seal** well, allowing a little **headspace** and freeze.

FREEZER LIFE: 3 months.

THAWING: allow to thaw in the container in a refrigerator for 2–3 hours; eat as soon as possible.

clementine A small sweet variety of **tangerinc**, which can be frozen in **syrup** or in a **dry sugar pack**.

FREEZING: remove the peel, pith and any pips and divide into segments. Either (a), pack in syrup, made with 250 g (8 oz) of sugar to every 600 ml (1 pint) of water, in **rigid containers**, leaving a 2.5 cm (1 inch) **headspace**; or (b), pack into rigid containers with alternate layers of **fruit** and sugar using 125 g (4 oz) of sugar to every 6 clementines.

FREEZER LIFE: 1 year.

THAWING: allow the fruit to thaw in containers for about 3 hours at room temperature before using.

clingfilm A type of plastic wrapping material used to cover food for storage purposes. Ordinary clingfilm is too thin to be used alone as a wrapping material for frozen goods, but used with **polythene bags** it can be very useful. **Freezer wrap** is a special type of clingfilm, manufactured specifically for use in the freezer because it is double the thickness of ordinary clingfilm, and is therefore a convenient way of wrapping many things such as **sandwiches** and **cakes** and for **overwrapping** containers without lids.

cloudberry An orange, berry-like fruit of a creeping Eurasian plant, which is very similar to a raspberry. Cloudberries can be used and frozen in the same way as the European **raspberry**.

coalfish See **coley**.

cockle A mollusc **shellfish** usually sold cooked and out of its shell. Only freeze very fresh cockles – within 12 hours of being caught.

FREEZING: rinse thoroughly in cold water, then allow to soak in fresh water for 2–3 hours. Cook in a little boiling water for about 5 minutes until the shells open. Remove cockles from their shells and continue to cook for a further 4 minutes. Cool completely, then pack in **rigid containers** leaving a 2.5 cm (1 inch) **headspace**. Then either freeze them dry or with a little of the cooking liquid poured over them.

FREEZER LIFE: 1 month.

THAWING: allow to thaw in their containers in a refrigerator for 2–3 hours.

coconut The white meat inside the fruit of the coconut palm. Fresh coconut can be frozen shredded, grated or toasted and then used for cooking purposes.

FREEZING: grate or shred the coconut and pack into **rigid containers** or **polythene bags**. It can then be moistened with the coconut milk if desired before freezing, which will help it retain its texture.

FREEZER LIFE: fresh, 6 months; toasted, 2 months.

THAWING: remove from wrappings or containers, allow to thaw at room temperature for about 2 hours and then drain it through a sieve. It can be used in a variety of foods, such as cakes, biscuits and curries.

cod A large **fish** with white flesh, which is available all year round. Cod is generally sold in steaks or fillets although whole fish can be purchased when small.

FREEZING: freeze steaks or fillets wrapped and interleaved in **freezer wrap**, then **overwrap** with **foil** or **polythene bags**. If freezing a whole fish, wash, remove the scales and then **ice glaze**. Wrap in freezer wrap and place in a freezer.

FREEZER LIFE: 3 months.

THAWING: steaks and fillets can be cooked from frozen, although they may be thawed in the refrigerator if desired. Whole fish should be allowed to thaw in a cool place for up to 24 hours. Fish should always be used as soon as possible after thawing.

cod's roe Cooked fresh cod's roe freezes very well. Smoked cod's roe can also be frozen as it is or when made into **taramasalata**.

FREEZING: cut freshly cooked cod's roe into slices and pack in **rigid containers**, interleaved with small sheets of **freezer wrap**. Smoked roe or taramasalata should be packed into small containers before freezing.

FREEZER LIFE: fresh cod's roe, 1 month; smoked roe and taramasalata, 3 months.

THAWING: fry fresh cod's roe from frozen until golden brown. Allow smoked roe and taramasalata to thaw in the refrigerator overnight.

coffee The beanlike seeds of the coffee tree and the beverage made from them. Fresh coffee beans can be frozen and so can freshly ground coffee provided it is absolutely fresh. Instant coffee may also be frozen as can liquid coffee.

FREEZING: pack coffee beans and freshly ground coffee into heavy-gauge **polythene bags** and expel as much air as possible. Coffee bought in plastic and **foil** packs can be frozen in those without the need to overwrap. Freeze instant coffee in polythene bags and liquid coffee in ice cube trays. Coffee ice cubes should then be stored in polythene bags.

FREEZER LIFE: coffee beans and freshly ground coffee, 1 year; packages of coffee and instant coffee, 3 months.

THAWING: it is possible to use coffee from frozen.

cold meat Cold, leftover cooked meat can be frozen in several ways: chopped up, sliced or sliced in **gravy**. Remember to freeze it as soon as possible after cooking and cooling.

FREEZING: chopped meat should be stored in **polythene bags**, sliced meat should be interleaved with **freezer wrap** and **overwrapped** in **foil** or in containers, and sliced meat in gravy should be placed in a foil dish and covered with foil.

FREEZER LIFE: 2 months.

THAWING: meat that is to be eaten cold should be allowed to thaw in the refrigerator for 2–3 hours. Meat with gravy should be reheated thoroughly from frozen at 200°C/400°F/Gas 6 for about 40 minutes.

coleslaw A mixed salad, usually consisting of raw shredded **cabbage**, **carrot** and **onion**, covered in a **mayonnaise** dressing. Coleslaw does not freeze satisfactorily because the mayonnaise separates during storage. If preparing coleslaw in advance it is best to prepare the vegetables and freeze them individually in **polythene bags**. After thawing, combine them with the mayonnaise.

coley (also called **coalfish** or **saithe**) A white **fish** that is similar to cod, but has a blue-black skin and is generally a cheap fish to buy. Coley is usually sold in fillets or cutlets, and it has a pink flesh that turns white after cooking. Freeze only very fresh coley.

FREEZING: wrap and interleave fillets or cutlets with **freezer wrap** and **overwrap** with **polythene bags**. If a whole fish is to be frozen **ice glaze** it first and then pack it in a polythene bag.

FREEZER LIFE: 3 months.

THAWING: fillets and cutlets can be cooked from frozen. Whole fish must be allowed to thaw in a cool place for up to 24 hours, then used promptly.

colour code If the freezer is going to be frequently used, it is helpful for every freezer owner to have a colour-code system. Each item is attached with a certain colour label or tie. For example, meat could be red and fish blue. This colour coding makes finding the correct foods quicker and easier, especially if it is a large chest freezer. Certain manufacturers make bags and containers with different coloured stripes or ties specifically for this purpose.

compressor A component within the freezer, usually a sealed unit, which alters the pressure of the liquid coolant and also pumps it round.

condenser A system of tubes that transfers the heat from the freezer to the outside, allowing the freezer to remain at a constantly cold temperature. It does this by condensing gas into liquid and allowing the heat given off to be dispersed into the air.

conger eel A type of eel with a long snake-like body and reduced fins. One of the two edible sea water eels, which is normally sold in thick slices and used in **soups** and **patés**. It can be satisfactorily frozen, providing it is very fresh.

FREEZING: pack slices of eel into **polythene bags**, **interleaving** each slice with a small piece of **freezer wrap**. Expel as much air as possible from the bags before **sealing**.

FREEZER LIFE: 2 months.

THAWING: allow the eel to thaw in the refrigerator overnight before using in soups, patés and terrines.

conservator A type of cold-storage cabinet used for storing previously frozen foods. A conservator is not capable of freezing fresh foods, and therefore is generally only used in large supermarkets and food stores rather than in the domestic home.

conserve See **jam**.

convenience food Any of a variety of foods that may be prepared quickly, with little cooking or **reheating**. Supermarkets are now rapidly expanding their production of ready-meals, which are generally precooked and then either chilled, canned or frozen. They are becoming increasingly popular today because often the housewife does not have the time to prepare nutritional family meals. It is important to read and follow the instructions carefully on convenience foods because as they are cooked they have a relatively short storage life. Some may be frozen in their packaging, but it is best to check the packet for freezing instructions, freezer life and thawing times. It is also important to get the food home quickly to avoid any thawing.

coriander The dried ripe seeds of a Eurasian shrub, which is used as a **herb** and is similar to continental **parsley** in appearance. Coriander is often used in curries and with **lamb** dishes. Because it does not dry particularly well it is useful to be able to freeze it.

FREEZING: wash and dry the coriander leaves. Chop up finely and pack into small cartons or **poly-**

thene bags, extracting as much air as possible before **sealing**.

FREEZER LIFE: 6 months.

THAWING: frozen coriander may be added to most dishes, straight from the freezer.

cornflour A fine, starchy flour made from maize and used to thicken foods. **Sauces** that are thickened with cornflour are less likely to separate when frozen than those thickened with ordinary flour. However, it is possible to restore other thickened sauces by whisking them thoroughly when completely defrosted.

corn on the cob Fresh unripe maize, which can be frozen whole or in kernels. Choose fresh corn that is bright yellow, but not overripe.

FREEZING: remove the husks and tassels and trim the ends. **Blanch** in boiling water for 4 minutes for small cobs or 8 minutes for large ones. Allow to cool completely and pack individual cobs in **freezer wrap**, then **overwrap** in **polythene bags**.

FREEZER LIFE: 1 year.

THAWING: allow to thaw in wrappings at room temperature for about 2 hours. Then cook in boiling water for 5–10 minutes until tender.

cottage cheese A low-fat soft **cheese** that does not freeze well because its texture, appearance and taste changes. It can be used in desserts and other dishes, such as **cheesecakes**, before freezing.

courgette A small variety of marrow, which freezes well. Choose young, unblemished small courgettes; larger ones do not freeze succesfully because they contain too much water.

FREEZING: wash and cut into 1 cm (½ inch) slices discarding both ends. **Blanch** for 1 minute, cool, drain and **open freeze** on trays until firm, then pack in **polythene bags**. Alternatively they can be sautéed in **butter** instead of blanched and packed into **rigid containers** when cool, leaving a 2.5 cm (1 inch) **headspace**.

FREEZER LIFE: 1 year.

THAWING: cook blanched courgettes from frozen. Finish cooking sautéed courgettes until golden brown and tender.

court-bouillon A type of **stock** made from simmering a mixture of root **vegetables**, water and **wine**. It can then be strained and reduced down to a concentrated form and frozen for use as a concentrated stock. Court-bouillon is then usually used to poach **fish**.

FREEZING: cook the court-bouillon as usual, then boil hard to reduce the quantity down to a minimum. Pour into an ice cube tray and allow to cool completely. Freeze until firm, then transfer the cubes into **polythene bags** for storage in the freezer.

FREEZER LIFE: 3 months.

THAWING: cubes may be gently reheated from frozen.

couscous A type of millet, which can be frozen after cooking.

FREEZING: pack loosely in a **polythene bag** and seal.

FREEZER LIFE: 6 months.

THAWING: allow to thaw at room temperature for 2–3 hours. Shake the bag when still half frozen so that the grains separate out.

crab A marine crustacean. Fresh cooked crab can be frozen, but it must be frozen within 24 hours of it being caught because it is highly perishable and can therefore be a source of **food poisoning** if not treated correctly.

FREEZING: cook and allow to cool, then remove all the edible meat from the crab, separating the brown meat from the white meat. Pack in a **rigid container**, cover with **freezer wrap** and seal with a lid if possible before **overwrapping** in **polythene bags**. Alternatively, the meat can be replaced in the cleaned shell and frozen, wrapped in freezer wrap and overwrapped in a polythene bag.

FREEZER LIFE: 1 month.

THAWING: allow to thaw for 6–8 hours in the refrigerator. Use immediately.

crab apple The small sour fruits of the crab apple tree, most frequently used to make **jams** and **jellies**.

FREEZING: wash and dry, then pack in **polythene bags**.

FREEZER LIFE: 8 months.

THAWING: cook from frozen, allowing a little extra time if following a particular recipe.

cracked wheat The wholewheat grain that has simply been cracked between rollers. It is normally soaked and boiled for 2 hours and then eaten in the same way as **rice** with **meat**, **vegetables** or in salads, or as a hot breakfast cereal. Once soaked and cooked it may be successfully frozen.

FREEZING: cook the cracked wheat as usual and allow to cool completely. Pack it loosely in a **polythene bag**, seal it and place in the freezer. When it is half frozen, squeeze the bag to separate out the grains and replace in the freezer.

FREEZER LIFE: 6 months.

THAWING: cracked wheat may be used from frozen if it is going to be reheated and used in a hot dish. If it is to be used in salads it should be allowed to thaw at room temperature for about 1 hour before using.

cranberry The sour red berry of a variety of trailing shrub, which is most frequently used to make cranberry **jelly** or **sauce**. Choose firm, red berries, which can either be frozen whole or as a sauce.

FREEZING: wash and dry the berries and allow to **open freeze** on trays before packing into **polythene bags**. If freezing cranberry sauce, allow to cool thoroughly before packing into **rigid containers**, leaving a 2.5 cm (1 inch) **headspace**.

FREEZER LIFE: 9 months.

THAWING: allow both the berries and sauce to thaw at room temperature for 2–3 hours.

crayfish (also called **crawfish**) A freshwater crustacean that looks like a small lobster and can be frozen within 24 hours of it being caught.

FREEZING: wash thoroughly and remove the central part of the tail and the intestines. Cook in boiling water for 10 mintues, cool and pack in **polythene bags**.

FREEZER LIFE: 1 month.

THAWING: allow to thaw in the refrigerator for 3–4 hours before serving cold, or thaw in boiling water and serve hot.

cream The yellow, fatty part of milk, which rises to the top when milk is left to stand. Pasteurized cream can be successfully frozen provided it has a butterfat content of at least 35–40%. The higher the **fat** content, the better the cream freezes. If possible it is best to whip the cream before freezing otherwise it tends to separate and become granular and heavy in texture. Adding a little sugar also helps to prevent it from separating during the freezing process. Cream can also be whipped and piped into shapes before freezing if required.

FREEZING: half whip the cream or add a little sugar and pour into **rigid containers**, leaving a 2.5 cm (1 inch) **headspace**. Commercially frozen cream can be frozen in its original container. Cover and seal securely. Pipe whipped cream onto trays covered with **foil**, **open freeze** until firm, then store in rigid containers.

FREEZER LIFE: Jersey, double and whipping cream, 3 months; clotted cream, 1 year; commercially frozen cream, 1 year. Single cream is not suitable for freezing.

THAWING: allow cream to thaw overnight in the refrigerator. Whisk for a short while again before using. Piped cream decorations take about 10 minutes to thaw at room temperature.

cream cheese A smooth, soft **cheese** that may be frozen for up to 6 weeks, but then it becomes yellow and hard. In order for it to freeze at all it must contain at least 40% butterfat. It can be successfully frozen within other dishes, such as **cheesecakes** and other **puddings**.

FREEZING: pack into cartons or small containers.

FREEZER LIFE: up to 6 weeks.

THAWING: allow to thaw overnight in the refrigerator.

crème fraiche **Cream** that has been allowed to sour. Crème fraiche is manufactured with different amounts of butterfat. Provided that it contains at least 35–40% butterfat it freezes satisfactorily. Ensure that commercially produced crème fraiche states on the container whether it is suitable for freezing because some manufacturers do not recommend it.

FREEZING: pack in cartons or **rigid containers**.

FREEZER LIFE: 3 months.

THAWING: allow to thaw overnight in the refrigerator.

croissant A crescent-shaped, flaky bread roll, which can be frozen baked or unbaked.

FREEZING: freeze cooked croissants in **polythene bags**. Home-baked croissants may need greater protection, so pack in **rigid containers** with sheets of **freezer wrap** between the layers. Unbaked dough can be frozen when it has been prepared up to the final rolling. Omit the last stage and freeze in polythene bags.

FREEZER LIFE: unbaked croissant dough, 4 weeks; baked croissants, 3 months.

THAWING: untie the bags containing uncooked dough and allow to thaw overnight in the refrigerator, complete the final rolling before baking as usual. Place frozen baked croissants in **foil** and reheat for 15 minutes.

cross-flavouring Foods that are highly spiced, seasoned or have a naturally strong flavour, such as fish, garlic, cheese, curries and onion, can transfer their flavour to other foods in the freezer. Cross-flavouring can be avoided by the use of extra thick wrapping materials, **overwrapping** and secure **sealing**.

crouton Small cubes of fried **bread** normally served with **soups** and **salads**, which freeze very well. This is a good way to store slightly stale bread.

FREEZING: cook, drain on absorbent paper and cool. Pack into **polythene bags** and freeze.

FREEZER LIFE: 1 month.

THAWING: remove from polythene bags, place on a baking tray and thaw under a grill for 5 minutes before using.

crumble A baked **pudding** made with any of a variety of fruits (e.g. apple), which can be frozen completely cooked or just prepared.

FREEZING: freeze cooked crumble in the dish it was cooked in. Freeze uncooked crumble mixture in **polythene bags**. The whole dish may be made up and frozen before cooking, so freeze in the container you choose.

FREEZER LIFE: 2 months.

THAWING: crumbles can be cooked from frozen allowing a little extra time.

crumpet Home-baked and commercially prepared crumpets can be easily stored in the freezer.

FREEZING: remove from packaging if bought, and pack into **polythene bags**.

FREEZER LIFE: 6 months.

THAWING: crumpets can be toasted straight from the freezer or allowed to thaw for 5–6 hours in an unsealed bag.

cucumber The long, thin fruit of a creeping plant. Cucumbers contain a high proportion of water and consequently do not freeze satisfactorily as a raw salad vegetable because they become very mushy. They can, however, be frozen either puréed or cooked.

FREEZING: either (a), peel a raw cucumber, cut into small pieces and place in a blender or liquidizer until smooth, then pour into **rigid containers** and freeze; or (b), place baked cucumber in rigid containers and freeze.

FREEZER LIFE: 2 months.

THAWING: allow to thaw at room temperature for 1–2 hours before adding to dishes, such as soups and sauces.

curd cheese A smooth, mild-tasting white cheese made from skimmed milk curds. Curd cheese does not freeze successfully unless it contains more than 40% butterfat.

currant A dried blackcurrant. See **dried fruit**.

curry Any of a variety of spicy dishes. Curries made from cooked **meat**, **poultry** or **vegetables** can be successfully frozen, as can curry **sauce**. Because many curries taste better when reheated they lend themselves well to freezing. The flavours of freshly-ground spices do mellow, and curry powder loses its piquancy after a few months and becomes peppery.

FREEZING: cook as the recipe states, allow to cool completely, then pack into **rigid containers** and freeze.

FREEZER LIFE: 2 months.

THAWING: allow to thaw overnight in the refrigerator before **reheating** thoroughly.

custard A term used to describe both a baked sweetened mixture of eggs and milk, and a sauce made of milk and sugar thickened with cornflour. Egg custard, caramel custard and vanilla custard separate during the freezing process so it is advisable to make them up freshly rather than try to freeze them.

dab A small European brown flatfish, which is similar to a small **plaice**. Dab is normally sold either whole or in fillets and can be frozen successfully. Only choose very fresh **fish** for freezing.

FREEZING: to freeze fillets, **interleave** them with small pieces of **freezer wrap**, then wrap several together in a **polythene bag**, extracting as much air as possible before **sealing**. If freezing whole fish, remove scales and gut and wrap tightly in a polythene bag. Place flat in the freezer until firm.

FREEZER LIFE: 3 months.

THAWING: fillets may be grilled or fried from frozen. Allow whole fish to thaw in a cool place for 4–6 hours depending on the size of the fish. Then consume as soon as possible.

dairy products Any of a variety of foods containing milk or milk products. Most dairy products can be frozen in some form or another, which is convenient if bulk buying. See **butter**; **cheese**; **cream**; **crème fraiche**; **eggs**; **fromage frais**; **milk**; **yoghurt**.

damson A small blue-black, plumlike fruit, which is generally sour tasting and is most often used either stewed with sugar or in **jams** and **jellies**. The skins tend to become tough during freezing and so damsons are best washed, halved, stoned and stewed before freezing. Choose firm, ripe fruit with no bruises.

FREEZING: wash, halve and stone the fruit. Either (a), sweeten and stew until tender; or (b), stew until a purée is formed, then blend until smooth; or (c), pack in cold syrup made with 500 g (1lb) of sugar to every 1 litre (2 pints) of water. Pack the fruit or purée into **rigid containers** to freeze.

FREEZER LIFE: 1 year.

THAWING: allow to thaw in their containers for 2–3 hours at room temperature, or cook from frozen and stew. The purée can be used to make a sauce or mixed with whipped cream to make a mousse or ice cream.

Danish pastry A sweet, puff pastry **cake**, which can be frozen as unbaked **dough**, home-baked or commercially baked. If home-baking, do not ice before placing in the freezer because the icing tends to become very sticky.

FREEZING: prepare the dough up to the final stage of rolling, then place in **polythene bags** and freeze. Pack home or commercially baked pastries into **rigid containers** or polythene bags if un-iced. Iced pastries should be allowed to **open freeze** until firm and then be packed into polythene bags.

FREEZER LIFE: unbaked dough, 6 weeks; baked pastries, 1 month.

THAWING: thaw the dough in its unsealed wrappings in a refrigerator overnight, before rolling and shaping and baking. Place frozen un-iced pastries in a moderate oven for 10 minutes. Remove iced pastries from their bags and allow to thaw at room temperature for 1–2 hours.

date The long oval fruit of the date palm. Fresh and dried dates may be stored in the freezer, which is an advantage as fresh ones tend to have a very limited season in the supermarkets.

FREEZING: remove stones from fresh dates, pack into **polythene bags** and freeze. Remove dried dates from their original packaging and freeze also in polythene bags.

FREEZER LIFE: fresh and dried dates, 1 year.

THAWING: allow to thaw at room temperature for about 2 hours.

defrosting The thawing of ice and **frost** that has formed on the wall and shelves of a freezer. This can be done most effectively by removing the contents of the freezer, switching the machine off and allowing it to become warmer. The ice can then be removed by hand, with a plastic or wooden spatula. It is important to defrost a freezer regularly to keep it operating effectively. A chest freezer generally needs only to be defrosted once or twice a year, but an upright may need to be defrosted three to four times a year.

dehydration The loss of water, which in frozen food is most often due to careless packaging. **Meat** is especially prone to drying out in the freezer, so care must be taken to ensure that it is closely wrapped in moisture- and vapour-proof packaging materials.

dill The leaves and seed-like fruits of a Eurasian plant, which are used fresh or dried as a **herb**, usually in **sauces** to accompany white **fish** and **potato** dishes. Dill can be successfully frozen and used straight from the freezer.

FREEZING: chop up the delicate fronds and freeze in small **polythene bags**. Extract as much air as possible before **sealing**.

FREEZER LIFE: 6 months.

THAWING: use straight from the freezer.

dips Many party dips can be prepared and frozen successfully. However, depending on what they contain they may separate a little on thawing, so mix thoroughly with a wooden spoon before serving. If there is any doubt as to their freezing capability, refer to the individual ingredients, e.g. cottage cheese.

FREEZING: prepare as the recipe states and pack into small containers.

FREEZER LIFE: 1 month.

THAWING: allow to thaw overnight in a refrigerator.

discoloration The loss or alteration of colour. Some **fruits**, such as **apples** and **peaches**, **vegetables**, such as **cauliflower**, and **fish** are likely to discolour during preparation, storing and **thawing**. This can be prevented by dipping them into a solution of **lemon juice** (1 lemon squeezed to 1 litre (2 pints) of water), in **ascorbic acid** or salted water. Fruit may be packed in syrup, which also prevents discoloration. The discoloration of meat or fish while in the freezer is usually due to careless packaging, which has allowed the food to come into contact with the air. The food will not be harmful, but it may taste a little **rancid**.

dogfish (also called **huss** or **rock salmon**) A variety of small, spotted European shark, which is commonly sold under the name of huss. Dogfish has firm, white flesh and is best fried in chunks or used in **pies**. It can be frozen providing it is very fresh. It is normally sold without its head and tail and skinned.

FREEZING: place large pieces or small chunks of the fish into a **polythene bag** and extract as much air as possible before **sealing**.

FREEZER LIFE: 3 months.

THAWING: allow the fish to thaw overnight before cooking.

dough A thick mixture of flour or meal and water or milk. Both **bread** dough and **pastry** dough can be satisfactorily frozen in their raw state.

FREEZING: make bread dough as the recipe states, but do not allow to rise. Grease the inside of **polythene bags** with oil and divide the dough into convenient quantities. Expel as much air as possible from the bags before sealing, leaving a little **headspace** for the dough to rise slightly before it freezes. Follow the recipe for preparing pastry dough, but do not roll out. Divide into suitable portions and pack into polythene bags withdrawing as much air as possbile.

FREEZER LIFE: bread dough, 1 month; pastry dough, 3 months.

THAWING: allow both bread and pastry dough to thaw in the refrigerator for 8–10 hours.

doughnut A small cake of sweetened dough, usually ring-shaped or filled with jam or cream. Both home-made and commercially made doughnuts can be frozen.

FREEZING: pack doughnuts into **polythene bags** and expel as much air as possible before sealing.

FREEZER LIFE: 1 month.

THAWING: heat from frozen in a hot oven for about 5–8 mintues.

Dover sole A particularly solid flatfish with brown-grey skin, white flesh and a good flavour, which is normally sold either whole or in fillets. It can be successfully frozen.

FREEZING: for a whole **fish** wash, remove the scales and gut. Freeze unwrappped until firm, then **ice glaze**. Wrap in **clingfilm** and **overwrap** in a **polythene bag**. Separate the fillets with clingfilm or **freezer wrap** and overwrap in **foil** before freezing.

FREEZER LIFE: 3 months.

THAWING: allow a whole fish to thaw in a cool place for up to 24 hours, then use as soon as possible. Fillets can be cooked from frozen or allowed to thaw in the refrigerator for 1–2 hours.

dried beans Most types of dried bean need to be soaked overnight and cooked for a considerable length of time before eating. Consequently, it can be useful to freeze already prepared dried beans for use in **pies** and **casseroles** and vegetarian dishes at a later stage.

FREEZING: soak thoroughly and cook the beans as usual until just undercooked. Allow to cool completely, then drain and pat dry and pack into **rigid containers**, leaving a small **headspace** before **sealing**.

FREEZER LIFE: 6 months.

THAWING: allow the beans to thaw at room temperature for 3–4 hours, then finish off cooking them either alone or with other foods.

dried fruit Any kind of fruit allowed to mature and dry or artificially dried. Most dried fruits, such as sultanas, figs and dates, can be successfully frozen. Although they normally store well in a cool, dry place, they do tend to dehydrate over time and lose their plump texture. Freezing keeps them moist and fresh for up to a year.

FREEZING: wrap the dried fruits tightly in **polythene bags** or small packages of **foil**, **sealing** them securely.

FREEZER LIFE: 1 year.

THAWING: allow the fruits to thaw at room temperature on a flat plate for about 2–3 hours, separating them as they thaw.

drip loss A term used to describe the liquid that exudes from frozen food during **thawing**. Drip loss can be reduced significantly by **fast freezing** and slow thawing. There is a certain amount of nutrient loss in the drip loss, which can be saved by using the liquid, especially in the case of meat, to make **gravy**.

dripping The fat that drips out of **meat** when it is being roasted, and is used for basting or for other cooking.

FREEZING: pour liquid dripping into small **rigid containers** and allow to become firm in the refrigerator. Seal and wrap in **foil** and freeze.

FREEZER LIFE: 3 months.

THAWING: allow to thaw in a refrigerator overnight.

dry freezing (also called **dry pack**) A method of freezing **fruits** without the use of sugar or syrup. Fruits that do not discolour badly, such as raspberries and strawberries, can be packed directly into **rigid containers** leaving a 1 cm ($\frac{1}{2}$ inch) **headspace**. See also **dry sugar pack**; **syrup pack**.

dry ice Solid carbon dioxide, used as a refrigerant when transporting food. Dry ice is generally used only in the commercial world and not in the home. It should never be allowed to come into direct contact with the food or its packaging.

dry pack See **dry freezing**.

dry sugar pack A method of packaging **fruit** in the freezer, using a combination of fruit mixed with dry sugar in a **rigid container**. A sugar pack is best suited for crushed or sliced fruit and for soft, juicy fruit, whose juices are easily drawn out. The fruit and sugar mix should be left to stand until the juice has formed and the sugar has dissolved.

Dublin bay prawns (also known as **langoustines**) A large prawn like a miniature lobster, which is usually sold ready frozen, but it can be home-frozen if bought absolutely fresh. As with all **shellfish**, it should be frozen within 12 hours of being caught to minimize the risk of **food poisoning**. Do not refreeze prawns that have already been frozen by the fishmonger. Fresh Dublin bay prawns are normally sold without their heads and claws and often pre-boiled.

FREEZING: raw prawns should be boiled gently in lightly salted water for about 8–10 minutes, then allowed to cool in their cooking liquid. Remove the shells and pack them tightly into **polythene bags**. Pre-boiled prawns should be shelled and packed tightly into polythene bags.

FREEZER LIFE: 1 month.

THAWING: if they are to be served in salads, the prawns should be allowed to thaw in the refrigerator for 3–4 hours before serving. Alternatively, they may be added to hot dishes from frozen, provided that they are heated through properly.

duck Any of a variety of aquatic birds and their meat, shot as game or raised domestically. Ducklings can be successfully frozen whole or in joints.

Older birds are best frozen when made into **casseroles** and **patés**. Choose young birds without too much **fat** because this may become **rancid** in the freezer.

FREEZING: remove **giblets** and pack separately in **polythene bags**. Wipe and dry whole ducklings and cover the legs in **foil**. Pack tightly in polythene bags, removing as much air as possible. Pack joints individually in **clingfilm**, then **overwrap** in polythene bags. Cold, cooked duckling may be frozen, wrapped in clingfilm and overwrapped in polythene bags.

FREEZER LIFE: duck, 6 months; giblets, 2 months; cold, cooked duckling, 2 months.

THAWING: it has now been suggested that **poultry** is better thawed in its wrappings at room temperature rather than in a refrigerator. A 1.4 kg (3lb) duckling needs about 9–10 hours, individual portions will need about 3–4 hours. Remember to thaw thoroughly before cooking. See **food poisoning**; **salmonella**.

duckling See **duck**.

dumpling A small ball of **dough** made from a mixture of flour, **suet** and seasonings. Savoury dumplings are added to **stews** and **casseroles** and may be frozen separately. **Fruit** dumplings, which are made with a piece of fresh fruit inside a dumpling case, are best frozen ready prepared, but not cooked.

FREEZING: prepare the dumplings in the usual way and place on baking trays. **Open freeze** until firm, then pack into **rigid containers**, separating the layers with small pieces of **greaseproof paper** or **freezer wrap**.

FREEZER LIFE: 3 months.

THAWING: fruit dumplings must be cooked from frozen in fast boiling water for up to 1 hour, depending on their size. Savoury dumplings must be defrosted overnight in the refrigerator before being added to other dishes.

duxelles A paste made from **mushrooms** including their stalks and peelings, which is used to flavour sauces, soups and casseroles, and in stuffings and savoury fillings. It can be frozen successfully.

FREEZING: make duxelles according to the recipe, then pack into small **rigid containers**. Seal securely leaving a small **headspace** for **expansion**.

FREEZER LIFE: 3 months.

THAWING: allow to thaw at room temperature in its container for 3–4 hours until soft enough to handle.

éclair A **cream cake** made from **choux pastry**, which can be frozen successfully, filled with cream and iced.

FREEZING: place both home-made and commercially baked éclairs without wrapping on trays in the freezer until firm. Then transfer to **rigid containers**, placing pieces of **freezer wrap** or **foil** between the layers.

FREEZER LIFE: up to 3 months.

THAWING: remove from containers and thaw in one layer on plates or trays at room temperature for about 1 hour.

eel A type of fish with a long snake-like body and reduced fins. The freshwater eel and **conger eel** can be frozen successfully, as can elvers (young eels).

FREEZING: skin, clean and remove the head. Cut into 5 cm (2 inch) slices, then wash again thoroughly and dry before packing into **polythene bags**. Wash and pack elvers in small quantities also in polythene bags.

FREEZER LIFE: 3 months.

THAWING: eels are best cooked from frozen.

egg The mature ovum of a chicken (or other poultry) protected by a calcified shell. Do not freeze eggs in their shells because they crack. Preferably, the yolks should be separated from the whites before freezing and only the freshest eggs used, although a whole egg mixture can be frozen and used in cooking. Hard-boiled eggs cannot be frozen because they become rubbery.

FREEZING: pack yolks and whites in **rigid containers**. For single egg yolks, add ½ teaspoon (2.5 ml) of salt or sugar. For every 6 egg yolks add 1 teaspoon (5 ml) of salt or 2 teaspoons (10 ml) of sugar. Freeze whole egg by beating eggs lightly together and adding 3 tbsp of sugar or ½ teaspoon salt to 900 ml (1½ pints) of mixture. Freeze in rigid containers with a 2.5 cm (1 inch) **headspace**.

FREEZER LIFE: 8–10 months for yolks and whites frozen separately; 6 months for whole egg mixture.

THAWING: allow the egg to thaw in a refrigerator for 4 hours for a 250 g (8 oz) block of egg yolk or white. Thaw egg mixture for 18–20 hours per pint (600 ml).

eggplant See **aubergine**.

elderberry The red, purple or black berry-like **fruit** of the elder shrub. Elderberries are not often found on sale commercially, but if enough can be found growing wild it is worthwhile to freeze them. They are best used to make elderberry syrup to supplement the fruit in **apple pies** and summer **puddings**.

FREEZING: spread the elderberries out on trays and **open freeze** until firm. Pack into **polythene bags**, extracting as much air as possible before **sealing**.

FREEZER LIFE: 6–8 months.

THAWING: allow whole **fruit** to thaw at room temperature for 3–4 hours. They can be used from frozen if the elderberries are to be cooked to make into a syrup.

elderflower The sprigs of cream-coloured flower heads of the elder shrub. Elderflowers can be dipped in **batter** and eaten as fritters. They are best eaten fresh because they do not freeze satisfactorily. Sec also **elderberry**.

elver See **eel**.

endive The crisp, curly leaves of a European plant with a bitter flavour. Due to its high water content endive does not freeze well. It stores perfectly well in plastic bags in the chilling compartment of the refrigerator.

enzyme A protein that acts as a catalyst in biochemical reactions. In **fruit** and **vegetables** the enzymes continue to be active during storage, causing **discoloration** and changes in flavour, unless a high temperature is introduced in the form of cooking or **blanching**. The enzymes present in other foods do not generally cause a problem except those in food with a high **fat** content, which eventually turn the fat **rancid**.

evaporator An integral part of a freezer, which consists of a system of coils that absorb the heat from frozen food, helping to keep the temperature at a constantly cold level.

expansion During the freezing process all foods and liquids expand, because the liquid within them expands as it turns into ice. It is most important when packing foods for the freezer that enough room is left in the top of the containers for this expansion to occur, otherwise the lids will be forced off, air will enter and cause the food to dry out, and lose its former texture and flavour. See **headspace**.

faggots A ball of chopped meat, usually pork liver, bound with cereal, **bacon**, **onion** and **spices**. Faggots can be purchased already made and ready frozen or home-made. They can be satisfactorily frozen.

FREEZING: prepare the faggots as usual and pack closely together into a freezer-proof dish. Cover with **foil** and **overwrap** in a **polythene bag**, extracting as much air as possible before **sealing**.

FREEZER LIFE: 2 months.

THAWING: allow to thaw in the refrigerator for 4–5 hours before cooking.

fast freezing A method whereby the temperature of new batches of fresh food introduced into the freezer is rapidly lowered. Most modern freezers have a fast-freeze switch or super-freeze switch, which overrides the freezer thermostat and takes the temperature down below –18°C. The newly introduced food is frozen quickly without affecting the temperature of the food already in the freezer. Food should reach 0°C in 24 hours and if it is frozen too slowly spoilage may result.

fat A large organic compound found in the body as body fat and as a nutrient in food with a high energy value. Fat within **meat** and **poultry** tends to turn **rancid** after freezing, so it is advisable to trim off as much fat as possible before freezing. Cooked dishes containing fat, such as **casseroles** and **stews** and **soups**, should be thoroughly cooled and skimmed of any excess fat before freezing.

Concentrated forms of fat, such as **butter**, **margarine**, **lard**, **dripping** and **suet**, can all be frozen successfully on their own for several months. However, do not freeze butter that has been made with unpasteurized milk. Wrap all fats well before freezing.

FREEZING: fats may be stored in their original wrappings, then overwrapped in **foil** or **freezer wrap**.

FREEZER LIFE: salted butter and margarine, 3 months, unsalted butter, lard and dripping, 6 months.

THAWING: allow to thaw in the refrigerator for about 4 hours per 250 g (8oz) block.

fennel The seeds and feathery leaves of a strong-smelling, yellow-flowered plant, which is used as a **herb** usually in **fish** dishes and **sauces**. The delicate fronds may be chopped up and frozen successfully.

FREEZING: wash and dry the fennel as thoroughly as possible. Chop finely and pack into **polythene bags**, extracting as much air as possible before **sealing**.

FREEZER LIFE: 6 months.

THAWING: fennel may be added to most dishes straight from the freezer.

fig The pear-shaped **fruit** pod of a tropical and sub-tropical tree, with smooth, fleshy, green or purple skin. Fresh and dried figs may be frozen, but choose only fresh, ripe undamaged figs.

FREEZING: wash fresh figs and remove the stems. Either **open freeze**, then pack in **polythene bags**, or peel, halve and slice and pack in syrup in **rigid containers**. Make the syrup with 250 g (8oz) of sugar to each 500 ml (1 pint) of water adding $\frac{3}{4}$ teaspoon of **ascorbic acid**. Allow a 2.5 cm (1 inch) **headspace** for expansion and hold the fruit under the syrup with crumpled **foil** before sealing. Dried figs freeze well if wrapped in foil or polythene bags.

FREEZER LIFE: fresh and dried figs, 1 year.

THAWING: allow to thaw at room temperature for about 2 hours.

filbert nut A flask-shaped nut with a firm husk, a variety of **hazelnut**. Filbert nuts can be satisfactorily frozen, keeping moist and fresh for up to a year. They may be frozen whole, chopped or flaked, but do not freeze salted nuts because they become **rancid** over time.

FREEZING: remove the husks from the nuts and pack into small containers or tight **foil** packages.

FREEZER LIFE: 1 year.

THAWING: allow the nuts to thaw at room temperature for 3 hours.

filo pastry A wafer-thin type of **pastry**, which is normally purchased already frozen. Fresh filo pastry may be frozen fully prepared if desired, or made up into cooked dishes.

FREEZING: pack uncooked pastry into **polythene bags**, extracting as much air as possible and seal securely.

FREEZER LIFE: uncooked pastry, 3 months.

THAWING: allow to thaw at room temperature for 2 hours or overnight in the refrigerator.

fish Any species of marine or freshwater cold-blooded aquatic vertebrates. All kinds of fresh fish may be frozen satisfactorily provided that they are absolutely fresh and have been caught and frozen within 24 hours. Most cooked fish dishes, such as pies, fish cakes, and kedgeree, can also be frozen successfully.

FREEZING: small fish should be washed, the gut, gills and fins removed, but the head and tail may be left on if desired. After washing and draining thoroughly, they should be wrapped tightly in **polythene bags**, excluding as much air as possible. Large fish, such as **haddock** and **cod**, are best cut into fillets and steaks and then frozen in individual packages in **clingfilm** and polythene bags. Large fish that are to be served whole, such as **salmon** and **trout**, should be **ice glazed**. Cooked dishes containing most types of fish can also be frozen successfully.

FREEZER LIFE: generally, white fish, 3 months; oily fish, 2 months; cooked fish dishes, 1 month.

THAWING: small fish, fillets and steaks can be cooked from frozen. Large ice glazed fish should be allowed to thaw in a cool place for 24 hours. Cooked fish dishes may be reheated from frozen. See **anchovy**; **bass**; **bloater**; **bream**; **brill**; **carp**; **catfish**; **coley**; **conger eel**; **dab**; **Dover sole**; **Dublin bay prawn**; **grey mullet**; **grouper**; **hake**; **hali-**

but; **herring**; **John Dory**; **lemon sole**; **mackerel**; **monkfish**; **perch**; **pike**; **pilchard**; **plaice**; **pollack**; **red mullet**; **red snapper**; **sea bass**; **skate**; **smelt**; **swordfish**; **tuna**; **turbot**; **whitebait**; **whiting**.

fish cake A type of **fish** rissole made from cooked white fish and **potato**. Fresh fish cakes or commercially prepared fish cakes can be frozen successfully.

FREEZING: pack in **rigid containers** with **interleaving** sheets of **freezer wrap** and **foil**. Or refer to the packaging for freezing instructions.

FREEZER LIFE: 3 months.

THAWING: best cooked from frozen.

fishfinger A rectangle of white **fish**, usually **cod**, covered with breadcrumbs, which is normally bought prepared and frozen. Fish fingers are a useful stand-by to have in the freezer, especially for children. Refer to packaging for storage times.

flan An open pastry or sponge tart, which may be filled with a sweet or savoury mixture. Cooked flans and flan cases can be useful items to store in the freezer. Savoury and sweet flan cases can be frozen, baked or unbaked, unfilled or filled.

FREEZING: allow unfilled, unbaked or baked, to **open freeze** in a flan ring or **foil** case until hard, remove ring or case and wrap in **polythene bags**. Pack carefully because they can easily become damaged. Filled flans, such as quiches should be baked and allowed to cool completely before open freezing and then placing in polythene bags.

FREEZER LIFE: unbaked, unfilled, 3 months; baked, unfilled, 6 months; baked and filled, 2 months.

THAWING: return unbaked flan cases to their original containers and bake from frozen. Allow baked flan cases to thaw at room temperature for 1 hour before filling. Thaw baked and filled flans for 2 hours at room temperature if they are to be served cold, or heat through from frozen if they are to be served hot.

flat-fold A particular way of wrapping **meat** or **fish** to ensure that no air is allowed to reach the food. The food is placed diagonally at one corner of a large sheet of **freezer wrap**. This corner is then folded over the food, and the package turned completely. The sides are then brought over the centre of the package and the package rolled to the opposite corner.

flavoured butter All types of savoury **butters** may be frozen.

FREEZING: beat the butter and chosen flavours together until well-mixed, then place on **freezer wrap** and shape into a roll. Roll the paper around the butter to cover it, then **overwrap** in a **polythene bag**.

FREEZER LIFE: 3 months.

THAWING: allow to thaw overnight in the refrigerator.

flavouring A substance added to food to give it a particular taste, which can be natural or artificial. Most artificial flavourings tend to become stronger in flavour during storage in the freezer, so it is best to use only half the recommended quantity. This particularly applies to synthetic **vanilla** flavouring, often used in **cakes** and **puddings**. See also **herb**; **spice**.

flounder (also called **fluke**) A European flatfish with a greyish-brown body and soft white flesh. Flounder can be frozen whole or in fillets.

FREEZING: for a whole fish, wash, remove the scales and gut then **ice glaze**. Place in **polythene bags** and return to the freezer. Fillets should be separated with **freezer wrap** and then also placed in polythene bags.

THAWING: allow whole fish to thaw for 24 hours in a cool place. Fillets may be cooked from frozen.

fluke See **flounder**.

foil A very thin sheet of aluminium for use in cooking and food storage. Aluminium foil can be used as a packaging material for frozen food, although it does tear easily. It is particularly useful for covering awkwardly shaped foods and bones in **meat** and **poultry**. Several thicknesses of foil are available and it is best to use the thickest for freezing. There are also many types of foil containers designed specifically for freezer use. These may be used to store cooked dishes, and can be washed and re-used many times. Most foil containers are sold with their own foil lids, if not it is necessary to **overwrap** them with **polythene bags**. Avoid storing **fruit** and other acidic foods in aluminium because the acid can react with the metal and cause pitting.

foil container See **foil**.

food poisoning An acute illness caused by foods or substances in them, and characterized by gastrointestinal inflammation, vomiting and diarrhoea. Food poisoning may be caused by **bacteria** (e.g. **listeria**), moulds, chemicals or toxic substances that occur naturally in foods.

Microorganisms are always present in food and they can survive at freezer temperatures, but they cannot multiply. They do multiply at higher temperatures, however, particularly over 10°C (50°F). It is vital that food is cooked and cooled as quickly as possible before freezing so that it does not stay at room temperature for longer than necessary. It is particularly important to keep cooked meat well-chilled because it can be susceptible to a particular bacteria, which produces toxins that are not destroyed by heat. Raw poultry may contain the **salmonella** bacteria and consequently it must always be thoroughly thawed and cooked, and not kept at room temperature for longer than necessary.

frankfurter A smoked sausage made of finely minced pork or beef, which can be frozen.

FREEZING: vacuum-packed frankfurters may be frozen in their own wrappings. Otherwise, pack into **polythene bags**.

FREEZER LIFE: 3 months.

FREEZER LIFE: allow to thaw overnight in the refrigerator.

free flow A method of freezing foods unwrapped to prevent large ice crystals from forming around the food. Commercially frozen items, such as minced **meat** and frozen **peas**, are often described as 'free-flow'. This method is also known as **open freezing**.

freezer bag A type of heavy-duty **polythene bag**, which is designed specifically for use in the freezer because it is strong and secure.

freezer burn A term used to describe grey-white patches that appear on food, particularly meat. Freezer burn is caused by exposure to the air, which is due to inadequate packaging. Freezer burn tends to dry out the meat, but it is still perfectly safe to use in cooked dishes, such as **casseroles** and **pies**. Other types of food may also suffer from freezer burn and this will result in loss of colour, flavour and texture.

freezer jam A **jam** with a low-sugar content, which makes it suitable for freezing. To prepare freezer jam, combine 1 kg (2lb) of fruit with 1.5 kg ($3\frac{1}{2}$lbs) of caster sugar and 4 tablespoons of lemon juice. Stir thoroughly and leave to stand until the sugar has completely dissolved. This may take from 20 minutes to 2 hours. Add 250 ml ($\frac{1}{2}$ pint) of commercially produced pectin and stir until the jam begins to set. Then pack into small freezer containers and seal securely. Do not use ordinary glass jam jars, because they may shatter.

freezer life A term that describes the length of time a food may be kept frozen without loss of flavour, texture and nutritional content. To ensure that the food is consumed in as good a condition as when it was first frozen it must be eaten within its recommended storage limits or freezer life. Food that is stored beyond its recommended freezer life is still perfectly safe to eat, but it will become poorer in quality.

freezer paper See **freezer wrap**.

freezer tape A special sticky tape designed for use in the freezer, which does not lose its adhesiveness at low temperatures. Freezer tape is used to seal bags, container lids and labels.

freezer wrap (also called **freezer paper**) 1. A type of strong, non-stick siliconized paper, similar to greaseproof and bakewell paper specially designed for wrapping foods that are to be stored in the freezer.

2. A type of heavy-duty **clingfilm**, designed specifically for use in the freezer.

freezing capacity The amount of fresh food that may be frozen successfully in any 24 hour period. It is usually about one tenth of the total storage capcity, although some modern machines may be able to cope with more than this. It is important to refer to the manufacturer's instructions in order to get the maximum benefits from the freezer.

French bean The slender, green pods of a small twining plant. French beans can be frozen satisfactorily. Young, thin beans freeze best, but bigger ones may also be frozen as long as they are not stringy.

FREEZING: wash, trim both ends and **blanch** for 1–2 minutes. Cool, drain and **open freeze** on trays. When firm, pack into **polythene bags**, expelling as much air as possible before sealing.

FREEZER LIFE: 1 year.

THAWING: cook from frozen in boiling water.

fridge-freezer A combination unit of a standard refrigerator with a freezer compartment attached. This type of unit is very useful if space is limited and for use by a single person or small families.

fromage frais (also called **fromage blanc**) A smooth, fluid, white **cheese**, which can be frozen provided it has a **fat** content of at least 35–40%. Always check the manufacturers, instructions because some brands of fromage frais may not be suitable for freezing.

FREEZING: fromage frais may be left in its original containers, as long as there is a little **headspace**, then **overwrapped** in a **polythene bag**. Alternatively, it may be transferred into a small **rigid container**, leaving a headspace of 2.5 cm (1 inch).

FREEZER LIFE: 1 month.

THAWING: allow to thaw in the refrigerator for about 4 hours. Whip well before using because it may separate out during the freezing and thawing process.

frost A white deposit of frozen moisture, which forms on the walls, shelves and items inside a freezer. Frost should be removed regularly so that the freezer can continue to work efficiently. If frost builds up on the inside of food packages, it is generally due to bad packaging. The package may not be airtight which allows air to enter, or the air was not expelled sufficiently before **sealing**. The air then picks up the moisture from the food, causing it to dry out.

fruit The fleshy, ripened ovary of a flowering plant, containing one or more seeds. Fruit tends to change in consistency more than any other food in the freezer. Generally, the juicier the fruit the more it will soften on **thawing**. The majority of fruits can be frozen in some form or another except for **melon** and **bananas**, which do not freeze well.

It is best to freeze fruit in **rigid containers** to avoid any leaking. It can be frozen in a **syrup pack**, a **dry sugar pack** or a **dry pack**. Most fruits that tend to discolour are best frozen in syrup, as are fruits that contain little juice. Fruits that are juicy are best stored in a dry sugar pack. The proportion of sugar to fruit is approximately 500 g (1lb) of sugar to every 1.5–2.25 kg (3–5 lb) of fruit, depending on the sweetness of the fruit. Other fruits, such as **grapes**, **gooseberries** and **rhubarb**, are most successfully frozen in a dry pack in rigid containers. **Ascorbic acid** is often added to fruit before freezing to prevent it from discolouring. See **apple**; **apricot**; **blackberry**; **blackcurrant**; **blueberry**; **cape gooseberry**; **cherry**; **clementine**; **crab apple**; **cranberry**; **damson**; **date**; **fig**; **grapefruit**; **greengage**; **guava**; **kiwi fruit**; **kumquat**; **lemon**; **lime**; **loganberry**; **lychee**; **mandarin**; **mango**; **nectarine**; **orange**; **papaya**; **passion fruit**; **peach**; **pear**;, **pineapple**; **plum**; **pomegranate**; **rambutan**; **raspberry**; **redcurrant**; **rowanberry**; **satsuma**; **star fruit**; **strawberry**; **tangerine**; **tayberry**; **ugli fruit**; **whortleberry**.

fruit juice Most fresh **fruit** juices can be frozen in **rigid containers** quite successfully, but do not freeze in plastic or glass containers.

FREEZING: mince or purée fruit until it is as liquid as possible. Strain through muslin or a fine sieve and allow to drip into a bowl. Sweeten to taste if desired and pack into rigid containers, allowing a 2 cm (¾ inch) **headspace**. Commerically prepared cartons of fresh fruit juice can be frozen in their containers, but it is preferable to transfer them into rigid containers because they tend to expand

and could therefore burst their original cartons. Fruit juices may also be frozen in ice cube trays, then packed in **polythene bags**.

FREEZER LIFE: home-made generally, 4–6 months; commercial juices should be frozen according to the manufacturer's instructions.

THAWING: allow to thaw at room temperatue for about 2 hours. See **apple juice**; **blackcurrant juice**; **grapefruit juice**; **lemon juice**; **orange juice**; **pineapple juice**; **tomato juice**.

fruit purée A smooth, thick pulp of stewed and sieved fruit. Fresh fruit purée can be frozen very successfully and can be used to make a variety of **puddings**, **sauces** and drinks.

FREEZING: stew the fruit with a little water, strain and then sieve to make a purée. Sweeten if desired. Pack the purée into **rigid containers**, leaving a 2.5 cm (1 inch) **headspace** before **sealing** and freeze upright until firm.

FREEZER LIFE: 1 year.

THAWING: allow the purée to thaw for several hours at room temperature in its container. As it begins to thaw, stir the purée to break up the large ice crystals.

fruit salad A dish consisting of fruits cut up and served in a syrup. Any fruits that are suitable for freezing may be combined in a sugar syrup and frozen as a fruit salad. This can be stored successfully for up to a year.

FREEZING: make a sugar syrup by dissolving 250 g (8 oz) of sugar in 500 ml (1 pint) of water. Bring it to the boil and then leave to cool. When freezing fruits that are likely to discolour, such as **apples**, **pears** and **peaches**, add the juice of one **lemon** or $\frac{1}{4}$ teaspoon of **ascorbic acid** to the syrup. Cut the fruit up into the syrup and pack into **rigid containers**. Leave a 2 cm (1 inch) **headspace** and place a piece of crumpled **foil** on top of the fruit to immerse it completely in the syrup. Seal securely and freeze upright until firm.

FREEZER LIFE: 1 year.

THAWING: allow the fruit salad to thaw overnight in the refrigerator.

fudge A soft sweet made from sugar, butter and cream and in a variety of flavours. It is possible to freeze all kinds of fudge.

FREEZING: prepare the fudge mixture as usual, but pour into **foil** containers to set. Cover with foil, seal and freeze. Ready made fudge can be stored in **rigid containers** with small sheets of **freezer wrap** dividing up the layers.

FREEZER LIFE: 3 months.

THAWING: allow to thaw at room temperature for about 30 minutes.

game Any animal or bird that is shot for sport and eaten. All kinds of game freeze satisfactorily, but it is important to hang it first to ensure maximum flavour, and to clean and prepare thoroughly. Choose young, plump animals and birds, and do not freeze any that have been damaged.

FREEZING: prepare game birds by removing their gut and trussing them, cover any bones with **foil**, then pack into **polythene bags**, freezing the **giblets** separately. Wrap **hare**, **rabbit** and **venison** in **freezer wrap**, then **overwrap** in polythene bags.

FREEZER LIFE: game birds, 9 months; hare and rabbit, 8 months; venison, 1 year.

THAWING: it has now been discovered that it is best to thaw game birds in their wrappings at room temperature rather than in the refrigerator. See **capercaillie**; **duck**; **grouse**; **partridge**; **pheasant**; **ptarmigan**; **quail**; **snipe**; **woodcock**.

gammon The cured leg of a pig. See **bacon**.

garlic The bulb of a small Asian plant made up of segments (cloves) and with a pungent flavour. Bulbs of garlic store quite adequately in a cool place, but can be frozen if necessary. However, do not freeze chopped or crushed garlic because it tends to develop an unpleasant flavour. Avoid using garlic in cooked dishes that are meant for the freezer as the flavour tends to deteriorate and affect the taste of the finished dish.

FREEZING: wrap bulbs of garlic in **foil** or **freezer wrap**, then **overwrap** in a **polythene bag**.

FREEZER LIFE: 3 months.

THAWING: allow to thaw for a few minutes at room temperature before using.

gateau Any of various elaborate, rich **cakes** usually made with cream. Gateau can be frozen complete or in parts, as sponge bases, fillings and toppings. Avoid using **fruit** prior to freezing because this tends to make the sponge soggy.

FREEZING: freeze sponges in **polythene bags** and **icings** and toppings in small containers. If freezing whole, completed gateaux, **open freeze** until firm then place in a polythene bag inside a **rigid container** to give it extra protection.

FREEZER LIFE: 3 months.

THAWING: remove gateaux from the wrappings and allow to thaw at room temperature for 2–6 hours, depending on size and thickness.

gelatin or **gelatine** A colourless or yellowish water-soluble protein. Desserts containing gelatin do not freeze very well because the gelatin tends to 'sweat' during the freezing and thawing process, although creamy mixtures containing sugar, such as **mousses**, freeze adequately.

FREEZING: mousses may be frozen in moulds or dishes, wrapped in **clingfilm** and **overwrapped** in a **polythene bag**.

FREEZER LIFE: 1 month.

THAWING: allow to thaw at room temperature for 4–6 hours.

ghee A type of **butter** clarified by boiling, used traditionally in Indian cooking. It can be frozen in a similar way to butter.

FREEZING: leave in original containers, but **overwrap** with **foil** or **freezer wrap**.

FREEZER LIFE: salted and unsalted, 6 months.

THAWING: allow to thaw in the refrigerator for 2 hours per 500 g (1 lb).

giblets The gizzard, liver, heart and neck of a fowl. **Poultry** and **game** should always be frozen without their giblets because these have shorter storage life. They may be frozen separately for a short while and then used in **patés**, **stocks** and **soups**.

FREEZING: clean thoroughly and pack into **polythene bags**.

FREEZER LIFE: 2 months.

THAWING: allow to thaw in the refrigerator overnight before using.

ginger The spicy, pungent underground stem of an Indian plant, which is used fresh or dried and powdered as a **spice** to give flavour to food. Ginger can be purchased either as root ginger, dried, or stem ginger. Root ginger stores well in a cool, dry place, but can be frozen if desired. Dried ginger stores well in an airtight jar for up to a year. If dried ginger is included in dishes that are to be frozen it may develop an unpleasant flavour or fade after 3–4 months, so it is best not to leave these dishes in the freezer for longer than 2 months. Stem ginger is usually preserved in syrup and stores well in an airtight jar in a cool dry place.

FREEZING: wrap ginger roots in **foil** or **freezer wrap** and **overwrap** in a **polythene bag**.

FREEZER LIFE: 3 months.

THAWING: allow the ginger to thaw for a few minutes at room temperature before using.

glacé fruit Any of various crystallized or candied fruit. All types of glacé fruits can normally be purchased around the Christmas season, so it is worth buying them and freezing a supply for future use. They remain moist and fresh in the freezer.

FREEZING: leave in the containers they were purchased and **overwrap** in **foil** or a **polythene bag**.

FREEZER LIFE: 1 year.

THAWING: thaw in their containers at room temperature for 3–4 hours.

glass Bottles and other glass containers should not be used in the freezer if possible. Glass is very likely to shatter because of the expansion of liquids on freezing and the uneven contraction of glass when thawing. There are, however, some glass containers that claim to be freezer-proof, but check that they are safe. Always overwrap any glass with polythene bags in case it breaks for any reason.

globe artichoke The large, thistle-like flower bud of an Asian plant, which can be frozen satisfactorily. Choose fresh green artichokes with no dry edges; the freshest ones generally have curled leaves rather than open ones.

FREEZING: remove outer leaves, wash thoroughly and trim the stems. **Blanch** in boiling water for 7 minutes, then plunge them immediately into ice cold water. Drain and cool completely, then pack into **polythene bags**.

FREEZER LIFE: 1 year.

THAWING: allow to thaw overnight in the refrigerator or for 4–5 hours at room temperature. Alternatively, cook from frozen in water with a little lemon juice (to prevent **discoloration**) for 10–15 minutes until tender.

gnocchi A dumpling made of semolina **pasta**, which are so simple to make fresh that there seems little point in freezing them. However, if cooked and finished with a **sauce** they are useful as a frozen ready meal.

FREEZING: cook gnocchi in boiling water for a few minutes until tender, make the sauce according to the recipe used and combine in a **foil** container. Allow to cool completely before **overwrapping** in a **polythene bag** and freezing.

FREEZER LIFE: cooked gnocchi with a sauce, 2–3 months.

THAWING: remove the lid from the foil container and heat from frozen, covering if necessary during cooking.

golden bass See **grouper**.

goose The rich, fatty flesh of the goose, a **poultry** bird. Geese are normally sold oven-ready or frozen. If freezing a fresh one choose a bird without too much **fat**.

FREEZING: cover the bones with **foil** and pack the whole bird in a **polythene bag**, extracting as much air as possible before sealing. Pack the **giblets** separately.

FREEZER LIFE: because it contains so much fat goose does not have a long storage life and should only be frozen for up to 4 months. Giblets may be frozen for 2 months.

THAWING: it is now believed that all poultry should be thawed at room temperature rather than in the refrigerator, so allow goose to thaw for approximatcly 18 24 hours for a bird weighing 6–7 kg (12–15 lb).

gooseberry The pale green or deep red **fruit** of a Eurasian shrub. Gooseberries may be frozen whole or puréed. Underripe gooseberries may be used if freezing for future jam-making, but otherwise choose firm, ripe fruit.

FREEZING: wash, dry, top and tail the fruit. Either (a), pack the fruit whole without **sugar** in **polythene bags**, for use in various desserts; or (b), stew with a little water and sugar until soft, then sieve, cool and pack in **rigid containers** allowing a ½ inch (1 cm) **headspace**.

FREEZER LIFE: 1 year.

THAWING: the whole fruit may be cooked from frozen, but the purée should be allowed to thaw overnight in the refrigerator.

granita A type of **sorbet** frozen in its granular state.

FREEZING: make as the recipe states, then pour into **rigid containers**, leaving a 2.5 cm (1 inch) **headspace**.

FREEZER LIFE: 2 months.

THAWING: allow to thaw at room temperature for about 10 minutes before serving.

grape The purple or green fruit of the grapevine. Most kinds of grape can be frozen although they do tend to become soft and can become mushy on **thawing**. Choose plump grapes with no bruising or blemishes.

FREEZING: seedless grapes can be frozen whole, but other types should be skinned, halved and the pips removed. Pack in a syrup, made with 250 g (8 oz) of sugar to every 600 ml (1 pint) of water, and place in **rigid containers** leaving a 2.5 cm (1 inch) **headspace**.

FREEZER LIFE: 1 year.

THAWING: allow to thaw at room temperature for about 2 hours.

grapefruit A large, yellow or pink (ruby) citrus **fruit**, which may be frozen successfuly.

FREEZING: peel the fruit, remove all the pith and divide into segments. Either (a), **dry sugar pack** the fruit by layering it with 125–175 g (4–6 oz) of sugar to every 500 g (1lb) of fruit, and placing into **rigid containers**; or (b), **syrup pack** it in a heavy syrup of 500 g (1lb) of sugar to every 600 ml (1 pint) of water, and pack in rigid containers leaving a 2.5 cm (1 inch) **headspace**.

FREEZER LIFE: whole fruit, 1 year.

THAWING: allow to thaw overnight in the refrigerator.

grapefruit juice The juice of the **grapefruit**. Fresh grapefruit juice can be frozen satisfactorily either sweetened or unsweetened. Both yellow and ruby grapefruits may be used.

FREEZING: halve the grapefruits and squeeze out as much juice as possible, taking care not to press too hard into the pith because this will give the juice a pithy flavour. Sweeten with sugar or syrup if desired and pour into **rigid containers** leaving a 2 cm (1 inch) **headspace** before **sealing**.

FREEZER LIFE: 4–6 months.

THAWING: allow the grapefruit juice to thaw overnight in the refrigerator before serving. See also **fruit juice**.

gravy The juices from roasting meat. Gravy can be frozen successfully, although it should be thoroughly whisked or liquidized on thawing before using again. Gravy can also be used to cover cold cooked **meat** that is to be frozen to prevent it from drying out and to provide a sauce for when it is thawed.

FREEZING: freeze in small quantities in **rigid containers**, allowing a 2.5 cm (1 inch) **headspace**.

FREEZER LIFE: 3 months.

THAWING: allow to thaw gently from frozen by **reheating** in a saucepan.

greaseproof paper A type of wrapping material that is not really suitable for using alone in the freezer. Greaseproof paper may be used to separate foods such as **beefburgers** and **chops**, and as an initial wrapping for bought goods such as **butter**, but these must then be **overwrapped** in **foil** or a **polythene bag**.

greengage A small, green plumlike **fruit**, which may be frozen either packed in syrup or stewed. It is also possible to freeze the fruit whole, but the skins become leathery and tough and the stones taint the fruit, so it is not recommended. Choose firm, ripe greengages with no bruises or blemishes.

FREEZING: wash the fruit thoroughly and dry. Either (a), halve and stone the fruit then pack into **rigid containers**, leaving a 2.5 cm (1 inch) **headspace**; or (b), halve, stone and stew the fruit, then pack in rigid containers leaving a little headpsace.

FREEZER LIFE: 1 year.

THAWING: allow the stewed fruit to thaw at room temperature. for about 2 hours. The uncooked fruit may be cooked from frozen.

grey mullet See **mullet**.

grouper A large white-fleshed fish, which is a delicacy in Mediterranean countries. Grouper is sold whole, weighing up to 6 kg (15lb), in steaks and fillets and can be frozen successfully. It is sometimes found under the name of golden bass.

FREEZING: for a whole fish, wash, remove the scales and gut, and dry as much as possible, then **ice glaze**. Transfer the fish to a large **polythene bag** or wrap in **foil** to store. **Interleave** steaks and fillets with small pieces of **freezer wrap** and **overwrap** in a polythene bag or piece of foil.

FREEZER LIFE: 3 months.

THAWING: allow the whole fish to thaw in a cool place for up to 24 hours, depending on its size, then use as soon as possible. Steaks and fillets can be cooked from frozen or allowed to thaw in the refrigerator for a few hours before using.

grouse A **game** bird that is available from 12th August to 10th December.

FREEZING: prepare the grouse by cleaning it thoroughly, inside and out, and removing the **giblets** to freeze separately. Pack in a **polythene bag**, extracting as much air as possible before sealing.

FREEZER LIFE: 6 months.

THAWING: allow to thaw in the refrigerator for about 5 hours per 500 g (1lb).

guava The small, pale yellow **fruit** of a tropical American tree. Guava is best frozen either as a purée or cooked in syrup.

FREEZING: either (a), purée the fruit and pack into **rigid containers**, leaving a 2.5 cm (1 inch) **headspace**; or (b), wash, peel and halve the fruit and cook in a syrup made with 250 g (8 oz) of sugar to every 500 ml (1 pint) of water, then pack in rigid containers, leaving a little headspace.

FREEZER LIFE: 1 year.

THAWING: allow to thaw at room temperature for about 2 hours.

guinea fowl A bird that can be frozen like chicken.

FREEZING: prepare guinea fowl by cleaning and removing **giblets** to freeze separately if desired. Do not stuff before freezing. Cover bones with small pieces of **foil** then place in a large **polythene bag**, extracting as much air as possible.

FREEZER LIFE: 10 months.

THAWING: allow to thaw in the refrigerator for 24 hours. The **meat** tends to be a little dry, so it is preferable to roast or **casserole** it using plenty of **fat** or liquid.

haddock An Atlantic white **fish**, similar to **cod**, which may be frozen either fresh or smoked, cooked or uncooked. It should be as fresh as possible.

FREEZING: fresh haddock should be washed thoroughly, then divided into fillets or steaks. These should be separated with small sheets of **freezer wrap** and then wrapped in **polythene bags**. Cooked haddock can be frozen very successfully in a variety of **sauces**. Raw or cooked smoked haddock should be wrapped in a polythene bag, extracting as much air as possible before sealing.

FREEZER LIFE: fresh and smoked haddock, 2 months; cooked haddock, 1 month.

THAWING: all types of haddock may be cooked from frozen.

haggis A traditional Scottish dish made with **offal**, oats and **suet** tightly packed into a skin made from the animal's stomach and boiled. A commercially produced haggis may be frozen for up to 2 months after which time it must be thawed and steamed thoroughly and consumed promptly.

FREEZING: pack haggis into a **polythene bag** and extract as much air as possible before **sealing**.

FREEZER LIFE: 1–2 months.

THAWING: allow to thaw completely, overnight in the refrigerator, then steam to reheat and eat while piping hot.

hake A marine **fish** similar to **cod**. Small hake are usually sold whole, but larger ones may be divided into steaks or fillets.

FREEZING: for a whole fish, first wash, remove the scales and gut, then **ice glaze**. Pack the fish in a **polythene bag** and expel as much air as possible. Separate fillets or steaks with **greaseproof paper** or **foil**, then pack tightly into polythene bags.

FREEZER LIFE: 3 months.

THAWING: allow whole fish to thaw in a cool place for about 24 hours. Steaks and fillets may be cooked from frozen.

halibut A North Atlantic white **fish** that is the largest flatfish and is sold in fillets or steaks.

FREEZING: separate fillets and steaks with small sheets of **greaseproof paper** or **foil**, then pack into **polythene bags**, extracting as much air as possible.

FREEZER LIFE: 3 months.

THAWING: fillets and steaks may be cooked from frozen.

ham The meat of the hindquarters of pig, which is cured and usually smoked. Raw and cooked ham may be frozen, but it has a limited freezer life because it contains a large amount of **salt**, which turns it **rancid** in a short time.

FREEZING: wrap raw ham in **freezer wrap**, then **overwrap** in a **polythene bag**, extracting as much air as possible. Cooked ham may be frozen in one whole piece or sliced and packed in polythene bags, **interleaving** the slices with freezer wrap. Chopped ham may also be frozen packed tightly into polythene bags for use in fillings and salads.

FREEZER LIFE: raw ham, 2 months; cooked ham, 1 month.

THAWING: allow joints of ham to thaw overnight in the refrigerator. Thaw slices in their wrappings in the refrigerator for about 3 hours.

hamburger See **beefburger**.

hare A **game** mammal, which is seasonal and is usually only available between August and February. Hare is normally sold hung and ready prepared, but if not it is important that it is hung by its feet for 7–10 days before freezing. A bowl should be placed underneath the hare so that the blood can be collected and used in the gravy, which is especially important in recipes for jugged hare.

FREEZING: skin the hare, remove intestines and clean thoroughly, inside and out, with a damp cloth. It can then be frozen either whole or cut into joints. Pack into **polythene bags** and extract as much air as possible before stealing. Freeze the blood separately if desired in small cartons.

FREEZER LIFE: 6 months; blood, 6 months.

THAWING: allow to thaw in its bags in the refrigerator for about 5 hours per 500 g (1lb). Thaw the blood overnight in the refrigerator.

hazelnut (also called **cob nut**) The small **nut** of the hazel shrub, which may be satisfactorily frozen, keeping moist and fresh for up to a year. Hazelnuts may be frozen either whole, chopped, flaked or toasted, but do not freeze salted nuts.

FREEZING: pack in small containers or tight **foil** packages.

FREEZER LIFE: 1 year; if buttered and toasted, 4 months.

THAWING: allow to thaw at room temperature for 3 hours.

headspace The air space that should be left between the lid of a **rigid container** and the food it contains in order to allow for the **expansion** of food when frozen. Liquid and semi-liquid foods expand by one-ninth of their volume when frozen. If there is no space the pack will burst open when the contents expand. Allow a headspace of between 1–2.5 cm (½–1 inch) for most items, but if more is left, fill the gap with crumpled **greaseproof paper** to block out the air. Cover purées likely to **discolour** with **clingfilm**.

heart A type of **offal**, usually calf or lamb. Hearts can be frozen either raw or cooked.

FREEZING: trim away any **fat** and blood vessels and wash thoroughly in cold water. Drain and pat dry before packing tightly in **polythene bags**. A cooked heart should be allowed to cool completely then packed into a **rigid container**.

FREEZER LIFE: raw, 3 months; cooked, 2 months.

THAWING: allow raw hearts to thaw in the refrigerator for about 5 hours per 500 g (1lb). Cooked hearts may be reheated from frozen.

heat sealer A machine that seals **polythene bags**, or can enable you to make your own size of bags from a sleeve of polythene. A similar effect can be achieved by placing a cool iron over a sheet of paper on a polythene bag in order to seal it.

herb Any of various aromatic plants used to add flavour to food. Most fresh herbs freeze very successfully, but for preference choose young and tender herbs and pack either in sprigs or chopped up.

FREEZING: wash and dry all herbs before freezing. Pack sprigs, when completely dry, into **polythene bags**. Otherwise, chop herbs finely and freeze in small plastic containers or bags. They can also be frozen in ice cube trays covered with a little water, then transferred into polythene bags.

FREEZER LIFE: 6 months.

THAWING: herbs can be added to most dishes, straight from the freezer. See **basil**; **bouquet garni**; **chervil**; **chive**; **coriander**; **dill**; **fennel**; **marjoram**; **mint**; **oregano**; **parsley**; **rosemary**; **sage**; **tarragon**; **thyme**.

herring A marine, soft-finned, fatty **fish**, which may be frozen if fresh.

FREEZING: remove scales, gut and wash thoroughly. The head and tail may be left on if desired. Remove the backbone and as many other bones as possible, then open out and pack in pairs in **polythene bags**, **interleaving** each fish with **freezer wrap**.

FREEZER LIFE: 3 months.

THAWING: herrings may be grilled or fried from frozen.

hollandaise sauce A rich **sauce** of butter and egg usually served with fish. Hollandaise is one of the few sauces that does not freeze successfully. It separates when frozen and thawed, and it cannot be whisked back to the same consistency.

horseradish The pungent white root of a Eurasian plant. Young horseradish roots may be frozen either grated or minced or made into horseradish **sauce**.

FREEZING: grate or mince roots, then sprinkle with white wine vinegar to prevent **discoloration**. Pack in small **rigid containers** and seal well. If preparing horseradish sauce for the freezer, grate or mince the roots, mix with **cream** and **lemon juice** and freeze in small rigid containers.

FREEZER LIFE: fresh horseradish, 6 months; horseradish sauce, 2 months.

THAWING: allow both fresh horseradish and horseradish sauce to thaw in their containers in the refrigerator for about 4–6 hours.

hot water pastry See **pastry**.

hummus, hoummos or houmous An off-white paste made from chickpeas, tahini and **garlic**, which can be frozen. It is better to leave the garlic out until it is thawed because this can develop an unpleasant taste in the freezer.

FREEZING: if freezing home-made hummus, pack into small **rigid containers** leaving a little **headspace**. Shop-bought hummus can develop an unpleasant taste after freezing due to the high garlic content, but if necessary it may be left in its original cartons and **overwrapped** in a **polythene bag**.

FREEZER LIFE: 1 month.

THAWING: allow to thaw overnight in the refrigerator.

ice cream A sweetened frozen liquid made either from cream and egg yolks or from milk or a custard base, flavoured in various ways. Both home-made ice creams and bought ice creams can be stored in the freezer, although they should not be stored for too long because the texture tends to become grainy. Avoid ice creams with synthetic flavouring if possible.

FREEZING: freeze home-made ice creams either in moulds or in **rigid containers** and **overwrap** in a **polythene bag**. Freeze bought ice creams in their containers, but overwrap with polythene bags.

FREEZER LIFE: home-made ice cream, 2–3 months; commercial ice cream, 1 month or as directed on the pack.

THAWING: allow to soften a little before serving. Soft-scoop ice cream can be used straight from the freezer as long as it has not been stored in the coldest part.

ice cubes Both plain ice cubes and flavoured ice cubes can be made in ice cube trays and transferred into **polythene bags** to provide a large stock.

FREEZING: freeze plain water, **fruit juice** or **coffee** in ice cube trays until solid. Add small pieces of **cherries**, **lemon** rind or a little food colouring if desired. When firm, tip the cubes into a polythene bag, extracting as much air as possible before **sealing** and return to the freezer as quickly as possible.

FREEZER LIFE: plain ice cubes, 1 month; flavoured ice cubes, 2 months.

iced lollies Unsweeetened **fruit juices** and diluted cordials can be frozen successfully to produce home-made iced lollies.

FREEZING: pour prepared fruit juice into iced lolly moulds and insert a stick. Place several on a tray and freeze at the top of the freezer until firm.

FREEZER LIFE: 2 months.

ice glaze A method of sealing a **fish** with ice to preserve its flavour and to protect it in the freezer. To ice-glaze a fish, clean and prepare it in the usual manner, then **open freeze** until solid. Remove it from the freezer and dip it into ice cold fresh water, which causes a thin film of ice to form over the fish. It should then be returned to the freezer to keep it solid. This procedure should then be repeated at about three or four half-hourly intervals until there is 0.5 cm ($\frac{1}{4}$ inch) of ice covering the fish. The whole fish should then be placed in a thick **polythene bag**, expelling as much air as possible, and stored in the freezer.

icing A variously flavoured sugar preparation used to coat foods, particularly **cakes**. The most satisfactory icing to freeze is **buttercream** because all flavours of buttercream freeze very well. Boiled icings, soft meringue icing, fondant and royal icing do not freeze well. They tend to become soft, dry and crumbly or sticky on thawing. Baked cakes filled with buttercream and iced with glacé icing can be successfully frozen although it is important to **open freeze** any cakes with glacé icing first, to prevent the icing from becomimg damaged.

FREEZING: pack icings into small containers to freeze. Iced cakes should be allowed to open freeze and then be packed in **polythene bags** , expelling as much air as possible.

FREEZER LIFE: icings and iced cakes, 3 months.

THAWING: remove iced cakes from their bags and allow to thaw at room temperature for about 2 hours. Thaw buttercream icing at room temperature for about 2–3 hours per 250 g (8 oz) in its containers.

insurance Freezer insurance is a sensible precaution to take if a freezer is used frequently for bulk, long-term storage. If the machine breaks down filled with food a great deal of money could be wasted. Freezer insurance covers the food and the servicing of the machine. It is important to check the smallprint of the insurance policy because if the freezer is unplugged or switched off by mistake, rather than suffering from an electrical fault or machine breakdown, the policy may not cover these circumstances. See also **breakdown**; **power cut**; **refreezing**.

interleaving A method of separating items, such as **chops**, **beefburgers** and fillets of **fish**, with small sheets of **clingfilm**, **foil** or **greaseproof paper** so that individual pieces can be removed from the freezer. Once frozen some items are impossible to separate, so interleaving avoids having to thaw more than is required.

jam (also called **conserve**) A confection of fresh fruit and sugar boiled together until set. Jam with a low-sugar content may be stored in the freezer and is sometimes known as **freezer jam**.

FREEZING: pack in small containers or plastic cartons. Do not use **glass** jam jars in the freezer because they are likely to shatter.

FREEZER LIFE: 3 months.

THAWING: allow to thaw in its container in a cool place overnight.

jelly A fruit-flavoured gel set with **gelatin**. Packets of jelly made up with **milk** or evaporated milk freeze well, but clear fruit jellies do not as they become granular and cloudy in the freezer.

FREEZING: make milk jellies in jelly moulds, cover with **clingfilm** and **overwrap** with a **polythene bag**.

FREEZER LIFE: 1 month.

THAWING: allow to thaw at room temperature for 3–4 hours.

Jerusalem artichoke The tuber of a variety of North American sunflower. It is a root **vegetable** best frozen as a purée.

FREEZING: scrub and peel the artichokes, cut up into small pieces and cook gently with **butter** and **stock** until tender. Purée in a liquidizer and pack into **rigid containers**, leaving a 2.5 cm (1 inch) **headspace**.

FREEZER LIFE: 3 months.

THAWING: the purée can be reheated from frozen.

John Dory A European flatfish sold either whole or in fillets.

FREEZING: for a whole fish, wash, remove the scales and intestines then **ice glaze**. Pack the fish in a **polythene bag** and return to the freezer. Separate fillets with **freezer wrap** and **overwrap** in a polythene bag.

FREEZER LIFE: 3 months.

THAWING: allow the whole fish to thaw in a cool place for 24 hours, then use as soon as possible. Fillets may be cooked from frozen.

juice, fruit See **fruit juice**.

juice, vegetable See **vegetable juice**.

kale A variety of cabbage with crinkled leaves. It can be frozen, but afterwards it is only suitable for use in **soups** and **purées**. Pick young, tender leaves.

FREEZING: wash thoroughly, then **blanch** in boiling water for 2 minutes. Cool, drain and pack into **polythene bags**, extracting as much air as possible before sealing.

FREEZER LIFE: 9 months.

THAWING: cook from frozen.

kebab (also called **shish kebab**) A dish of cubed pieces of **meat** and **vegetables** threaded onto skewers. The meat and vegetable cubes can be marinated and frozen ready for use.

FREEZING: chop up the required meat and vegetables and marinate for 2–4 hours. Remove from the marinade and thread onto skewers. Cover the sharp ends with **foil**, then wrap each kebab completely in foil, then **overwrap** several together in a **polythene bag** to freeze. Pour the marinade into a **rigid container** to freeze. Alternatively, the meat and vegetables can be packed, unskewered in rigid containers in the marinade and frozen, allowing a 2.5 cm (1 inch) **headspace**.

FREEZER LIFE: lamb kebabs, 3 months; pork kebabs, 2 months.

THAWING: thaw marinade and baste kebabs. Cook skewered kebabs from frozen. Allow unskewered kebabs to thaw in the marinade overnight in the refrigerator.

kedgeree A cooked dish of **rice**, flaked **fish** and hard-boiled eggs, which freezes very well.

FREEZING: cook 500 g (1lb) of fish to every 175 g (6 oz) of long grain rice. When cooked flake the fish into the rice and stir in 25 g (1 oz) of melted **butter** and 1–2 tablespoons of chopped fresh **parsley**. Allow to cool completely then pack into **polythene bags**, expelling as much air as possible before **sealing**.

FREEZER LIFE: 1 month.

THAWING: kedgeree may be cooked from frozen. Melt a little butter in a pan and tip the frozen kedgeree into it. Heat gently, breaking it up with a fork, then add chopped hard boiled **eggs**, seasoning and serve.

kidney A type of **offal**, from a calf, lamb, pig or ox, which can be frozen successfully.

FREEZING: trim the kidneys of any **fat** and thin skin and wash and dry well. **Open freeze** on trays until firm, then pack them into **polythene bags**, extracting as much air as possible. Kidneys can also be bought ready-frozen, and these must be put in the home freezer as soon as possible after purchase.

FREEZER LIFE: 3 months.

THAWING: allow to thaw in the refrigerator for 3–4 hours.

kipper A salted smoked **herring**. Freshly smoked kippers can be frozen satisfactorily.

FREEZING: pack the kippers individually in **clingfilm**, then **overwrap** in **polythene bags**. They have a strong smell so seal securely to avoid **cross-flavouring**.

FREEZER LIFE: 2–3 months.

THAWING: cook from frozen.

kiwi fruit (also called **Chinese gooseberry**) The oval **fruit** of an Asian climbing plant. Kiwi fruit may be frozen in syrup, but, as with most fruits, it becomes soft during the freezing and thawing processes and is only suitable for use in dishes.

FREEZING: peel and slice the **fruit** into a syrup made with 250 g (8 oz) of sugar to every 600 ml (1 pint) of water. Pack in **rigid containers**, leaving a 2.5 cm (1 inch) **headspace**.

FREEZER LIFE: 1 year.

THAWING: allow to thaw at room temperature for 2–3 hours.

kohlrabi The thickened white stem of a variety of **cabbage**. Young, tender kohlrabi may be **blanched** and frozen.

FREEZING: trim the bases, leaves and stalks and wash well. Blanch whole in boiling water for 3 minutes, cool and drain. **Open freeze** on trays until firm, then transfer into **polythene bags** and freeze.

FREEZER LIFE: 1 year.

THAWING: cook from frozen in boiling water.

kumquat The small, round, orange fruit of a Chinese tree. These bitter-sweet fruits can be frozen whole for use in desserts or chopped up for use in preserves.

FREEZING: either allow to **open freeze** on trays, then transfer into **polythene bags**, or pack in syrup in **rigid containers** leaving a 2.5 cm (1 inch) **head-space**. Use a cold syrup of 250 g (8 oz) of sugar to every 500 ml (1 pint) of water.

FREEZER LIFE: **dry pack**, 2 months; **syrup pack**, 1 year.

THAWING: allow to thaw overnight in the refrigerator or for about 3 hours at room temperature.

labelling It is important to label food that is to be frozen, because when ice forms on the packages it is very difficult to identify the food (particularly meat and fish). It is also important to write on the label the date that the food was placed in the freezer so that it is not stored for longer than its own particular **storage life** and does not deteriorate. It is also helpful to add the quantity of food that you have frozen and any extra cooking instructions that might be needed after **thawing**. Use adhesive labels suitable for freezer use and write clearly with a **Chinagraph pencil** or wax crayon. Alternatively use labels that can be tied securely round the package.

ladies' fingers See **okra**.

lamb The **meat** of young sheep, which can be frozen successfully in joints. Choose good quality, fresh lamb. It is possible to buy a complete lamb and have it divided into suitable cuts and joints by a butcher. Joints may be roasted and then frozen to serve later as **cold meat**. Reheated joints and sliced meat are not very satisfactory because they tend to dry out.

FREEZING: pack into heavy duty **polythene bags** and **overwrap** with **butcher's muslin** or **freezer wrap**. Make sure that the meat is sealed securely and labelled clearly.

FREEZER LIFE: raw lamb, 6 months; cooked lamb, 2 months.

THAWING: it is best to thaw lamb before cooking although it is possible to cook meat for **casseroles** and **stews** from the frozen state. However, extra care must be taken that the meat is cooked properly and cooking time must be increased a great deal. Allow joints to thaw in the refrigerator for about 6–8 hours per 500g (1lb) or at room temperature for about 2–3 hours per 500 g (1lb). Thaw cooked meat in its wrappings for about 4 hours per 500 g (1lb) at room temperature. Never **refreeze** raw or cooked meat that has thawed.

langoustine See **Dublin bay prawn**.

lard Rendered and clarified pig **fat**, especially from the abdomen. Lard stores very well in the refrigerator, but it can be frozen if required.

FREEZING: freeze in its original wrappings, then **overwrap** securely with **foil** or **freezer wrap**.

FREEZER LIFE: 5 months.

THAWING: allow to thaw in the refrigerator overnight.

laver bread A type of reddish purple seaweed, which is traditionally boiled until it is similar to a spinach purée. The boiled laver bread is then mixed with oatmeal and made into small flat cakes. These can be frozen prior to cooking.

FREEZING: boil the laver down to a thick purée, mix with oatmeal and form into flat cakes. Allow to cool completely, then place on a sheet of **greaseproof paper** and pack flat in a **rigid container**, separating the layers with small sheets of greaseproof paper or **freezer wrap**. Seal securely.

FREEZER LIFE: 6 months.

THAWING: allow to thaw in the refrigerator overnight. Then fry in a little oil and butter as part of a cooked breakfast.

leaching The draining of vitamins and minerals into the drip water during **thawing**, or into the cooking water during cooking. It is difficult to prevent this loss, especially when thawing meat and fish, and it is best not to use the drip water. However, the loss can be minimized with **fruit** and **vegetables** because their drip water can be used.

leek A **vegetable** with a slender white bulb, cylindrical stem, and broad, flat leaves. It may be frozen, but it is then only suitable for use in cooking, such as in **casseroles** and **soups**. Choose young, even-sized leeks.

FREEZING: trim ends and outer leaves, then wash thoroughly. **Blanch** whole in boiling water for 3–4 minutes, then cool, drain and pack into **polythene bags**. Thicker leeks can be sliced into chunks and blanched for 2 minutes, before packing into polythene bags.

FREEZER LIFE: 6 months.

THAWING: cook from frozen in boiling water for 7–10 minutes or add to dishes such as stews. They may also be made into vegetable soups.

leftovers Any leftovers may be frozen to avoid waste, and provided the food is cooled quickly and then frozen immediately there is little chance of **bacteria** growing and causing **food poisoning**. Do not allow cooked food to remain at room temperature for any longer than necessary, because it is the optimum temperature for bacteria growth. Leftovers should be stored for a maximum of two months.

legumes See **pulses**.

lemon A small, yellow citrus **fruit**, which may be frozen whole, sliced or as rind for decorations and flavourings.

FREEZING: wash and dry whole lemons and pack into **polythene bags**. Alternatively, slice the lemons, spread onto trays and **open freeze**. Then transfer into polythene bags, seal and return to the freezer. Grated lemon rind may be packed into small cartons and frozen.

FREEZER LIFE: 1 year.

THAWING: unwrap whole lemons and allow to thaw at room temperature for 1–2 hours. Use lemon slices frozen in drinks or allow to thaw at room temperature for about 1 hour. Use grated rind from frozen, or allow to thaw at room temperature for 30 minutes. See also **lemon juice**.

lemonade A drink made from lemon juice, sugar and water, which may be carbonated. Fresh lemonade may be frozen successfully, but do not freeze carbonated lemonade.

FREEZING: prepare fresh lemonade as desired and pour into **rigid containers**, leaving a 2.5 cm (1 inch) **headspace**. Freeze upright until firm.

FREEZER LIFE: 1 year.

THAWING: allow to thaw overnight in the refrigerator.

lemon grass See **herb**.

lemon juice A **fruit juice** that can be frozen to use as a drink or for use in cooking and the preparation of foods.

FREEZING: halve and squeeze the juice from the lemons, then freeze either sweetened or unsweetened into **rigid containers** or ice cube trays. If lemon ice cubes are made, these can then be packed into **polythene bags**.

FREEZER LIFE: 4–6 months.

THAWING: allow to thaw at room temperature for 2–3 hours before using.

lemon sole A European flatfish, which is sold either whole or in fillets and freezes satisfactorily.

FREEZING: for a whole fish, wash, remove the scales and gut, then **ice glaze**. Wrap in **freezer wrap** and **overwrap** in a **polythene bag**. Separate fillets with freezer wrap, then pack into polythene bags.

FREEZER LIFE: 3 months.

THAWING: allow the whole fish to thaw in a cool place for up to 24 hours then use as soon as possible. Fillets may be cooked from frozen or allowed to thaw in the refrigerator overnight.

lentil A nutritious **pulse** originating from South West Asia. Dried black, green or orange lentils take a long time to soak and cook, so it may be helpful to freeze them after cooking for future use in dishes, such as **casseroles**. Choose only the freshest lentils because older lentils become musty and stale.

FREEZING: soak the lentils and cook in the usual manner, undercooking them slightly. Allow to cool completely, drain and pat dry and pack into **rigid containers**.

FREEZER LIFE: 6 months.

THAWING: allow the lentils to thaw at room temperature for 3–4 hours, then add to other foods and continue cooking until soft. Alternatively, continue to cook the lentils, until completely soft then add to **soups**.

lettuce The leaves of a variety of leafy green plants. Lettuce does not freeze well, because it has a very high water content and consequently loses all its crisp texture during the freezing and thawing process. It can, however, be used in **soups** that can then be frozen successfully.

lime A small, round or oval, greenish citrus **fruit**, which is not always widely available so it may be useful to freeze. Lime slices and lime juice can also be frozen.

FREEZING: pack whole limes tightly into **polythene bags**. Pour lime juice into small **rigid containers** or ice cube trays for use in cold drinks. **Open freeze** slices of lime, then pack into polythene bags for use in drinks.

FREEZER LIFE: 1 year.

THAWING: allow whole fruit and juice to thaw overnight at room temperature. Slices may be used from frozen in drinks, or left to thaw for about one hour, if using as decorations.

listeria A type of **bacteria** commonly found in soil, water, and the digestive system of animals. Food sources from which it may enter the human body are unwashed **vegetables**, some soft **cheeses**, **patés**, and pre-cooked chilled foods, which may result in the disease listeriosis. Generally, listeria does not harm those who may come into contact with it, but pregnant woman, the sick and the elderly are at risk and can become seriously ill because they have less immunity to infection. It can, in severe cases, lead to miscarriage, meningitis and even death. It is therefore important for those people who are at risk to avoid these particular foods.

Listeria can survive the freezing process although it lies dormant while the food is frozen, but because it can start reproducing as soon as that food is thawed it is vital that food is prepared in a most hygienic way prior to freezing, and food that is already cooked and then chilled before purchase, should never be frozen.

liver A type of **offal**, from lamb, calf, pig, ox, and poultry. All types of liver can be frozen successfully either raw or cooked.

FREEZING: wash raw liver thoroughly and cut into slices. Pat dry, then pack into **polythene bags**, **interleaving** the slices with **freezer wrap**. Cooked liver should be packed with **gravy** in **foil** containers and sealed with a lid or freezer wrap. Chicken livers should be washed, dried and packed into small containers or polythene bags.

FREEZER LIFE: raw, 3 months; cooked, 2 months.

THAWING: allow raw liver to thaw in the refrigerator overnight. Reheat cooked liver from frozen and covered with foil. Chicken livers should be allowed to thaw in the refrigerator then rinsed thoroughly and used as required.

liver sausage A type of soft sausage generally used as a **paté** for spreading onto toast or crackers. Liver sausage may be frozen successfully, but if it contains **bacon** it cannot be stored for longer than 1 month.

FREEZING: place slices of liver sausage in a **polythene bag interleaving** them with small pieces of **freezer wrap**. Extract as much air as possible from the bag before **sealing**.

FREEZER LIFE: liver sausage containing bacon, 1 month; other types of liver sausage, 3 months.

THAWING: allow the liver sausage to thaw for 4–5 hours in a refrigerator, before serving.

lobster Any of various crustacean **shellfish**. Lobster must be caught, boiled and frozen within 12 hours because it can be a source of **food poisoning** if not served absolutely fresh.

FREEZING: boil the lobster, allow it to cool completely, then wrap tightly in **foil** and freeze. Alternatively, the meat may be removed from the shell after cooking and packed into **polythene bags** or small cartons before freezing.

FREEZER LIFE: 1 month.

THAWING: allow to thaw in its wrappings for 6–8 hours in the refrigerator.

loganberry The dark, purplish-red **fruit** of a trailing prickly shrub. Loganberries are best frozen either unwrapped on trays or as a purée. Choose ripe, dry fruit, and do not wash unless absolutely necessary.

FREEZING: **open freeze** on trays and when the fruit is firm transfer it into **polythene bags**. Fruit that is not suitable for freezing whole can be puréed and sweetened and then packed into **rigid containers**, leaving a 2.5 cm (1 inch) **headspace**.

FREEZER LIFE: 1 year.

THAWING: allow the fruit to thaw in the refrigerator for about 6 hours. Leave the purée to thaw at room temperature for about 3 hours.

loose pack A method of freezing food unwrapped, so that the food does not freeze in one solid mass of ice. When firm the food is then usually transferred to **polythene bags** to store in the freezer. This method is also called **open freezing**.

luncheon meat A meat product made from ground pork and cereals. Luncheon meat is usually sold in cans, but it is possible to buy it in slices at delicatessens. It may be frozen for a short period of time.

FREEZING: pack slices of luncheon meat tightly into **polythene bags, interleaved** with small sheets of **freezer wrap**.

FREEZER LIFE: 2 months.

THAWING: allow to thaw in its wrappings for about 3 hours in the refrigerator.

lychee, litchi, lichee, or **lichi** A small Chinese fruit, similar to a **plum**, with dry pink skin and white, sweet flesh. Lychees can be frozen, but avoid choosing fruit with dry, shrivelled skins.

FREEZING: pare off the skin with a small knife. Pack the fruit into **rigid containers** with a cold syrup consisting of 500 g (1lb) of sugar to every 1 litre (2 pints) of water. Leave a 2.5 cm (1 inch) **headspace** and seal well.

FREEZER LIFE: 1 year.

THAWING: allow to thaw in containers in the refrigerator for 3–4 hours.

mackerel An oily, spiny-finned **fish** normally sold whole, which can be frozen successfully, but only when very fresh. Smoked mackerel may also be frozen satisfactorily.

FREEZING: clean thoroughly, remove the scales and gut. Wash well in cold water and allow to drain. Then either wrap each fish individually in **polythene bags**, or **ice glaze** each fish before wrapping in polythene bags. Smoked mackerel should also be wrapped in polythene bags, expelling as much air as possible before **sealing**.

FREEZER LIFE: both fresh and smoked mackerel, 2 months.

THAWING: mackerel may be cooked from frozen or allowed to thaw in the refrigerator overnight. Smoked mackerel should be allowed to thaw for 4–5 hours in the refrigerator.

malt loaf An enriched fruit teabread, which can be frozen successfully.

FREEZING: commercially produced malt loaves may be kept in their original wrappings and over-wrapped in a **polythene bag**. Allow a home-made malt loaf to cool completely after cooking, then pack tightly into a polythene bag, extracting as much as air as possible before **sealing**.

FREEZER LIFE: commercially produced and home-made, 4 months.

THAWING: allow the loaf to thaw in its wrappings at room temperature for 3–6 hours.

mandarin (also called **mandarin orange**) A small orange-like **fruit** with sweet, juicy flesh. Mandarins are in the shops from November to January, and can be frozen for use in desserts.

FREEZING: peel and remove the pith from the mandarins. Prepare a cold sugar syrup with 250 g (8 oz) of sugar to every 600 ml (1 pint) of water and pack the mandarin segments into **rigid containers** covered with the syrup. Leave a 2.5 cm (1 inch) **headspace** before **sealing**.

FREEZER LIFE: 1 year.

THAWING: allow the mandarins to thaw in the refrigerator overnight or for 3–4 hours at room temperature.

mangetout (also called **sugar pea**) The immature pod of the garden pea. Mangetout can be frozen provided that the pods are still flat, tender and young.

FREEZING: trim the ends and remove any strings attached, then **blanch** in boiling water for 2 minutes. Cool and drain, and pack in **rigid containers** or **polythene bags**.

FREEZER LIFE: 1 year.

THAWING: cook from frozen in boiling water.

mango A tropical **fruit** with sweet, orange-yellow flesh. Mangoes can be frozen successfully in syrup. Choose ripe fruit only, which feel soft when gently squeezed.

FREEZING: peel the fruit, remove the stones and slice. Pack in **rigid containers** covered with a cold syrup made with 500 g (1lb) of sugar to every 1 litre (2 pints) of water. Place a piece of crumpled **foil** on top of the fruit to keep it immersed in the syrup, so that it does not **discolour**. Leave a 2.5 cm (1 inch) **headspace** and seal securely.

FREEZER LIFE: 1 year.

THAWING: allow to thaw at room temperature for 3–4 hours or overnight in the refrigerator.

margarine A butter substitute made from vegetable or animal oils. Margarine can be frozen successfully for convenience and if **bulk buying**.

FREEZING: leave the margarine in its original wrappings, but **overwrap** tightly with **foil** or a **polythene bag**.

FREEZER LIFE: 5 months.

THAWING: allow to thaw overnight in the refrigerator.

marinade A highly seasoned liquid that is used to tenderize **meat** and **fish** before cooking. The food may be marinaded for 24 hours before freezing, or the marinade can be prepared and frozen separately and used at a later date with fresh meat or fish.

FREEZING: prepare the marinade as usual and cool if necessary. Pour into a small **rigid container** and seal securely, leaving a 2.5 cm (1 inch) **headspace**. If it is very highly seasoned, **overwrap** in a

polythene bag to prevent **cross-flavouring** with other foods in the freezer occurring.

FREEZER LIFE: 3 months.

THAWING: allow the marinade to thaw overnight in the refrigerator before using with fresh food.

marjoram The leaves of a small Mediterranean plant, which are used as a **herb** usually in **lamb** and **tomato** dishes and in salads. Marjoram may be frozen satisfactorily.

FREEZING: wash and dry the marjoram leaves thoroughly. Chop finely and pack into small **polythene bags**, extracting as much air as possible before **sealing**.

FREEZER LIFE: 6 months.

THAWING: frozen marjoram may be added to most dishes straight from the freezer.

marmalade A preserve made by boiling the pulp and rind of citrus **fruits** (especially **oranges**) with sugar. It is unnecessary to freeze marmalade because it stores well in a cool dry place. But it is possible to freeze fruit in preparation for making marmalade at a later stage. The best oranges for making marmalade are Seville oranges and these only have a short season in the shops, so it is useful to be able to freeze them either whole or in pulp form. The only point to remember if making marmalade from frozen oranges is that freezing lowers the pectin level in the fruit, so either add commercial liquid pectin or an additional one-eighth extra weight of oranges.

FREEZING: whole fruit should be washed, dried and frozen in **polythene bags**. Make the orange pulp by cutting up whole fruit and cooking without sugar until they are reduced to a pulp. Pack into **rigid containers** and label stating the quantity of oranges initially used, so the correct amount of sugar can be added later.

FREEZER LIFE: 6 months.

THAWING: allow fruit pulp to thaw overnight in the refrigerator before using. Place frozen whole fruit in a pan with the required amount of water, simmer until soft, then continue following a standard recipe.

marrow The large green fruit of a creeping plant. Young marrows can be frozen, but because of their high water content they do become very soft. Particular care must be taken when preparing after freezing not to overcook them. Older marrows are best cooked or made into other dishes before freezing.

FREEZING: peel and cut marrows into 2.5 cm (1 inch) slices, and **blanch** in boiling water for 3 minutes. Then allow them to drain and cool before packing them into **polythene bags**.

FREEZER LIFE: 6 months.

THAWING: cook from frozen and heat very gently to prevent them from falling apart.

marzipan A paste made from **almond paste**, sugar, and egg whites. Commercial marzipan does not freeze very well because of its high oil content.

It is also manufactured in blocks that tend to crumble when thawed and cannot be worked very easily. It can be frozen when as a topping for a **cake**, or when previously made into decorations.

mayonnaise A thick sauce made from egg yolks, oil, and vinegar or lemon juice. It does not freeze satisfactorily because it separates on **thawing** and cannot be beaten back into an emulsion again.

meat The flesh of mammals used for food as distinguished from that of birds and fish. Fresh, good quality meat can be frozen successfully, and freezing may even tenderize it slightly although it will not improve quality or taste. It may be frozen raw in joints, **chops**, **steaks**, cut up or minced up. It does not matter if it is boned or not although removing bones does mean that there is more space available in the freezer. Bones must be padded with **foil** or **freezer wrap** so that they do not puncture the outer wrappings, allowing air to enter. Raw meat must be well wrapped with as much air as possible expelled to avoid **freezer burn** and the meat drying out and losing its former texture and flavour.

Meat should always be frozen as rapidly as possible in order to retain its texture and flavour. Switch the freezer on to fast freeze for 24 hours before freezing, and do not freeze more than one tenth of the freezer's capacity in any 24 hours. Pack the meat as close to the freezer walls as possible so that it freezes quickly. It is preferable to thaw meat thoroughly before cooking, but it is possible to cook chops and steaks successfully and safely from frozen. Cured and **smoked meats** can be frozen for a short time only. Meat made up into dishes such as **casseroles**, **pies**, and **stews** freezes very well. See **bacon**; **beef**; **beefburger**; **cold meat**; **ham**; **lamb**; **luncheon meat**; **pork**; **sausage**; **sausagemeat**; **veal**.

melon The fruit of a variety of twining plants. Most types of melon tend to lose their flavour and crisp texture if frozen, but it can be frozen for use in desserts. The best varieties for freezing are Charantais and Ogen, because they are firm and sweet. **Watermelon** is difficult to prepare for freezing because it has so many seeds.

FREEZING: either (a), cut the melon in half, remove the seeds and cut the flesh into balls, cubes or slices, then wrap in **polythene bags** with a little sugar sprinkled over it; or (b), make a syrup using 500 g (1 lb) of sugar to every 1 litre (2 pints) of water, and pack into **rigid containers** covering with the syrup. Place a piece of crumpled **foil** on top of the fruit to keep it immersed in the syrup and seal securely.

FREEZER LIFE: 6 months.

THAWING: allow the melon to thaw in the refrigerator overnight or at room temperature for 2–3 hours. Use when still slightly frosted.

meringue A baked mixture of beaten **egg** whites and sugar. Although very fragile, meringues freeze very successfully. Do not freeze soft meringue **icing** because it tends to become soft and crumbly.

FREEZING: make meringues according to the recipe used and allow them to cool completely. Pack into **rigid containers**, separating the layers with small sheets of **greaseproof paper**. Seal, then place near the top of the freezer and do not place anything heavy on top of them.

FREEZER LIFE: 1 year.

THAWING: allow to thaw at room temperature for about 1–2 hours before filling.

microorganism Organisms that are microscopic in size, such as **bacteria**, moulds, and yeasts. They are present in foods and may cause **food poisoning** or spoil its quality. They multiply at temperatures over 10°C (50°F), but are dormant at freezer temperatures. Freezing does not kill them, so it is important that frozen foods are correctly thawed, properly cooked or **reheated** and consumed as soon as possible. It is important to cool **blanched** and cooked foods quickly before freezing them, so that they do not remain at room temperature for long. Cooked **meat** is particularly susceptible to a particular bacteria that produces toxins not destroyed by cooking. With raw **poultry** there is always the risk that a bird may be carrying **salmonella**. Moulds and yeasts may change the quality and taste of the food, but they do not render it unsafe to eat. See also **listeria**; **refreezing**.

microwave thawing A microwave enables frozen food to be thawed, cooked and consumed extremely quickly. For example, some frozen **meat** can be defrosted in 5–10 minutes per pound and a loaf of **bread** in about 5 minutes (depending on the size and output of the microwave). Most microwaves now have an automatic defrosting setting, which only thaws and not cooks the food. Special containers are now available that can be used for both freezing and microwave cooking. Readers are recommended to consult the Collins *Gem Food for Microwaving*.

milk Pasteurized milk does not freeze particularly well because the **fat** separates out during the freezing process and the milk becomes flaky. Homogenized, semi-skimmed and skimmed milk can be frozen successfully, although only for about one month. Never freeze milk in a glass bottle because it cracks and may shatter.

FREEZING: pour milk into **rigid containers**, waxed, or plastic cartons, leaving a 2.5 cm (1 inch) **headspace** for expansion. Commercial cartons of milk may be frozen.

FREEZER LIFE: up to 1 month.

THAWING: allow to thaw in the refrigerator for 18–24 hours per pint. If the milk is to be used for cooking, it may be thawed by heating it gently from frozen. Stir thoroughly before using.

mincemeat A mixture usually made with dried fruit and spices. Mincemeat recipes generally recommend that it is left to mature for at least 2 weeks in a cool, dry place before use. As long as it contains brandy, there is no point in freezing it unless it is going to be stored for longer than about 6 weeks. In this case there are recipes specifically for freezer mincemeat that omit the brandy, which can be added once it has thawed and is ready to use.

FREEZING: pack freezer mincemeat in plastic containers or small **polythene bags** in 250g (8oz) quantities, leaving a little **headspace**.

FREEZER LIFE: up to 3 months.

THAWING: allow to thaw in the refrigerator overnight before using.

mince pie A small pastry tart filled with mincemeat. It is a good idea to prepare and freeze plenty of mince pies before the Christmas rush. They freeze well and can be stored for up to 3 months, but they are best stored uncooked.

FREEZING: prepare pastry in patty tins and fill with mincemeat. Place the tins in the freezer and freeze until the **pastry** is firm. Then remove them from the tins and pack them into **rigid containers**, **interleaving** with small sheets of **greaseproof paper**. Seal securely and return them to the freezer.

FREEZER LIFE: 3 months.

THAWING: replace in patty tins and bake from frozen.

mint The aromatic leaves of a temperate shrub used as a **herb**, which can grow in abundance and is well worth freezing. Mint can also be made into **mint sauce** before freezing if preferred.

FREEZING: pack whole springs of mint into **polythene bags** to freeze. Chopped mint can be frozen with a little water in ice cube trays. When solid, transfer the mint cubes into polythene bags to store.

FREEZER LIFE: whole and chopped mint, 6 months.

THAWING: crumble whole sprigs while frozen into **sauces** and cooked dishes. Allow mint cubes to thaw a little before adding to prepared dishes.

mint sauce Fresh **mint** can be easily made into mint sauce and frozen satisfactorily for up to 6 months.

FREEZING: prepare the mint sauce according to the recipe used, and pour carefully into ice cube trays. When hard transfer the cubes into **polythene bags** to store.

FREEZER LIFE: 6 months.

THAWING: allow mint sauce cubes to thaw at room temperature for 30 minutes before thinning down with a little water.

monkfish A round white **fish** with a very large, ugly head. Only the tail is eaten and it is sold as fillets. The flesh is firm and white and similar in texture to lobster.

FREEZING: separate the fillets with **freezer wrap**, then **overwrap** several fillets together in **foil** or a **polythene bag**; alternatively **ice glaze**.

FREEZER LIFE: 3 months.

THAWING: monkfish fillets may be cooked from frozen or allowed to thaw in the refrigerator overnight.

mousse A light creamy dessert made with eggs and cream and in a variety of flavours. Mousse freezes well, but it is best to decorate it after thawing.

FREEZING: prepare mousse according to the recipe used, pour into a plastic or freezer-proof mould or bowl and chill until firm. Cover the top of the container with **clingfilm**, then **overwrap** with **foil**.

FREEZER LIFE: 2 months.

THAWING: remove outer wrapping and allow to thaw in the refrigerator overnight.

muffin A thick round baked roll, which is normally eaten toasted with butter. Muffins are generally more widely available in the winter months so it is useful to be able to store them in the freezer.

FREEZING: freeze muffins in their original wrappings and **overwrap** in a **polythene bag**, expelling as much air as possible before sealing.

FREEZER LIFE: 6 months.

THAWING: muffins may be toasted from frozen or allowed to thaw in their wrappings for about 6 hours at room temperature.

mulberry The blackberry-like fruit of a temperate tree. Mulberries may be frozen with or without sugar.

FREEZING: either (a), **open freeze** whole mulberries on trays until firm, then transfer into **polythene bags**, expelling as much air as possible before **sealing**. Or (b), pack straight into polythene bags adding approximately 125 g (4 oz) of sugar to every 500 g (1 lb) of **fruit**.

FREEZER LIFE: 1 year.

THAWING: allow the mulberries to thaw at room temperature for about 3 hours before using. Alternatively, the fruit may be used straight from the freezer if it is to be used for decoration.

mullet (grey and red) A small white **fish** of two distinct varieties. Grey mullet is sold whole or in fillets. Red mullet is much smaller, pinky red in colour with a delicate flavour and is sold whole. They can both be frozen using the same method.

FREEZING: for a whole fish, wash, remove the scales and gut, then **ice glaze**. Place the frozen fish in a **polythene bag** expelling as much air as possible and store in the freezer. Wrap fillets in **foil** or a polythene bag **interleaving** them with **freezer wrap** to keep them separate.

FREEZER LIFE: 3 months.

THAWING: allow the whole fish to thaw in a cool place for up to 24 hours. Use as soon as possible after it is thawed. Fillets may be cooked from frozen.

mushroom Any of a variety of edible fungi. Mushrooms are available all year, but they can be frozen successfully if required. Choose clean, unblemished mushrooms and freeze button mushrooms whole and larger ones sliced up for use in cooked dishes.

FREEZING: wipe with a damp cloth until as clean as possible. Spread whole button mushrooms on trays and **open freeze** until firm. Transfer into **polythene bags** and seal, expelling as much air as possible, and return to the freezer. Slice larger mushrooms and sauté in a little **butter** for one minute. Pack into small **rigid containers** with their cooking liquid, allow to cool completely and freeze.

FREEZER LIFE: raw, 1 month; cooked, 3 months.

THAWING: mushrooms can be used from frozen if used in **stews**, **soups** and **sauces** or sautéed in butter and used as a **vegetable**. Alternatively, allow them to thaw in the refrigerator in their containers for about 6 hours. See also **duxelles**.

mushy peas A type of processed pea, normally purchased in cans. If there are some left over in the tin they may be frozen satisfactorily. Do not allow them to stand in the opened tin for long before freezing because they may lose their flavour and texture.

FREEZING: transfer the contents into small **rigid containers** and seal well, leaving a little **headspace**.

FREEZER LIFE: 4 months.

THAWING: allow to thaw in the refrigerator for 3–4 hours before using.

mussel A mollusc **shellfish**. Mussels freeze very well, but they must be absolutely fresh and ideally they should be frozen within 12 hours of being caught. They should always be cooked before freezing. If preparing live mussels, ensure that the shells are tightly shut and discard any that are open or broken.

FREEZING: wash thoroughly and scrub under cold running water. Place in a large pan, cover and cook until the shells open. Discard any that do not open. Leave them to cool completely, then pack into **rigid containers** with their cooking juices.

Alternatively, the mussels may be cooked with wine, **onions**, **garlic** and **herbs** for 3–5 minutes until the shells open. Allow them to cool completely then pack, either with or without their shells, into rigid containers. Pour over the juices leaving a little **headspace** before **sealing**.

FREEZER LIFE: 1 month.

THAWING: allow the mussels to thaw overnight in their wrappings in the refrigerator and use as soon as possible.

mustard A condiment made from the powdered seeds of the mustard plant. Mustard stores very well in a cool, dry cupboard or in the refrigerator. There is therefore no point in freezing it.

mutton The meat of a mature sheep. See **lamb**.

naan bread A type of slightly leavened Indian **bread**, which can be stored successfully in the freezer if frozen when really fresh.

FREEZING: leave the naan bread in its original packaging and **overwrap** in a **polythene bag**, excluding as much air as possible before sealing.

FREEZER LIFE: 3 months.

THAWING: remove from the polythene bag and allow to thaw in original wrappings at room temperature for 3–4 hours.

nectarine A soft, juicy, smooth-skinned **fruit**, which is a variety of **peach**. Nectarines are best frozen in **sugar syrup**. They tend to discolour easily and this can be avoided by adding either $\frac{1}{4}$ teaspoon of **ascorbic acid** or 1 tablespoon of **lemon juice** to every 600 ml (1 pint) of syrup.

FREEZING: plunge the nectarines into boiling water for 1 minute to loosen their skins, then cool immediately in cold water. Rub or peel off the skins and slice directly into a sugar syrup consisting of 250 g (8 oz) of sugar to every 600 ml (1 pint) of water. Remove the stones and pack the fruit into **rigid containers**. Make sure that the fruit is immersed in the syrup by placing a piece of crumpled **foil** on top of the fruit before **sealing**. Allow a 1–2.5 cm ($\frac{1}{2}$–1 inch) **headspace**.

FREEZER LIFE: 1 year.

THAWING: allow the fruit to thaw in the refrigerator for 4–5 hours and serve while still a little frosty.

non-freezing items There are certain food items that simply cannot be frozen because their texture alters to an unacceptable degree. **Mayonnaise**, egg

custards, single, double or unpasteurized **cream**, **milk** (except homogenized), soured cream and **cottage cheese** do not freeze successfully because they tend to separate out and cannot be whisked back into their former state once thawed. **Bananas** become soft and black when frozen. Crisp salad greens, such as **lettuce**, cucumber, and also **radishes** become mushy if frozen due to their high water content. Soft **meringue icings** and fillings will crumble and fall apart after freezing. Hard boiled **eggs** should not be frozen because the whites become tough and leathery, although fresh egg can be frozen.

noodle A ribbon-like strip of **pasta**. Cooked noodles can be frozen successfully, as can most types of pasta and pasta dishes. However, because noodles can be prepared in such a short time it does not seem necessary to freeze them. They can also be incorporated into dishes, such as chow mein, prior to freezing, which can then be taken straight from the freezer for a quick **ready meal**.

FREEZING: cook the noodles as directed, drain and cool in a sieve under runnning water, then allow to dry. Pack into **polythene bags**, expelling as much air as possible, and freeze. Alternatively, pack complete meals into **foil** containers or other suitable dishes, cover with a lid or foil and **overwrap** in a polythene bag.

FREEZER LIFE: cooked noodles, 1 month; composite dishes, 2–3 months.

THAWING: place frozen noodles in a pan of boiling water. As soon as the water begins to boil once more, remove the noodles, drain and serve. Remove the polythene bag and lid from ready meals and cook from frozen until thoroughly heated.

nuts The edible kernels of various hard, woody fruits. Most types of nut keep fresh and moist in the freezer for up to a year, but it is important to remember not to freeze salted nuts because these quickly become **rancid**. Nuts may be frozen in shells, whole, chopped, flaked or toasted. They can also be made into nut butter (e.g. peanut butter), which can be satisfactorily frozen for up to 3 months.

FREEZING: pack whole or chopped nuts in **polythene bags** or small **rigid containers** and seal well. Pack nut butters into small cartons and **overwrap** with a polythene bag.

FREEZER LIFE: nut butters, 3 months; whole and chopped nuts, 1 year; toasted nuts, 4 months.

THAWING: allow to thaw at room temperature for about 3–4 hours in containers or bags.

octopus A soft-bodied mollusc with eight tentacled legs. Small octopuses can be bought whole, but generally they are sold already cut into rings or small pieces. The bag of ink that is part of the whole octopus is not usually used for cooking because it has rather a strong, musky flavour.

FREEZING: for a whole octopus, rinse thoroughly, then remove the head and the tentacles. Rinse the body and the tentacles and beat with a wooden mallet. **Blanch** in boiling water for 2 minutes, then plunge into ice cold water. Remove the skin and pack the flesh into **polythene bags**, expelling as much air as possible before sealing. If rings or pieces are to be frozen, simply rinse, then blanch and continue as above.

FREEZER LIFE: 3 months.

THAWING: allow to thaw in the refrigerator for 3–4 hours in its wrappings.

offal A general term that describes everything that is removed when dressing the carcase, leaving only the meat and bone. All offal that is to be frozen must be very fresh.

FREEZING: clean and trim and pack into **polythene bags** or containers.

FREEZER LIFE: 3 months.

THAWING: allow all offal to thaw in the refrigerator for about 8 hours or overnight. See **brain**; **heart**; **kidneys**; **liver**; **oxtail**; **tongue**; **tripe**; **sweetbreads**.

okra (also called **ladies' fingers**) The long tapering, green seed pod of an African and Asian plant, which has juicy green flesh and thick gluey sap. Okra is often used to thicken **stews** and **casseroles** as well as a **vegetable**. Choose only small green okra, up to about 7.5 cm (3 inches) long.

FREEZING: remove the stems and **blanch** in boiling water for 3–4 minutes. Cool, drain and pack into **polythene bags**, expelling as much air as possible before sealing.

FREEZER LIFE: 1 year.

THAWING: okra may be cooked from frozen or added to other dishes straight from the freezer.

olive A small green or black **fruit** of a Mediterranean tree. Olives are generally used as an appetizer and for garnishes. It is most economical to buy them in a large jar and then either keep them in the refrigerator or freezer. They store satisfactorily in the refrigerator or freezer for up to 6 months. Add a few drops of **lemon juice** to the brine to prevent them from discolouring.

FREEZING: transfer the olives into small cartons and cover with cold water, adding a few drops of lemon juice. Leave a 2.5 cm (1 inch) **headspace** and seal securely.

FREEZER LIFE: 6 months.

THAWING: allow to thaw at room temperature for 3–4 hours, then consume within three days.

onion A bulb with a pungent odour and taste. Large onions are available all year, but it can be useful to have a store of chopped onions in the freezer. Small pickling onions are not always available and can be stored whole for use in dishes such as **casseroles**.

FREEZING: peel, chop or slice large onions and pack into **rigid containers**. **Overwrap** carefully with plastic wrap or a polythene bag, so that they do not taint other foods in the freezer with their strong smell. Peel and **blanch** small onions for 3 minutes. Cool, drain and pack into **polythene bags**. Overwrap with another bag in order to prevent **cross-flavouring**.

FREEZER LIFE: chopped onions, 3 months; whole baby onions, 6 months.

THAWING: allow chopped onions to thaw in their wrappings for 15 minutes at room temperature before using. Use whole onions from frozen.

open freezing A method of freezing whereby foods are frozen before they are wrapped, so that the food is not frozen in one solid mass. This method is also known as **loose pack**. Commercially prepared frozen foods, such as frozen peas and minced meat, are sometimes described as **free-flow**, which means that they have been open frozen so that the food can flow freely out of the package.

The open freezing method also means that large ice crystals do not have the opportunity to form in foods with a high water content, such as soft fruits. Such foods then retain as firm a texture as possible after thawing. Iced **cakes** and **meringues** can also benefit from open freezing because they are less likely to be damaged when firm.

To open freeze food, spread it out on trays or plastic plates allowing a little space between every piece. Freeze until firm, then transfer into **polythene bags** or other suitable containers. It is important to remove delicate items, such as iced cakes, from their wrappings prior to thawing so that they do not become damaged.

orange A citrus **fruit**, with three main varieties, the sweet Valencia, the thick-skinned navel, and the bitter Seville. Oranges can be successfully frozen in a **dry sugar pack** or a **syrup pack**. Grate off the rind before freezing and pack it into small cartons or pieces of **foil** and freeze for future use as a flavouring or decoration. Seville oranges may be frozen for making **marmalade**, although it is important to remember that freezing destroys some pectin in the fruit and this must be allowed for.

FREEZING: if the oranges are to be used for marmalade, freeze them whole in **polythene bags**. Otherwise, remove peel, pith and pips from the oranges and cut into slices or segments. Either (a), place alternate layers of fruit and sugar into **rigid containers**, using about 175 g (6 oz) of sugar to every 4 oranges and freeze; or (b), pack the prepared oranges into rigid containers in a sugar syrup made with 250 g (8 oz) of sugar to every 600 ml (1 pint) of water. Leave a 2.5 cm (1 inch) **headspace** before **sealing**.

FREEZER LIFE: 1 year.

THAWING: allow the fruit to thaw in its containers for about 3 hours at room temperature.

orange juice The juice of **oranges**, which may be frozen successfully for 4–6 months.

FREEZING: squeeze the juice from the oranges and strain into **rigid containers**. Leave a 2 cm **head-**

space before **sealing**, and freeze upright until firm. Commercially prepared cartons of orange juice may be frozen, but it is preferable to transfer the juice into another rigid container because when the juice expands it may burst the original carton if there is not enough headspace.

FREEZER LIFE: 4–6 months.

THAWING: allow the juice to thaw at room temperature for 2–3 hours before serving. See also **fruit juice**.

oregano The leaves of a Mediterranean variety of marjoram, which is most often used to flavour **pizzas**, **tomato** dishes and **fish**. It can be frozen successfully.

FREEZING: wash and dry the oregano leaves thoroughly. Chop finely and pack into small cartons or **polythene bags**, extracting as much air as possible before **sealing**

FREEZER LIFE: 6 months.

THAWING: frozen oregano may be added to most dishes straight from the freezer.

ortanique A cross between a **tangerine** and an **orange**, similar in size to a Navel orange. Ortaniques are very good for making **marmalade** and also in a **fruit salad**. They can be frozen either whole, with sugar or syrup.

FREEZING: if the fruit is to be used for marmalade, freeze it whole in **polythene bags**. Otherwise, remove peel, pith and pips from the fruit and cut into slices or segments. Either (a), place alternate layers of fruit and sugar in **rigid containers**, using about 175 g (6 oz) of sugar to every 6 ortaniques and freeze; or (b), pack the prepared fruit into rigid containers in a sugar syrup made with 250 g (8 oz) of sugar to every 500 ml (1 pint) of water. Leave a 2.5 cm (1 inch) **headspace** before **sealing**.

FREEZER LIFE: 1 year.

THAWING: allow the fruit to thaw in its containers for about 3 hours at room temperature.

overwrapping A method of wrapping food in an additional layer of packaging material in order to protect it against **cross-flavouring**, **dehydration**, **freezer burn** and **oxidation**. The most effective overwrapping material is polythene either in the form of sheeting or bags. Air must be eliminated as much as possible from the packages before overwrapping and **sealing**.

oxidation A term used, in a freezing context, to describe the undesirable process of oxygen being absorbed into frozen food. Oxidation alters the texture of the food and can cause it to dry out. The presence of air will cause **fats** to become **rancid** and **meat** and **poultry** to suffer from **freezer burn**. It can be prevented easily by **packaging** and wrapping all food items that are to be frozen securely and thoroughly. Low-temperature storage gradually dehydrates food over time and so the packaging materials used must be strong and moisture- and vapour-proof.

oxtail The skinned tail of an ox, a type of **offal**. Oxtail can be frozen either raw or cooked, or it may be braised and made into **soup** before freezing.

FREEZING: chop raw oxtail into joints, trim off surplus **fat** and pack into **polythene bags**. Cooked oxtail must be thoroughly cooled and the fat skimmed off before freezing in **rigid containers**. Soup must be chilled and stored upright in rigid containers until solid.

FREEZER LIFE: raw oxtail, 3 months; cooked, 1 month.

THAWING: allow raw oxtail to thaw overnight in the refrigerator before using. Reheat cooked oxtail slowly from frozen, or allow to thaw in the refrigerator overnight.

oyster A marine mollusc **shellfish**, which must be frozen within 12 hours of being caught.

FREEZING: scrub the shells, then prise them open, reserving the juice. Remove the oysters and wash in salted water using about 1 tblsp of salt to 600 ml (1 pint) of water. Drain, then pack in **rigid containers** adding the reserved juices. Leave a 2.5 cm (1 inch) **headspace** before **sealing**.

FREEZER LIFE: 1 month.

THAWING: allow to thaw in the refrigerator in the unopened container for 6–8 hours then consume as soon as possible. Cooked oysters may be added frozen to **soups** and **sauces** and cooked gently until thoroughly heated through.

packaging It is important when freezing to ensure that food is packaged correctly and that as much air as possible is excluded from the packages. The presence of air causes **oxidation**, which results in food drying out, **fats** quickly become **rancid** and **fruit** losing its colour. Every item must be securely sealed and wrapped in material strong enough to withstand handling and storage.

Bags and containers are available that are designed specifically for freezer use. However, many other items may be used, for example, ice cream containers, margarine tubs and yoghurt pots, but they should be **overwrapped** with a **polythene bag** for extra protection. See **clingfilm**; **foil**; **freezer wrap**; **polythene sheeting**; **rigid containers**; **sealing**; **waxed cartons**.

palm heart The bud of a **cabbage** palm tree, which needs to be **blanched** before cooking to get rid of its bitter flavour. Palm hearts may be frozen either blanched or fully cooked.

FREEZING: blanch the palm hearts for 2–3 minutes, drain and allow to cool completely. Pack into **polythene bags**, extracting as much air as possible before **sealing**. Alternatively, after blanching, cook the palm hearts until tender in wine or stock and allow to cool completely. Turn into **rigid containers** and cover with a lid, allowing a 2.5 cm (1 inch) **headspace** for **expansion**.

FREEZER LIFE: 6 months.

THAWING: allow to thaw in the refrigerator overnight before using.

pancake A flat cake made from a batter. Both cooked pancakes (filled or unfilled) and the batter freeze well. Make sure, however, that the fillings only contain ingredients that may be frozen.

FREEZING: cook the pancakes in the usual way and allow to cool. **Interleave** unfilled pancakes with **freezer wrap** or **clingfilm** and pack in **foil** or **polythene bags**. If freezing filled pancakes, make the filling and allow to cool before stuffing pancakes. Place in **rigid containers** or foil containers, cover and **overwrap** with a polythene bag.

FREEZER LIFE: unfilled, 6 months; filled, 1–2 months.

THAWING: unwrap unfilled pancakes and separate out. Allow to thaw at room temperature for about 20 mintues, then reheat for about 30 seconds in a lightly oiled frying pan. Alternatively, when the pancakes are thawed stack them and place in a piece of **foil** and reheat in the oven 190°C/375°F/Gas 5 for 20–30 minutes until heated through. Those pancakes that have been frozen already containing their fillings may be cooked from frozen with a sauce.

papaya (also called **pawpaw**) A pear-shaped tropical **fruit** with smooth yellow skin and orange flesh, similar in taste and texture to a small **melon**.

FREEZING: peel the skin away, remove the seeds and slice into a cold syrup made with 500 g (1lb) of sugar to every litre (2 pints) of water. Stir in 2 tablespoons of **lemon juice** to each litre (2 pints) of syrup and pack in **rigid containers**.

FREEZER LIFE: 9–12 months.

THAWING: allow the fruit to thaw in its container at room temperature for about 1–2 hours.

parsley A small herbaceous European plant used as a **herb**, which freezes very well either in sprigs or chopped up.

FREEZING: wash and dry sprigs of parsley and pack into **polythene bags** or little parcels of **foil**. Chopped parsley is best frozen in small cartons or packed into ice cube trays and frozen with a little water. The frozen cubes should then be transferred into polythene bags for storage.

FREEZER LIFE: 6 months.

THAWING: use from frozen and crumble directly into dishes, such as **casseroles** and **sauces**.

parsley sauce A sauce that freezes very well because it is made with a roux base. It is important to whisk or blend parsley sauce thoroughly when thawed to regain its former smooth texture.

FREEZING: make sauce according to the recipe used and cool quickly, placing a small sheet of **greaseproof paper** directly on the top of it to prevent a skin from forming. Pack into small **rigid containers**, leaving a little **headspace**.

FREEZER LIFE: 6 months.

THAWING: reheat slowly from frozen in a solid pan and beat thoroughly with a wooden spoon until smooth.

parsnip A long root **vegetable** with white flesh, which can be frozen successfully. Choose young and tender parsnips.

FREEZING: wash, trim and peel the parsnips and cut into small narrow strips. **Blanch** in boiling water for 2 minutes, cool, drain and **open freeze** on trays until firm. When firm, transfer the parsnips into **polythene bags** to store.

FREEZER LIFE: 1 year.

THAWING: if the parsnips are to be boiled they may be cooked from frozen. If they are to be roasted, allow them to thaw at room temperature for 3–4 hours before cooking.

partridge A **game** bird that should be hung before freezing. Partridges are normally hung from 3 to 7 days, depending on taste.

FREEZING: remove the gut, clean thoroughly and dry. Then pack into **polythene bags**, extracting as much air as possible before sealing. Pack the **giblets** separately in polythene bags or small cartons.

FREEZER LIFE: partridge, 6 months; giblets, 2 months.

THAWING: allow the partridge to thaw in the refrigerator for about 5 hours per 500 g (1lb). After freezing, young birds may be roasted, but older birds should be used in dishes such as **casseroles**.

passion fruit A small, olive green or black tropical **fruit** with wrinkled skin and sweet juicy flesh with small, edible seeds. Choose fruit with hard wrinkled skins because this indicates that the fruit is ripe.

FREEZING: scoop out the juice and flesh from the passion fruit. Make a cold syrup using 500 g (1lb) of sugar to every 1 litre (2 pints) of water. Add 30 ml (2 tablespoons) of **lemon juice** and stir in the passion fruit. Pack into **rigid containers** and freeze upright until firm.

FREEZER LIFE: 1 year.

THAWING: allow the fruit to thaw in its container at room temperature for about 1–2 hours. Use with other fruits in **puddings**, such as **fruit salads**.

pasta (dried/fresh) A dough made from flour and water (sometimes egg and milk) moulded into a variety of shapes, such as spaghetti and macaroni. All types of cooked pasta may be frozen successfully, whether dried, fresh or made up into cooked dishes.

FREEZING: cook the pasta in boiling water until just tender or just slightly undercooked, drain and cool in a sieve under running water. Shake dry as thoroughly as possible, before packing into **polythene bags**. Dishes made with pasta, such as lasagne or stuffed cannelloni, can be cooked and frozen in freezer- and oven-proof dishes to provide quick ready meals. Allow them to cool, then cover with a lid and **overwrap** in polythene bags.

FREEZER LIFE: cooked pasta, 1 month; composite dishes, 2–3 months.

THAWING: place frozen, cooked pasta in a pan of boiling salted water and simmer for a few minutes until tender and heated through. Remove the bag and lid from composite dishes, and cook from frozen until thoroughly heated through. If it appears that the dish is drying out cover with a piece of **greaseproof paper** or **foil** to keep it moist.

pastry A dough of flour, water and shortening, which may include eggs, sugar or cheese. All kinds of pastry freeze very well, particularly shortcrust, puff and flaky pastry. It can be either uncooked or cooked or made into **pies** or **flan** cases. It is sometimes thought that shortcrust pastry actually improves in flavour and texture if frozen when uncooked.

FREEZING: freeze uncooked shortcrust pastry in rolled out sheets if possible. (A ball of pastry takes a long time to thaw and knead again.) Wrap each sheet in **foil** or **greaseproof paper** and **overwrap** several together in a **polythene bag**, expelling as much air as possible.

Prepare flaky and puff pastry up to the final rolling, then wrap in foil and overwrap in a polythene bag. The pastry can be shaped into flan or tartlet cases if required before freezing. These should be frozen either baked or unbaked, without wrapping until they are firm, removed from their tins or containers, then transferred into polythene bags. Take care not to damage the pastry cases because they are still very fragile even when frozen. If there is space in the freezer stack several in a box to avoid the risk of damage.

FREEZER LIFE: unbaked pastry, 3 months; baked pastry, 6 months.

THAWING: allow unbaked pastry dough to thaw at room temperature for 2–3 hours until it is soft enough to knead and roll out again. Unbaked pastry cases should be placed in their original tins or containers and baked from frozen, allowing a little extra cooking time. Baked pastry cases should be allowed to thaw at room temperature for about an hour, then refreshed in a hot oven for about 5 minutes. See also **choux pastry**.

paté A spread of finely minced meat, poultry, offal, fish or vegetable matter. Patés freeze very well, but a paté containing **bacon** can be frozen only for a short period.

FREEZING: make paté according to the recipe used, allow it to cool completely, then place in a freezer-proof dish and cover with **foil**. **Overwrap** with a **polythene bag** before freezing. If the paté is purchased in slices, **interleave** each slice with **greaseproof paper** or **clingfilm**, and overwrap all the slices with foil.

FREEZER LIFE: patés containing bacon, 1 month; other types of paté, 3 months.

THAWING: allow the paté to thaw overnight in the refrigerator, or for 6 hours at room temperature.

pawpaw See **papaya**.

pea The bright green seed of the garden pea. Young, sweet garden peas can be frozen successfully. Commercially frozen peas are readily available and retain a good flavour and texture after freezing.

FREEZING: remove the shells from fresh peas, then **blanch** in boiling water for 1–2 minutes. Cool quickly in ice-cold water, drain and **open freeze** on trays until firm. Pack into **polythene bags**, expelling as much air as possible.

FREEZER LIFE: fresh and commercially frozen peas, 1 year.

THAWING: cook from frozen in boiling water.

peach A reddish-yellow, downy-skinned **fruit** with sweet, orange-yellow flesh. Peaches are best frozen either in a cold **sugar syrup** or as a purée. Choose slightly soft, ripe peaches, with no bruises. Peaches discolour rapidly, so it is best to put them directly into a sugar syrup.

FREEZING: peel the peaches either under a cold tap, or **blanch** them for a few seconds if their skins are difficult to remove. Either (a), remove the stones, and slice the peaches into a syrup made with 250 g (8 oz) of sugar to every 600 ml (1 pint) of water. Add $\frac{1}{4}$ teaspoon of **ascorbic acid** or 1 tablespoon of **lemon juice** to help prevent **discoloration**. Pack into **rigid containers** and place a piece of crumpled **foil** on top of the fruit to keep it immersed in the syrup. Leave a 0.5 cm (1 inch) **headspace** before **sealing** with a lid; or (b), purée the stoned peaches, add 1 tablespoon of lemon juice and 125 g (4 oz) of sugar to each 500 g (1 lb) of fruit and pack into rigid containers.

FREEZER LIFE: peaches in syrup, 9–12 months; purée, 6–8 months.

THAWING: allow the peaches to thaw at room temperature in their containers for 3–4 hours, then serve while still frosty. Allow purée to thaw at room temperature for 3 hours before serving as a sauce.

peanut (also called **groundnut** or **monkey nut**) The seed of a small leguminous plant. Peanuts can be successfully frozen either whole, chopped or roasted, but salted peanuts do not freeze well because they tend to become **rancid**. Peanut butter can also be frozen.

FREEZING: pack nuts in small pieces of **foil** and peanut butter in small cartons.

FREEZER LIFE: unsalted nuts, 1 year; buttered and roasted, 4 months; peanut butter, 3 months.

THAWING: allow to thaw at room temperature for 2–3 hours.

peanut butter See **peanut**.

pear A rounded or elongated bell-shaped **fruit** with yellow, green or pinkish fruit. Pears are best frozen lightly cooked because raw pears tend to discolour quickly and lose their crisp texture and flavour. Choose firm pears, which are just ripe. Most varieties of pear freeze well, but Comice are the best to use.

FREEZING: peel, quarter and core the **fruit**. Dip into **lemon juice** immediately to prevent **discoloration**. Prepare a syrup with 250 g (8 oz) of sugar to 600 ml (1 pint) of water and poach the pears in this for $1\frac{1}{2}$ minutes. Cool and pack the fruit into **rigid containers**. Cover with the syrup and place a piece of crumpled **foil** on the top to immerse the pears in the syrup. Leave a 2.5 cm (1 inch) **headspace** before **sealing** with a lid.

FREEZER LIFE: 8 months.

THAWING: allow the pears to thaw in their container at room temperature, for about 3 hours.

pecan nut A smooth, dark red **nut**, which may be frozen whole or chopped, but not salted because they tend to become **rancid**.

FREEZING: pack the pecan nuts tightly in small pieces of **foil** or in small cartons and **overwrap** with a **polythene bag**.

FREEZER LIFE: 1 year.

THAWING: allow to thaw at room temperature for 2–3 hours.

peppers (also called **pimientos** or **sweet peppers**) A species of **capsicum** with green (unripe), red, yellow or orange fruits. All the different coloured peppers may be frozen. Make sure that the skins are firm and glossy with no blemishes or bruising.

FREEZING: wash thoroughly, cut off the stems and remove all the seeds and inner membranes. Cut into halves, slices or rings, depending on their intended use. **Blanch** the halves in boiling water for 3 minutes, the rings and slices for 2 minutes, then cool in ice cold water and drain. Pack into **polythene bags**, expelling as much air as possible.

FREEZER LIFE: 1 year.

THAWING: either allow the peppers to thaw in their wrappings for 1–2 hours at room temperature or use directly from the freezer in dishes such as **casseroles**.

perch A large, round freshwater **fish** with firm flesh. Perch is normally sold whole, and must be cleaned and frozen within 12 hours of being caught.

FREEZING: wash thoroughly, remove the scales and gut, then **ice glaze**. Wrap the fish in **freezer wrap** and **overwrap** in a **polythene bag**, expelling as much air as possible before sealing.

FREEZER LIFE: 3 months.

THAWING: allow the perch to thaw in its wrappings in a cool place for up to 24 hours. Once it has thawed it should be cooked and consumed as quickly as possible.

persimmon A large, orange-red tropical **fruit**, similar to a large tomato, with tough sweet and sharp orange flesh. Choose soft and ripe persimmons for freezing.

FREEZING: wash and dry the fruit, remove the stems and peel. Make a syrup using 250 g (8 oz) of sugar to 600 ml (1 pint) of water and add 1 tablespoon of **lemon juice**. Pack the persimmons, either whole or cut in to quarters, into **rigid containers** and cover with the cold syrup. Leave a 2.5 cm (1 inch) **headspace** before **sealing** with a lid.

FREEZER LIFE: 1 year.

THAWING: allow the fruit to thaw in its container for about 3–4 hours at room temperature. Fruit that is to be eaten without further preparation should be used as soon as it has thawed. Alternatively, persimmons may be gently stewed from frozen in their syrup.

pesto sauce A **sauce** made with fresh **basil** and **pine kernels**, which is most often used as a sauce to accompany **pasta** dishes. It normally contains **garlic**, which tends to develop an unpleasant taste when frozen, so it is advisable to omit this prior to freezing and add it later.

FREEZING: make the pesto sauce as directed, omitting the garlic. Pack into small cartons and seal well. **Overwrap** with a **polythene bag** so that the strong smell of the basil does not taint other foods in the freezer.

THAWING: allow the pesto sauce to thaw in its container at room temperature for 2–3 hours, then mix in the crushed garlic before using.

pheasant A popular, seasonal **game** bird. Hen birds are thought to be more flavoursome and succulent than cock birds, but both may be frozen. Pheasants should be hung before freezing to tenderize them.

FREEZING: pluck the pheasants, remove the gut and clean thoroughly inside and out. Dry as much as possible, then pad the legs and any protruding bones with **foil**. Pack into **polythene bags**, extracting as much air as possible. Freeze the

giblets, if required, separately in polythene bags.

FREEZER LIFE: 6 months; giblets, 3 months.

THAWING: allow the pheasant to thaw in its wrapping at a maximum room temperature of 16°C (65°F) for approximately 8–9 hours until completely defrosted inside and out. Always remember to thaw poultry and game thoroughly to avoid the risk of **food poisoning**.

pickle Vegetables preserved in vinegar or brine. Pickle does not require freezing because the vinegar content ensures that it can be stored in a cool dry place for a considerable length of time. Commercially produced pickles may advise on the packaging that the product is stored in the refrigerator once it has been opened.

pies Most types of pie freeze well, either baked or unbaked.

FREEZING: make large and small pies in **foil** dishes or flan tins. If they are to be frozen unbaked do not make a steam vent. **Open freeze** all pies until they are firm. Cover the foil dishes with foil and **overwrap** in a **polythene bag**. Remove pies from tins and pack in **freezer wrap** and polythene bags. If the pies are to be baked before freezing, remember to undercook them a little so that they do not over-brown when **reheated**. Cool completely, then cover with foil and overwrap in a polythene bag, expelling as much air as possible. If making double crusted **fruit** pies, it can be helpful to add a little cornflour to the sugar, which thickens the juices and prevents the bottom layer of pastry from becoming soggy.

FREEZER LIFE: unbaked, 3 months; baked **meat** pies, 3–4 months; baked fruit pies, up to 6 months.

THAWING: unwrap, frozen unbaked pies and place in the oven at 220°C/425°F/Gas 7 for 40–60 minutes, depending on their size. Pies with a pastry top and base should have a small vent cut into the top because they begin to thaw in the oven. If oven- and freezer-proof **glass** dishes are used it is important to allow them to stand at room temperature for 10 minutes before being placed into a hot oven.

Alternatively, allow the pies to thaw in the refrigerator overnight and bake as usual. Allow baked pies to thaw at room temperature for 3–4 hours before reheating at 180°C/350°F/Gas 4. A filled biscuit pie crust, which is to be served cold, should be allowed to thaw at room temperature for 6 hours before serving.

pigeon A small **game** bird, which can be successfully frozen. Do not stuff before freezing, and freeze the **giblets** separately as they have a short storage life. Only freeze young, plump tender birds. Older birds should be made into **pies** or **patés** before freezing.

FREEZING: pluck, clean and dry thoroughly, and pad the legs and any protruding bones with **foil**. Then pack into **polythene bags**, extracting as much air as possible before sealing.

FREEZER LIFE: 1 year; giblets, 3 months.

THAWING: allow the birds to thaw at room temperature overnight, then cook and consume promptly.

pilchard A small, oily, **fish** of the herring family (known as a **sardine** when immature). Pilchards must be frozen within a day of being caught.

FREEZING: wash, remove the scales and gut. Dry and pack into **polythene bags**, expelling as much air as possible.

FREEZER LIFE: 2 months.

THAWING: pilchards may be cooked from frozen or allowed to thaw on a plate in the refrigerator for 3–4 hours before cooking.

pimiento See **peppers**.

pineapple A tropical **fruit** with yellow flesh and a hard scratchy skin. Pineapple can be obtained quite cheaply during the summer. They freeze very well either in a **dry sugar pack** or in a **syrup pack**. A pineapple is ripe when the inner leaves on the end of it can be pulled out easily. Choose ripe fruit for freezing, with a fruity smell and pale yellow base.

FREEZING: peel off all the hard skin, remove the hard core and slice or dice the fruit. Either (a), pack in sugar (approximately 125 g (4 oz) of sugar to every 500 g (1 lb) of fruit in **polythene bags**, expelling as much air as possible; or (b), pack pieces of pineapple in **rigid containers** and cover with a cold syrup made with 250 g (8 oz) of sugar to each 600 ml (1 pint) of water. Cover with crumpled **foil** in order to completely immerse the fruit in the liquid, and leave a 2.5 cm (1 inch) **headspace** before **sealing** with a lid. Crushed pineapple can also be frozen in this way, using approximately 125 g (4 oz) of sugar to every 375 g (12 oz) of fruit.

FREEZER LIFE: crushed pineapple, 8 months; pineapple in syrup, up to 1 year.

THAWING: allow to thaw in its container for 3–4 hours at room temperature.

pineapple juice The juice of the **pineapple**, which can be successfully frozen for 4–6 months.

FREEZING: remove the outer hard skin and spots from the pineapple and take out the central hard core. Chop up the flesh and purée in a blender or food processor. Strain through a sieve and pour into **rigid containers**, allowing a 2 cm **headspace** before **sealing**. Commercially prepared cartons of pineapple juice may be frozen, but it is preferable to transfer the contents into another container in case the carton bursts due to expansion of the juice in the freezer.

FREEZER LIFE: 4–6 months.

THAWING: allow to thaw at room temperature for about 2 hours before serving. See also **fruit juice**.

pine kernel The oily, aromatic seed of certain varieties of pine tree. Pine kernels contain a great deal of resinous oil, so they should not be stored for too long because they begin to develop a musty taste. They can be frozen whole for a short period of time.

FREEZING: pack tightly in little parcels of **foil** or in small cartons.

FREEZER LIFE: 1–2 months.

THAWING: allow to thaw at room temperature for 1–2 hours before using.

pistachio nut A small, hard-shelled **nut** with a green kernel. It may be frozen shelled, either whole or chopped up. Do not freeze salted pistachios because they quickly turn **rancid**.

FREEZING: pack shelled pistachios in small **foil** packages, expelling all the air, or in small cartons.

FREEZER LIFE: 1 year.

THAWING: allow the pistachios to thaw at room temperature for 2–3 hours.

pitta bread A flat, rounded, unleavened **bread**, which is now widely available and can be frozen successfully, providing that it is very fresh and soft. Slightly stale pitta bread becomes hard and leathery if frozen.

FREEZING: leave the pitta bread in the packaging it was bought in and **overwrap** in a **polythene bag** to exclude the air.

FREEZER LIFE: 6 months.

THAWING: allow to thaw in its wrappings at room temperature for 2–3 hours before warming in the oven. Or use from frozen, reheating under a hot grill and turning frequently.

pizza A disc of dough usually topped with tomatoes, cheese and any of a variety of other ingredients. Both home-made and commercially bought pizzas freeze well and are a useful standby for a quick and easy snack or meal.

FREEZING: home-made pizzas can be frozen unbaked or baked, but allow to cool completely before freezing. **Open freeze** pizzas until firm, then wrap each one in **foil** and **overwrap** several together in a **polythene bag**. Observe manufacturers' instructions for freezing commercially prepared pizzas.

FREEZER LIFE: unbaked, 1 month; baked, 3 months.

THAWING: bake or heat from frozen in a hot oven for about 30 minutes. Alternatively allow the pizzas to thaw at room temperature for 2–3 hours before baking or reheating in a warm oven for 15 minutes.

plaice A white flatfish with brown skin and red or orange spots. Plaice freezes well either whole or in fillets. Choose only the freshest fish for freezing.

FREEZING: wash and dry the fish thoroughly, remove the scales, roe (if present) and gut. Pack small whole plaice in **polythene bags**, expelling as much air as possible. **Open freeze** larger fish by freezing until firm, then **ice glaze**. Pack the fish into polythene bags and return them to the freezer. Separate fillets with **freezer wrap** and pack several together in **foil** or a polythene bag.

FREEZER LIFE: 3 months.

THAWING: cook small whole fish and fillets from frozen. Larger fish should be allowed to thaw in a cool place for 4–6 hours depending on the size of the fish. Then consume as soon as possible.

plastic containers These can be purchased in a variety of shapes and sizes, and are either made of flexible or rigid plastic (see **rigid containers**). Plastic containers that contain foods, such as **ice cream**, **margarine** and **yoghurt**, can be invaluable for use in the freezer. They save the cost of buying special freezer containers and are just as convenient to store and are generally just as airtight. However, they should be used with **polythene bags** to ensure that as much air as possible is excluded.

plum A small, thin-skinned **fruit** that may be purple, green or yellow. Most varieties of plum will freeze well. Choose firm, ripe fruit with no bruising, blemishes or splits in them. If stored for a long time the skins tend to become tough and the stones taint the flesh, so it is best to remove the stones and gently stew them or pack them in syrup.

FREEZING: wash, halve and remove the stones. Either (a), pack into **rigid containers** and cover with sugar syrup made with 250 g (8 oz) of sugar to every 600 ml (1 pint) of water. Place a piece of crumpled **foil** on top of the fruit to keep it immersed in the syrup; or (b), gently stew the fruit with sugar and allow it to cool completely, then pack into rigid containers leaving a 2.5 cm (1 inch) **headspace**.

FREEZER LIFE: 1 year.

THAWING: plums stored in syrup may be cooked from frozen. Allow stewed fruit to thaw at room temperature in its container for 2–4 hours.

pollack (also called **lythe**) A North Atlantic **fish** similar to **cod**, but with less flavour. Pollack is sold either whole, in steaks or fillets and can be frozen successfully. Always choose fresh fish that have been caught the same day.

FREEZING: **interleave** fillets or steaks with small pieces of **freezer wrap**, then **overwrap** several together in a **polythene bag**. Extract as much air as possible from the bag before **sealing**. For a whole fish, gut and clean then **ice glaze**.

FREEZER LIFE: 3 months.

THAWING: steaks and fillets can be cooked from frozen, although they may be thawed in the refrigerator if desired. Whole fish should be allowed to thaw in a cool place overnight, then cooked and consumed promptly.

polystyrene trays **Convenience foods** are often available in polystyrene packaging with a wax coating, which can then be transferred from the freezer to the microwave. These containers are available from supermarkets and other freezer specialists for use in the home freezer. They are useful for microwave cooking, but are not suitable for use in a conventional oven.

polythene bags These are available in a range of sizes for use in the freezer. It is important to use heavy-gauge polythene, designed specifically for freezer use, because the bags must be strong and airtight. Polythene bags are cheaper to use than **rigid containers** and can be used to freeze liquids as well as solids, by placing the bag inside a solid container until the liquid is frozen. It is possible to buy 'boil-in-the-bag' type bags in which ready cooked foods can be frozen, and then reheated by immersing the bags in boiling water. It is important to leave a **headspace** at the top of these bags for **expansion**, but as much air as possible must be expelled from ordinary polythene bags before **sealing**, so that the food is not spoiled by contact with the air.

polythene sheeting This material may be bought in one long sheet or as a sleeve for making different sized bags according to use. Polythene sheeting is also useful for wrapping **meat**, for **overwrapping foil** and packages of highly flavoured foods.

pomegranate A round tropical **fruit** with a hard reddish skin and pink flesh containing many small seeds. The seeds are edible and it is quite difficult and time consuming to separate the flesh from the seeds, so it is best to scoop out the insides and to freeze the pomegranate in sugar syrup. Choose ripe fruit.

FREEZING: cut the fruit in half, scoop out the insides and pack into **rigid containers**. Cover with a sugar syrup made with 250 g (8 oz) of sugar dissolved in 600 ml (1 pint) of water. Leave a 2.5 cm (1 inch) **headspace** before **sealing**.

FREEZER LIFE: 1 year.

THAWING: allow the fruit to thaw in its container for 2–4 hours at room temperature.

pork Pig **meat**, which has a relatively short freezer life (6 months) due to its high fat content, but joints, **chops** and diced or minced pork may be frozen successfully. Choose firm, pink, lean meat with firm, creamy white **fat**. Reheated cooked pork tends to dry out and become tough, so it is best to freeze raw rather than cooked pork.

FREEZING: trim off the surplus fat, pad any bones with small pieces of **foil**, or remove bones altogether if desired. **Interleave** chops with **freezer wrap** and **overwrap** several together in foil or **polythene bags**. Pack whole joints in freezer wrap then overwrap in polythene bags, expelling as much air as possible before sealing. Remember to label the packages clearly with a **Chinagraph pencil** or permanent ink felt-tip pen, because the **frost** that covers the packages makes it difficult to identify items.

FREEZER LIFE: 6 months.

THAWING: allow the meat to thaw in its wrappings for about 5 hours per 500 g (1lb), or cook from frozen. Chops, cubed and minced meat can be cooked from frozen, but allow about twice as long a cooking time at a reduced temperature, increasing the temperature towards the end of the cooking time. The cooking time for frozen joints can be difficult to calculate, so it is advisable to thaw them before cooking.

pork pie A pie made with minced, seasoned **pork**. Pork pies are not suitable for freezing because of their high fat content and jelly filling.

porridge A smooth paste made with oats cooked in milk or water. It is not advisable to freeze cooked porridge because it thickens and becomes solid and gluey in texture. It does not take long to cook fresh porridge and porridge oats may be stored in a cool dry place for up to 3 months, as long as they are kept in an airtight container.

potato A starchy, white tuber with brown or red skin. Most potatoes can be frozen successfully either fully or partially cooked. **Chips**, duchesse potatoes and croquettes are best frozen partially cooked, new and roast potatoes should be fully cooked. Leftover jacket potatoes may be split and stuffed with a cheese and potato mixture and frozen.

FREEZING: prepare duchesse and croquette potatoes in the usual manner, shape and then **open freeze** on trays until solid. Transfer into **rigid containers** separating the layers with **greaseproof paper**. Partially fry home-made chips until just soft (about 2 minutes), cool, open freeze, then pack into **polythene bags**, expelling as much air as possible. New potatoes should be small and all similar in size. Cook until just undercooked, drain and cool and pack into polythene bags. Roast potatoes in the usual way, drain on absorbent paper, cool and pack into polythene bags.

FREEZER LIFE: chips, 6 months; all other types of potato, 3 months.

THAWING: allow croquettes to thaw at room temperature for about 1 hour, then deep-fry or bake. Glaze duchesse potatoes with **egg** and reheat in a hot oven. Deep-fry chips from frozen. Cook roast potatoes from frozen in a fairly hot oven; fry them quickly in a little oil to make then crisp again. Small new potatoes can be cooked from frozen, but larger ones should be thawed.

potato dishes Cooked potato dishes, such as potatoes boulangere and lyonnaise, may be frozen and then simply reheated.

FREEZING: prepare potato dishes according to the recipe used and place in freezer-proof dishes or **foil** containers. Cook completely, allow to cool, and then cover with foil and **overwrap** with a large **polythene bag**.

THAWING: cooked dishes may be reheated from frozen.

poultry The meat of domestic fowls. Most kinds of fresh poultry freeze satisfactorily, if prepared and cleaned in the usual manner beforehand. Always choose young, plump tender birds. If you buy ready trussed poultry, remember to remove the bag of **giblets** before freezing because they have a far shorter freezer life and must be frozen separately. Do not stuff before freezing because this slows up freezing and thawing, which allows time for **microorganisms** (especially **salmonella**) to grow and may lead to **food poisoning**.

Always thaw poultry thoroughly because it is a fruitful source of salmonella. Freezing does not destroy harmful bacteria it only makes it dormant. Bacteria can only be destroyed by cooking the birds thoroughly, right through to the inside. Almost all bacteria found in raw poultry are destroyed by careful and adequate cooking. To test if a bird is thoroughly cooked pierce the thickest part with a skewer. If the juices run clear then the bird is cooked, but if they are pink (which means blood is still present) it needs to cook for longer. Never refreeze cooked poultry, this can lead to food poisoning. See **chicken**; **duck**; **goose**; **poussin**; **turkey**.

poussin A young **chicken** usually weighing a maximum of 500 g (1 lb) and sold whole.

FREEZING: clean thoroughly, inside and out, and remove the **giblets**. Do not stuff before freezing. Cover any protruding bones with small pieces of **foil**, then pack in a **polythene bag** and extract as much air as possible before **sealing**.

FREEZER LIFE: 1 year.

THAWING: allow the poussin to thaw in the refrigerator, in its wrappings, overnight.

power cut A power cut generally does not affect the contents of a freezer too much. The food keeps solid and perfectly safe for 16–24 hours, providing that the door or lid is not opened.

If given an advanced warning of a power cut certain precautions may be taken. Ice cream should be moved to the bottom or back of the freezer and dense food items, such as meat or poultry, should be placed on the top or at the front. Fill the freezer to the brim, padding out any gaps with screwed up newspapers. Turn on the fast-freeze switch for 2–4 hours before the power cut, and leave it on for several hours after the cut until the temperature has returned to normal. If the power cut lasts longer than 24 hours check for any food that has started to thaw and either cook it immediately, or throw it away if it has deteriorated in any way.

prawn Any of various small, mild-tasting **shellfish**. Prawns must be exceptionally fresh if they are to be frozen, to minimize the risk of **food poisoning**. Ideally they should be frozen within 12 hours of being caught.

FREEZING: wash thoroughly, then boil in lightly salted water for 2–4 minutes until they turn pink. Cool in their cooking liquid. Remove the shells and pack the prawns tightly into **polythene bags**. It is also possible to freeze raw prawns by simply washing them, removing their heads and packing tightly into polythene bags.

FREEZER LIFE: 1 month.

THAWING: allow cooked prawns to thaw in the refrigerator if they are to be served in salads. They may be added to hot dishes while still frozen and allowed to heat completely through. Raw frozen prawns should be dropped in boiling salted water and simmered for 2–4 minutes.

prunes A dried plum. See **dried fruit**

puddings Most types of hot and cold puddings freeze successfully with the exception of clear **jellies**, which become granular and rubbery in texture. Steamed, baked and **milk** puddings freeze well, as do **crumbles**, **pies**, **mousses** and **soufflés**.

FREEZING: make steamed puddings in the usual way and pack into **foil** basins or freezer-proof basins after cooking and cooling. Cover with foil and **overwrap** with a **polythene bag**. Do not put **jam** or syrup in the base of any of the puddings, this will become soggy when thawing. Make baked sponge puddings in the usual way, turn out of the tin, cool and **open freeze**. When hard, wrap in foil and return to the freezer. Crumbles can be either made up completely in freezer-proof dishes, or the filling and the crumble may be frozen separately in **rigid containers**. Make and freeze **fruit** pies in foil containers, wrapping them in foil and overwrapping in polythene bags. Cook milk puddings and allow to cool, then cover in foil and overwrap in a polythene bag. Cold puddings, such as mousses and cold soufflés, can be frozen in their moulds or freezer-proof dishes and covered in foil or **freezer wrap**.

FREEZER LIFE: 3 months for most puddings.

THAWING: reheat steamed puddings from frozen by boiling for approximately 1 hour in a large saucepan until thoroughly heated through. Thaw baked puddings at room temperature for 3–4 hours if to be served cold. Or thaw them at room temperature for approximately 2 hours and then reheat at 190°C/375°F/Gas 5 for 30 minutes.

Crumbles may be baked from frozen at 190°C/375°F/Gas 5 for about an hour. Alternatively sprinkle frozen crumble mixture over fresh fruit and bake in the usual way. Raw fruit pies can be baked from frozen at 200°C/400°F/ Gas 6. Cooked pies should be reheated at 190°C/375°F/Gas 5 for 30–40 minutes.

To thaw milk puddings, add a little extra milk and reheat very gently in a pan, stirring frequently. Cold puddings, such as mousses and soufflés, should be allowed to thaw in the refrigerator for 2–4 hours.

pulses (also called **legumes**) The edible seeds of leguminous plants. Certain pulses, such as **lentils**, dried peas and beans, take a long time to soak and then cook, so it can be quite useful to soak and cook them in bulk and store them after cooking for future use. They need to be fresh because older pulses tend to become musty and stale.

FREEZING: soak and cook all pulses in the usual way, but remove from the heat when still slightly undercooked and allow to cool completely. Drain, pat dry and pack into **rigid containers**.

FREEZER LIFE: 6 months.

THAWING: allow the pulses to thaw at room temperature for 3–4 hours, then add to other foods giving them enough time to finish cooking. Alternatively, they may then be puréed and added to dishes, such as **soups**.

pumpernickel A type of coarse, black, sour-tasting **bread** made with wholemeal rye flour. Pumpernickel may be frozen successfully either on its own or combined with various fillings as a **sandwich**.

FREEZING: wrap both filled and unfilled pumpernickel in **freezer wrap** and **overwrap** in a **polythene bag**, extracting as much air as possible before **sealing**.

FREEZER LIFE: 4 months.

THAWING: allow to thaw at room temperature for 3–4 hours before using.

pumpkin A large round **fruit** with a tough orange rind and pulpy orange flesh. Pumpkins are generally only available from September to December. Consequently, it can be very useful to buy fresh pumpkin and freeze it for future use.

FREEZING: wash the pumpkin, peel, cut in half and remove all the seeds. Cut into small peices and either steam or boil until tender. Either drain and allow to cool, or mash with **butter** until thoroughly puréed and allow to cool. Pack in **rigid containers** and leave a 2.5 cm (1 inch) **headspace**.

FREEZER LIFE: 1 year.

THAWING: allow pumpkin pieces to thaw in the refrigerator for 3–4 hours before using. Pumpkin purée may be reheated gently from frozen before using.

pyrosil See **china**.

quail A small **game** bird, which may be frozen satisfactorily.

FREEZING: remove feathers, head, neck and giblet. Clean well and pack into **polythene bags** or onto **foil** trays, **overwrapped** with polythene bags.

FREEZER LIFE: 6 months.

THAWING: allow the quail to thaw in the refrigerator for 5 hours per 500 g (1lb) before roasting.

quark A very low-fat soft **cheese**, made with skimmed **milk**. It does not freeze well alone, because it has such a low butterfat content, but it can be frozen when made into other composite dishes, such as **paté** and **cheesecake**.

quiche A savoury **flan** that is invaluable to keep in the freezer to provide a quick and easy snack or meal. Quiches should be completely baked before freezing.

FREEZING: after baking allow to become completely cold, then **open freeze** until firm. When hard remove from the flan tin (if used) wrap in **foil**, then **overwrap** in a **polythene bag**. If the quiches have been baked in foil containers, simply cover with foil and overwrap with a polythene bag.

FREEZER LIFE: 2 months.

THAWING: if the quiche is to be served cold allow it to thaw at room temperature for about 2 hours loosely wrapped. If it is to be served hot it may be cooked from frozen at 180°C/350°F/Gas 4 for approximately 20 minutes.

quince A pear-shaped, brownish-yellow **fruit** with hard, sour flesh. Quince is most commonly used either on its own or combined with **apples** or **pears** in **jellies**, **preserves**, **pies** and **puddings**. It can be satisfactorily frozen for this purpose.

FREEZING: peel, quarter and core the fruit and remove any hard pieces of flesh around the core. Slice into small pieces and **blanch** in boiling water for 2 minutes. Cool the fruit, drain and **open freeze** on trays. When hard, transfer into **polythene bags**.

FREEZER LIFE: 1 year.

THAWING: stew the quince gently from frozen with a little sugar and water until tender, then combine with other fruit.

quorn A **vegetable** protein that is now becoming widely available as a substitute for **meat** in cooked dishes and in **convenience foods**. It may be frozen or chilled successfully.

FREEZING: freeze quorn either alone or made up into composite dishes in the container it is purchased in and **overwrap** it in a **polythene bag** to prevent air from reaching it.

FREEZER LIFE: up to 3 months.

THAWING: quorn can be used straight from the freezer or allowed to thaw in the refrigerator for up 2–3 hours before using as required.

rabbit A small **game** mammal, which freezes well providing it is absolutely fresh and has not been hung.

FREEZING: skin the rabbit, remove the gut and clean thoroughly (inside and out), and dry with a cloth. Cut it into joints and pack tightly into **polythene bags**.

FREEZER LIFE: raw, 6 months; cooked, 2 months.

THAWING: allow the rabbit to thaw in the refrigerator for about 5 hours per 500 g (1lb). Young rabbits can be roasted after freezing, but it is best to braise or **casserole** older rabbits or make them into a **pie**.

radish A small rounded root with pink skin and pungent, white flesh. As with many other salad **vegetables**, due to their high water content, radishes do not freeze well, becoming soft and mushy. They store quite satisfactorily for a few weeks in a cool, dry place.

raisin A dried black grape. See **dried fruit**

rambutan A small, red, hairy skinned **fruit**, very similar to a **lychee**. Rambutans are best frozen in syrup.

FREEZING: remove the outer skin, halve and stone the fruit. Pack into **rigid containers** and cover with a sugar syrup made with 250 g (8 oz) of sugar to every 600 ml (1 pint) of water. Leave a 2.5 cm (1 inch) **headspace** before **sealing**.

FREEZER LIFE: 1 year.

THAWING: allow the fruit to thaw in its container at room temperature for 3–4 hours before serving.

rancid A term used to describe food with an unpleasant stale taste or smell due to decomposition. Over a length of time foods containing a high proportion of **fat** may become rancid. Fatty **meats**, oily **fish**, **butter** and **pastry** are the foods that are likely to become rancid most quickly. It is a result of oxygen in the air reacting with the acids in the fat cells. Rancidity is not harmful, but the taste and smell of foods are greatly affected. Salt speeds up rancidity, so foods with a high salt content should not be stored for long. Careful and thorough packing prior to freezing foods can help a great deal to prevent rancidity occurring, especially in the case of **bacon** and fish. See **oxidation**.

raspberry The red, soft **fruit** of the raspberry plant. Rasberries freeze extremely well, retaining their colour and flavour. They may be frozen with or without sugar or as a purée. Do not freeze any damaged or squashed fruit if freezing whole.

FREEZING: **open freeze** whole raspberries on trays until firm, then transfer into **polythene bags** to store. Alternatively, they may be packed with sugar, adding 125 g (4 oz) of sugar to every 500 g (1lb) of fruit, and put into polythene bags. Make raspberry purée with sugar to taste and pour the purée into **rigid containers**, leaving a 2.5 cm (1 inch) **headspace** before **sealing**.

FREEZER LIFE: 1 year.

THAWING: allow whole fruit and purée to thaw at room temperature for about 3 hours. Fruit that has been open frozen may be used straight from the freezer.

ratatouille A **vegetable** dish containing a combination of **onion**, **tomato**, **aubergine**, **courgettes** and **peppers**, which can be made up and cooked thoroughly and frozen satisfactorily.

FREEZING: make the ratatouille as usual, then place in **foil** freezer containers or oven-to-freezer dishes and allow to cool completely. Cover with foil or a lid and **overwrap** with a **polythene bag**.

FREEZER LIFE: 6 months.

THAWING: ratatouille may be reheated from frozen or allowed to thaw at room temperature for 3–4 hours before using.

ravioli See **pasta**.

ready meal See **convenience foods**.

red cabbage A **vegetable** that is not always available in the shops, so it can be worthwhile freezing. Red cabbage can either be **blanched** and frozen or cooked completely, for example by braising, before freezing.

FREEZING: wash the cabbage thoroughly, slice it up and blanch in boiling water for $1\frac{1}{2}$ minutes.

Plunge immediately into ice cold water, then drain and pat dry and pack into **polythene bags**, expelling as much air as possible before sealing. If the cabbage is to be cooked, cook in a freezer-to-oven container and allow to cool. Cover with the lid or a sheet of **foil** and **overwrap** with a polythene bag.

FREEZER LIFE: blanched or cooked, 6 months.

THAWING: it may be cooked or reheated from frozen.

redcurrant A small, rounded, red **fruit**, which is best frozen by the **dry pack** method and preferably without any wrapping until firm.

FREEZING: remove all the stalks, wash and dry the fruit. **Open freeze** on trays. When firm, transfer into **polythene bags** and extract as much air as possible before **sealing**. Alternatively, they may be packed with sugar, using about 125 g (4 oz) of sugar to every 500 g (1lb) of fruit. Mix the fruit well with the sugar and pack into polythene bags to freeze.

FREEZER LIFE: 1 year.

THAWING: allow the fruit to thaw at room temperature for about 3 hours or cook from frozen if preferred. Fruit that has been open frozen first can be used as decoration.

red mullet See **mullet**.

red snapper A round, red, marine **fish** with white flesh. Red snappers are usually sold whole, in steaks or fillets. They must be fresh when bought for home freezing because they should not be refrozen.

FREEZING: wash, remove the scales and the gut. Small whole fish may be wrapped in **polythene bags**, with as much air extracted as possible. **Open freeze** large fish until firm, then dip into cold water to **ice glaze**. Then wrap tightly in a polythene bag and store in the freezer. **Interleave** steaks and fillets with **freezer wrap** and **overwrap** several together in **foil** or a polythene bag.

FREEZER LIFE: 3 months.

THAWING: allow whole fish to thaw in a cool place for up to 24 hours, then use as soon as possible.

refreezing The main problems associated with refreezing are loss of texture and bacterial growth. The latter can be a cause of **food poisoning** so it is important to be very careful when refreezing. Generally, it is best never to refreeze food that has been thawed. However, if it has only softened a little on the outside, for instance when transporting from shop to home, it may be refrozen, although it may lose a little colour and texture. Also such food should be refrozen using the super-freeze switch, if possible.

Fruit and **vegetables** tend to thaw very quickly and consequently should be cooked first before refreezing. Their texture may change, but they can always be used in dishes such as soups and sauces. Vegetables that have thawed are particularly susceptible to bacterial growth, so half-thawed items should not be refrozen. Bacterial activity increases in frozen foods once they become warm, so **fish**, **meat** and **poultry** must be cooked immediately once they have thawed, but if they deteriorate in any way they must be thrown away.

If there is a **breakdown** or **power cut** care must be taken that only certain foods are refrozen. The food must still be fresh, if it has deteriorated at all it may cause food poisoning because freezing does not kill the **bacteria** that would have grown. When food is thawed and refrozen there is likely to be a loss of colour, texture, flavour and nutritional value, but providing that certain foods have been well wrapped there are many that may be saved. Fruit and vegetables should be cooked and puréed before refreezing. **Bread**, plain, unfilled **cakes** and **pastry** can be refrozen, but they may be become a little stale. Never refreeze raw meat, poultry or fish. If they have just thawed and not deteriorated they can be cooked and then refrozen in dishes such as casseroles. Never refreeze **ready meals**, **ice cream** or **cream** (including synthetic cream). It is also important that with every food that has thawed and been refrozen it should not be stored for very long and eaten as soon as possible.

reheating Once frozen food has completely thawed it is important to reheat it as quickly and thoroughly as possible. **Convenience foods** and **ready meals** can sometimes be reheated from frozen, but it is necessary to ensure that they are heated right through at a high temperature to prevent bacterial growth and the risk of **food poisoning**. Always consume reheated food as soon as possible. If reheating in a microwave remember to stir and turn dishes regularly, to distribute the heat evenly.

rhubarb The sour, pink leafstalk of the rhubarb plant. Early rhubarb has tender stalks, but later rhubarb is tougher and stronger. Both may be frozen successfully, but avoid limp stalks.

FREEZING: wash, remove the leaves and thick stalk bases. Cut into 2.5 cm (1 inch) lengths and **blanch** in boiling water for 1 minute. Plunge into cold water, drain and cool. Either (a), **open freeze** on trays and pack into **polythene bags**, expelling as much air as possible before sealing; or (b), pack in **rigid containers** and cover with a sugar syrup made with 250 g (8 oz) of sugar to every 600 ml (1 pint) of water. Cover with a lid leaving a 2.5 cm (1 inch) **headspace**. The rhubarb may also be stewed, sweetened and frozen as purée in rigid containers.

FREEZER LIFE: dry pack, 6–8 months; syrup pack, 9–12 months; purée, 1 year.

THAWING: rhubarb in syrup should be gently reheated until thawed before cooking. Dry pack rhubarb can be partially thawed at room temperature for a few hours or thawed gently with a little water and sugar before cooking in **pies** and **crumbles**. Thaw purée at room temperature for about 3 hours.

rice The grains of a grass, which can be successfully frozen. Rice can be quickly cooked, so there is not much point in freezing it specifically to save time later on, but it may be worthwhile for saving leftovers.

FREEZING: pack the rice loosely in a **polythene bag**, **seal** it and place in the freezer. When it is half frozen, squeeze the bag to separate out the grains and replace in the freezer.

FREEZER LIFE: on its own, 6 months; in made-up dishes containing other foods, 3 months.

THAWING: rice may be used from frozen if it is to be used in hot dishes such as **soups**. If it is to be used as a stuffing ingredient, allow it to thaw at room temperature for about 1 hour before using.

rice pudding See **pudding**.

rigid container These are containers, normally made of hard plastic, that are sold specifically for use in the freezer. They are manufactured with well-fitting lids so that the food is sealed in securely, and they are washable and can be used many times. Rigid containers are invaluable in the freezer because they help to protect delicate foods and their shapes make them convenient for stacking (especially square ones), which helps to save space. It is also possible to freeze liquids in them.

risotto A rice dish made with a variety of **meat** and **vegetable** ingredients.

FREEZING: cook as usual, allow to cool, then pack into **rigid containers**.

FREEZER LIFE: 2 months.

THAWING: allow the risotto to thaw overnight in the refrigerator, then reheat gently before consuming.

rissole A savoury flat cake made with **meat**, **fish** or **nuts** combined with mashed **potato** and seasonings. Rissoles freeze satisfactorily for up to 3 months.

FREEZING: make the rissoles according to the recipe and then pack them into **rigid containers**. Separate the layers with small pieces of **foil** or **greaseproof paper** and seal securely.

FREEZER LIFE: 3 months.

THAWING: rissoles are best fried, grilled or baked when still frozen.

rock salmon See **dogfish**.

roe The milt or testis of the male fish (soft roe) or the eggs of the female fish (hard roe). Cod's roe, smoked cod's roe and herring roe must be really fresh if it is to be frozen. Do not refreeze roe from the fishmonger if it has already been frozen.

FREEZING: slice cooked cod's roe into 1 cm ($\frac{1}{2}$ inch) slices and **interleave** slices with **freezer wrap**. Pack into **rigid containers**. Pack smoked cod's roe into **polythene bags** and exclude as much air as possible before sealing. Soft and hard herring's roe should be washed, dried and packed into rigid containers.

FREEZER LIFE: cooked cod's roe, 1 month; herring roe, 2 months; smoked cod's roe, 3 months.

THAWING: allow to thaw at room temperature for about 2–3 hours. Once it has thawed, it should be cooked and used as soon as possible. See also **taramasalata**.

rosehip The scarlet, berry-like fruit of a rose plant. Rosehips are normally used to make rosehip syrup, which has always been a popular syrup to give to children because it contains a high proportion of vitamin C. Alternatively, they may be made into rosehip jelly. Rosehip juice may be satisfactorily frozen for 4–6 months.

FREEZING: chop up the rosehips and steep in boiling water. Pass the liquid 2 or 3 times through a muslin cloth or **jelly** bag, making sure that all the sharp, prickly hairs surrounding the seeds are removed. Pour into **rigid containers** leaving a 2.5 cm (1 inch) **headspace** and freeze upright until firm.

FREEZER LIFE: 4–6 months.

THAWING: allow the juice to thaw in its container at room temperature for 3–4 hours before using to make rosehip syrup or jelly.

rosemary The aromatic grey-green leaves of a small European shrub. Rosemary is a strong **herb** that has a particular affinity with **lamb** dishes. It can be successfully dried or frozen.

FREEZING: wash and dry the rosemary thoroughly, and strip the leaves off the hard stalks and chop finely. Then either (a), place in small cartons or **polythene bags** and extract as much air as possible before **sealing**; or (b), pack sprigs of rosemary into small polythene bags to freeze.

FREEZER LIFE: 6 months.

THAWING: frozen rosemary may be added to most dishes straight from the freezer without thawing.

roulade A sponge **cake** that can be made into a savoury roulade or sweet swiss roll. It is best to freeze the sponge before filling, if possible, because it may become soggy when thawed.

FREEZING: roll up the roulade with a little cornflour sprinkled on it to prevent it from sticking. Pack carefully into a **polythene bag**, expelling as much air as possible. Filled roulade should be **open frozen** before packing in **freezer wrap** and **overwrapping** in a polythene bag.

FREEZER LIFE: unfilled roulades, 4 months; filled roulades 2–3 months, depending on the ingredients in the filling.

THAWING: allow unfilled roulades to thaw at room temperature for about 2 hours before carefully unrolling and filling. Filled roulades should be unwrapped and thawed at room temperature for 2–3 hours.

rowanberry The orange-scarlet, berry-like **fruit** of the mountain ash tree. Rowanberries are bittersweet and normally made into a **jelly** to serve as an accompaniment to **venison** or **lamb**. They are not usually available in the shops, but they can be frozen successfully.

FREEZING: wash and dry, then **open freeze** on trays until firm. Transfer into **polythene bags** and expel as much air as possible before sealing.

FREEZER LIFE: 6–8 months.

THAWING: allow to thaw in the bag for 2–3 hours before using in **jams** and jellies.

rum babas Individual sponge-type **puddings** made from a yeast dough. Rum babas are best frozen baked, but not soaked in syrup. This can be done after thawing.

FREEZING: bake as usual and allow to cool completely. Pack into **polythene bags**, expelling as much air as possible before sealing.

FREEZER LIFE: 3 months.

THAWING: remove the rum babas from their wrappings and stand on a plate. Allow to thaw at room temperature for about 45 minutes before soaking with hot syrup.

runner bean (also called **string bean**) The immature pod of the scarlet runner bean plant. Runner beans freeze successfully, but choose young, fresh beans for the best results.

FREEZING: cut off the ends and remove strings if necessary. Slice thickly because they lose their taste and texture if sliced too finely. **Blanch** in boiling water for 2 minutes, cool in cold water, drain and **open freeze** on trays in the freezer. When firm, transfer the beans into **polythene bags** and withdraw as much air as possible before **sealing**.

FREEZER LIFE: 1 year.

THAWING: runner beans are best cooked from frozen in boiling water.

sage The grey-green leaves of a perennial Mediterranean plant, which are used as a **herb**. Sage can be frozen simply chopped up or with a little water.

FREEZING: wash, dry and chop up the sage leaves. Pack them into small plastic cartons or into ice cube trays with a little water. Tip the frozen cubes into **polythene bags** to store.

FREEZER LIFE: 6 months.

THAWING: allow to thaw at room temperature for 1–2 hours before using, such as in **stuffings** and **pork** dishes.

sago A starchy cereal obtained from the pith of the sago palm. Sago is commonly used to make a **milk pudding**, which can be frozen if necessary.

FREEZING: freeze leftover sago pudding in a **foil** or a plastic **rigid container** and cover with foil or a lid.

FREEZER LIFE: 3 months.

THAWING: add a little more milk and allow to thaw slowly. Once thawed increase the heat so that the pudding is heated through thoroughly.

salad vegetables A general term used to describe certain **vegetables** commonly used in salads, such as **cucumbers, lettuce, tomatoes, radishes, watercress** and **spring onions**. Most salad vegetables contain a high proportion of water, which means that they do not freeze successfully because they become soft and mushy. Therefore, they are not suitable for freezing if they are to be eaten raw.

salami A type of sausage, highly spiced and usually flavoured with garlic. Salami may be frozen for a short time, so if there is some left over it may be worthwhile to freeze it, but there is not much point in preparing it especially for freezing.

FREEZING: wrap tightly in **freezer wrap** or **clingfilm** and **overwrap** in a **polythene bag**, expelling as much air as possible before sealing.

FREEZER LIFE: 1 month.

THAWING: allow the salami to thaw in its wrappings for 2–3 hours at room temperature and consume within a few days.

salmon A soft-finned fatty **fish** native to the Atlantic and Pacific Oceans. Salmon must be frozen when absolutely fresh. Ideally it should be caught and frozen on the same day.

FREEZING: wash, remove the scales and gut, then wash thoroughly again under running cold water, drain and dry. It may be left whole or divided into steaks for freezing. Whole fish should be **ice glazed** and wrapped in a large **polythene bag** or polythene sheeting. **Interleave** steaks or fillets with **freezer wrap** and wrap several together in **foil** or a polythene bag.

FREEZER LIFE: 2 months.

THAWING: allow whole fish to thaw in a cool place for up to 24 hours, then cook and consume as soon as possible. Salmon steaks may be cooked from frozen or allowed to thaw in the refrigerator overnight.

salmon, smoked See **smoked fish**.

salmonella A type of **bacteria** that can lead to severe **food poisoning**. Salmonella's symptoms are characterized by diarrhoea, vomiting, abdomenal pain and feverishness. It should always be diagnosed and treated by a doctor.

Salmonella is most often found in **poultry** and so it is vitally important that **chicken**, **turkey** and **goose** are thawed thoroughly after freezing and then cooked properly, so that the heat penetrates right through to the inside. This should ensure that any salmonella bacteria that might be present in the cavity of the carcass is completely destroyed. It is destroyed by temperatures above 60°C, so boiling foods is an effective way of ensuring that they are safe to eat.

Raw **milk**, **eggs** and **meat** can also be contaminated by the salmonella bacteria, so it is important to always cook these items thoroughly. Salmonella also breeds rapidly at room temperature so no food should be kept at this temperature for any longer than necessary.

salsify A root **vegetable** with a delicate, oyster-like flavour. Salsify may be frozen, but use young and tender roots.

FREEZING: scrub the salsify, but do not peel. **Blanch** in boiling water for 2 minutes, cut into 5–6 cm (2–3 inch) lengths and peel while still warm. Allow to cool completely and pack into **polythene bags**, expelling as much air as possible, seal and freeze.

FREEZER LIFE: 1 year.

THAWING: cook from frozen in boiling water.

salt A white powder or crystalline solid consisting mainly of sodium chloride. Salt becomes stronger in taste during the freezing process, so it is advisable not to over-season food that is to be frozen. It also accelerates the speed at which certain foods, such as **nuts** and **butter** and other fatty foods, turn **rancid**. Generally, it is best to avoid using it if possible.

samosa A small, spicy triangular Indian **pastry** containing either **meat** or **vegetables** and served fried. Samosas may be cooked and frozen, but only for a short time. Due to the high **fat** content they become **rancid** if stored for too long.

FREEZING: pack the samosas into a **polythene bag** and expel as much air as possible before **sealing**.

FREEZER LIFE: 1 month.

THAWING: allow to thaw at room temperature for 2–3 hours before either serving cold or **reheating**.

sandwich Two or more slices of **bread** filled with a variety of fillings. Sandwiches are worth freezing if they are required frequently, for example, for packed lunches, picnics, and parties. However, the bread should be fresh and only filled with ingredients that can be frozen for up to 2 months. Avoid hard-boiled **eggs**, **mayonnaise** or **salad vegetables**.

FREEZING: make sandwiches as usual and stack them in piles of up to six or eight together. Wrap in **foil** and **overwrap** in a **polythene bag**, expelling as much air as possible, then seal and freeze. Open sandwiches can be frozen unwrapped without garnishes on trays in the freezer and then packed into **rigid containers**, **interleaving** them with **freezer wrap** between the layers. Pinwheel and ribbon sandwiches should be frozen before slicing, and they can be cut as required when partially thawed.

FREEZER LIFE: 2 months.

THAWING: allow the sandwiches to thaw in their wrappings at room temperature for about 3 hours.

sardine A small, immature fatty **fish** of the herring family (usually a **pilchard**). Sardines that are intended for freezing must be fresh. Leftover canned sardines may be transferred to small containers and frozen if desired.

FREEZING: wipe the sardine with a damp cloth and remove the head and gut. Rinse thoroughly, drain and dry, then wrap tightly in **polythene bags**.

FREEZER LIFE: 2 months.

THAWING: sardines may be cooked from frozen.

satsuma A small citrus **fruit** similar to a **tangerine**, with a loose rind and without any pips. Satsumas may be frozen in a number of ways.

FREEZING: peel, remove the pith and separate into segments. Then either (a), pack the fruit into **rigid containers** and cover with a cold syrup made with 500 g (1lb) of sugar to every 1 litre (2 pints) of water; or (b), pack into rigid containers and mix with 250 g (8 oz) of sugar to every 500 g (1lb) of fruit until the juices begin to run, then seal and freeze; or (c), squeeze the juice from the satsumas and pack into ice cube trays. When frozen pack into polythene bags, expelling as much air as possible before sealing.

FREEZER LIFE: fruit, 1 year; fruit juice, 4–6 months.

THAWING: allow both the fruit and fruit juice to thaw in their containers for 3 hours at room temperature.

sauces Any liquid or semi-liquid preparation eaten with food to improve or add flavour. Sauces, such as white, bolognese, curry, apple and bread, can all be successfully frozen.

FREEZING: make the sauce according to the recipe and cool completely, covering with **greaseproof paper** if a skin is likely to form. When cool, beat thoroughly and pack into **rigid containers**, leaving a little **headspace** before **sealing**.

FREEZER LIFE: white sauce and meat sauces, 3 months; fruit sauces, 12 months.

THAWING: most sauces may be reheated gently from frozen. Beat well during heating, adding a little extra liquid if necessary.

sausage Finely minced meat, especially pork or beef, mixed with fat, cereal or bread, and seasonings. Only fresh sausages and sausage meat may be frozen. Avoid **garlic** sausages because their flavour may deteriorate during the freezing process.

FREEZING: pack sausages and sausage meat in small quantities into **polythene bags** and extract as much air as possible before **sealing**.

FREEZER LIFE: 2 months.

THAWING: allow the sausages to thaw in the refrigerator for 3–4 hours before using or cook gently and thoroughly from frozen if necessary. Allow sausage meat to thaw in the refrigerator for 4–5 hours before using.

sausage roll A roll of sausage meat encased in **pastry**. Sausage rolls made with shortcrust or puff pastry can be successfully frozen, either baked or unbaked.

FREEZING: **open freeze** unbaked sausage rolls on trays in the freezer. When firm, transfer in to **polythene bags** to store, expelling as much air as possible before **sealing**. Part-baked or completely baked sausage rolls may be frozen in **rigid containers**, separating the layers with sheets of **foil** or **freezer wrap**.

FREEZER LIFE: 2 months.

THAWING: unbaked sausage rolls may be cooked from frozen. Place them on a baking sheet and brush with a little beaten egg or milk. Cook at 220°C/425°F/Gas 7 for approximately 30 minutes, until they are puffed up and golden brown. Baked sausage rolls should be left to thaw in the refrigerator for several hours, then 'refreshed' in a moderate oven for a few minutes.

savarin A sponge dessert made from the same yeast **dough** as **rum babas**, but which is baked in a large ring mould. Savarin can be frozen baked, but it is advisable not to soak it in syrup or decorate it before freezing.

FREEZING: make and bake as usual and allow to cool without soaking in syrup. Pack in **freezer wrap** and freeze until firm. Then **overwrap** in a **polythene bag** to store.

FREEZER LIFE: 3 months.

THAWING: unwrap the savarin and stand on a plate to thaw for 1–2 hours before soaking with syrup and decorating.

scallop Any of various edible molluscs. Scallops can only be frozen if they are really fresh. Ideally they should be caught and frozen on the same day.

FREEZING: scrub the shells thoroughly, then place in boiling water until the shells open. Remove the scallops and the orange **roe** as soon as the shells open. Wash thoroughly in salted water, rinse well and pat dry. Pack into **rigid containers** and freeze. Scallops may also be frozen when cooked in a **sauce** and simply **reheated** after thawing.

FREEZER LIFE: 1 month.

THAWING: allow the scallops to thaw in the refrigerator overnight and use as fresh scallops. They can also be heated in water or a sauce from frozen if necessary. Composite dishes may also be reheated from frozen.

scampi A large prawn that must be really fresh if it is to be frozen. Ideally scampi should be caught and frozen on the same day.

FREEZING: remove the heads and shells from the scampi and place the flesh in a sieve under running water. The unshelled tails may also be frozen complete. Wash well and pack into **rigid containers** or **polythene bags** to freeze.

FREEZER LIFE: 1 month.

THAWING: place frozen scampi into boiling water and simmer gently for 4–6 minutes, depending on their size.

scone A small doughy cake. Scones freeze well and because they quickly become stale it is worth freezing any leftover scones.

FREEZING: bake as usual and allow to cool completely. Pack into **polythene bags**, expelling as much air as possible before **sealing**.

FREEZER LIFE: plain scones, 6 months; cheese scones, 3 months.

THAWING: allow the scones to thaw in their bags at room temperature for about 1 hour before using. Or spread frozen scones on a baking tray and reheat for 10 minutes at 200°C/400°F/Gas 6.

scorzonera The black rooted variety of **salsify**. Prepare and freeze as for salsify.

Scotch egg A hard-boiled **egg** encased in a layer of meat covered with egg and breadcrumbs. Do not freeze either commercially prepared or home-made Scotch eggs because the eggs become hard and rubbery.

sea bass A large round **fish** native to the American coast. Sea bass is sold whole or as steaks and fillets, and it can be frozen successfully.

FREEZING: wash, remove the scales and the gut from whole fish, and dry as much as possible. **Ice glaze** and then transfer the fish to a large **polythene bag** or wrap in **foil** to store. **Interleave** steaks and fillets with small pieces of **freezer wrap** and **over-wrap** in a polythene bag or with foil.

FREEZER LIFE: 3 months.

THAWING: allow the whole fish to thaw in a cool place for up to 24 hours, then use as soon as possible. Steaks and fillets can be cooked from frozen or allowed to thaw in the refrigerator for a few hours before using.

seakale beet (also called **chard** or **leaf beet**) A form of beet grown for its stalks and leaves, which are similar to spinach. Seakale beet grows continuously throughout the summer months if it is constantly picked. Consequently it is worthwhile freezing it.

FREEZING: remove the leaves from the stalks and **blanch** the green leaves for 2 minutes in boiling water. Cool, drain and pack tightly into **polythene bags**. Cut the stalks into short lengths and blanch in boiling water for 3 minutes. Cool, drain and pack tightly into polythene bags or **rigid containers**.

FREEZER LIFE: 1 year.

THAWING: cook both the leaves and the stalks from frozen in boiling water.

sealing The correct and secure sealing of all packages of food is crucial in ensuring that food retains as much of its colour, flavour, texture and nutritional content as possible. If air enters the package moisture escapes causing the food to dry out. Bags can be sealed with a simple knot, a wire tie, string, adhesive **freezer tape** or clips. Rubber bands, however, should not be used because they perish in the freezer. It is also possible to seal **polythene bags** with a **heat sealer**. **Rigid containers** and other cartons and containers should have well-fitting lids and, for complete security, be sealed with **freezer tape**. See also **cross-flavouring**; **oxidation**; **packaging**.

semolina A grainy powder made from hard or durum wheat, which is traditionally made into a **milk pudding**. Semolina pudding can be frozen if necessary, but it takes just as long to thaw and reheat frozen semolina as it does to make it fresh.

FREEZING: freeze leftover semolina in a **foil** container or **rigid container** and cover with foil. **Overwrap** with **clingfilm** or a **polythene bag**.

FREEZER LIFE: 3 months.

THAWING: add a little more milk and thaw slowly from frozen until thawed, then increase the heat to cook through completely.

shallot A small bulb related to the **onion**, which it may be useful to store in the freezer either whole or chopped up. Remember to seal the packages well to avoid **cross-flavouring**.

FREEZING: peel and **blanch** whole shallots for 2 minutes in boiling water, plunge into cold water, drain and pack into **polythene bags**. Blanch chopped shallots in boiling water, drain and pack into polythene bags. **Overwrap** in both cases with another polythene bag or sheet of **foil** to prevent cross-flavouring with other foods.

FREEZER LIFE: 6 months.

THAWING: shallots may be added straight from the freezer into dishes, such as **stews**, **casseroles**, and **sauces**, or fried from frozen.

shellfish A general term for edible crustaceans and molluscs. It is vitally important that shellfish are frozen only if they are absolutely fresh. They quickly deteriorate and are one of the most common causes of **food poisoning**. It is recommended that frozen shellfish is only ever stored for up to 1 month and consumed promptly after **thawing**. See **clam**; **cockles**; **crab**; **crawfish**; **crayfish**; **lobster**; **mussels**; **oyster**; **prawn**; **scallops**; **scampi**; **shrimp**.

shortbread A rich crumbly biscuit made with a high proportion of fat. Shortbread freezes successfully, although it does store well in an airtight tin for 1–2 weeks.

FREEZING: prepare and bake the shortbread according to the recipe used. Allow it to cool completely, then wrap in **foil**, **overwrap** in a **polythene bag** and freeze.

FREEZER LIFE: 3 months.

THAWING: allow the shortbread to thaw at room temperature for 3–4 hours.

shrimp Any of various crustacean **shellfish**. Shrimps can be frozen successfully, but they must be absolutely fresh.

FREEZING: shrimps may be frozen either raw or cooked. Remove heads and shells from raw shrimps, wash in salted water and drain. Pack tightly into **polythene bags** and freeze.

Cook shrimps in boiling water until pink, then allow them to cool in the cooking liquid. Remove the shells if desired and then pack into polythene bags and freeze.

Alternatively, they may be frozen as potted shrimps. Pack cooked and shelled shrimps into small cartons and then season with **lemon** juice, salt and black pepper. Cover with melted **butter**, using 25 g (1 oz) of butter for every 125 g (4 oz) of shrimps. Allow to cool completely then cover with **foil** and seal securely.

FREEZER LIFE: raw, cooked and potted shrimps, 1 month.

THAWING: raw shrimps may be cooked from frozen in a pan of boiling water or allowed to thaw in a cool place for 2–3 hours, then used as soon as possible. Cooked, frozen shrimps may be added to hot dishes straight from the freezer and heated through, or allowed to thaw in the refrigerator for 4–5 hours before use. Potted shrimps should be allowed to thaw in the refrigerator overnight before serving.

skate A large, fatty **fish** of the ray family. Skate is normally sold as skate wings, which have been cut away from the body, and these can be frozen satisfactorily. They must be frozen when absolutely fresh because skate deteriorates rapidly.

FREEZING: wrap the wings individually in **freezer wrap** and pack several together in a **polythene bag**, expelling as much air as possible before sealing.

FREEZER LIFE: 3 months.

THAWING: skate may be cooked from frozen or allowed to thaw for several hours in the refrigerator before cooking. Use immediately.

sloe The small, sour, blue-black fruit of the blackthorn, traditionally used to make sloe gin. Sloes may be frozen and stored for this purpose.

FREEZING: **open freeze** the sloes on trays in the freezer. When firm transfer to **polythene bags** and expel as much air as possible before **sealing**.

FREEZER LIFE: 6 months.

THAWING: allow to thaw in the refrigerator overnight before using.

smelt A small, bright, silver-coloured **fish** about 17 cm (7 inches) long. Smelt is traditionally skewered, dipped in **milk** and flour and deep fried. They can be frozen, but they must be extremely fresh.

FREEZING: clean thoroughly, but leave the head and tail on. Dry as much as possible, then pack several together in a **polythene bag**, extracting as much air as possible before **sealing**. It is a good idea to wrap each fish individually in **clingfilm** first, so that they can be easily separated for **thawing** purposes.

FREEZER LIFE: 2 months.

THAWING: allow the smelts to thaw in a cool place for 2–3 hours before using, then fry as usual.

smoked fish Fish that has been preserved by hanging it in smoke. Most smoked fish can be satisfactorily frozen. Smoked **salmon** can be frozen provided that it has not already been frozen at the fishmonger's. Smoked **haddock** can be frozen either raw or cooked.

FREEZING: freeze whole, unopened vacuum-sealed packs, or **interleave** slices of smoked salmon with **freezer wrap** and **overwrap** in **polythene bags** or **foil**. Wrap smoked haddock, either raw or cooked, in polythene bags and expel all the air before **sealing**.

FREEZER LIFE: smoked salmon, 2–3 months; smoked haddock, 2 months; other smoked fish, up to 2 months.

THAWING: allow smoked salmon slices to thaw at room temperature for ½–1 hour. Smoked haddock and other smoked fish may be cooked from frozen. Cooked frozen fish should be allowed to thaw in the refrigerator for 4–5 hours before using.

smoked meat Meat that has been preserved by hanging it in smoke. Smoked meat may be frozen for only 1 month, and it is probably only worthwhile to store leftovers this way.

FREEZING: pack in slices **interleaved** with **freezer wrap** into **polythene bags** or sheets of **foil**. Seal securely.

FREEZER LIFE: 1 month.

THAWING: allow the meat to thaw in the refrigerator for 4–5 hours.

snail A mollusc with a spirally coiled shell. Snails should only be consumed fresh or from cans. They do not freeze well because of their rubbery texture and they quickly lose their flavour.

snipe A tiny **game** bird. Snipe is often prepared with its long beak skewered through its body. It may be frozen raw for up to 6 months.

FREEZING: pack whole birds into **polythene bags** and expel as much air as possible form the bags before **sealing**.

FREEZER LIFE: 6 months.

THAWING: allow to thaw overnight in the refrigerator in its wrappings before cooking. It is traditionally roasted inside a hollowed out baked **potato** to seal in all the juices.

sole Any white flatfish, which can be frozen provided that it is absolutely fresh.

FREEZING: remove the skin, scales and gut, wash thoroughly in cold water, then drain and pat dry. Sole may be frozen whole or cut into fillets. Freeze a whole fish in a **polythene bag**. **Interleave** fillets with small pieces of **freezer wrap** and place in a polythene bag. Expel as much air as possible from the bags before **sealing**.

FREEZER LIFE: 3 months.

THAWING: sole may be cooked from frozen or allowed to thaw in the refrigerator for about 5 hours per 500 g (1lb).

sorbet A water ice that is prepared from **fruit juice** or purée, sugar, **egg** white and water. Both home-made or commercially prepared sorbet may be frozen.

FREEZING: prepare and freeze sorbets according to the recipe used, whisking at intervals during the freezing process.

Alternatively, make a fresh fruit sorbet. Combine 250 ml (½ pint) of water with 75 g (3 oz) of sugar in a pan, then boil it for 5 minutes to make a syrup. Stir in 250 ml (½ pint) of fresh fruit purée or fruit juice and mix thoroughly. Allow to cool completely, then freeze in a **rigid container** until just solid. Remove the sorbet from the freezer and fold in a stiffly whisked egg white, then return it and freeze until firm.

FREEZER LIFE: home-made and commercially prepared, 2–3 months.

THAWING: allow the sorbet to thaw at room temperature for about 10 minutes before serving to allow it to soften a little. Replace the remaining sorbet in the freezer as soon as possible.

sorrel A leafy **vegetable** that is similar to **spinach** and used in salads, **sauces** and **soups**.

FREEZING: remove the leaves and discard the stalks. Place in a saucepan with a tiny amount of water. Simmer gently until tender, then squeeze out the moisture and drain throughly. Cool, chop and pack into **polythene bags**.

FREEZER LIFE: 1 year.

THAWING: sorrel may be reheated gently from frozen.

soufflé A very light dish made with egg yolks and stiffly beaten egg whites combined with various ingredients, such as fish or cheese. Sweet and savoury soufflés, to be served hot or cold, all freeze extremely well. However, soufflés should be frozen without any decoration.

FREEZING: prepare the soufflé dish in the usual way, but use **foil** instead of **greaseproof paper** as a collar, and make sure that the dish is freezer proof. Secure it firmly with **freezer tape**. Pour the soufflé mixture into the prepared dish and **open freeze** on a tray until hard. Place the dish, with the collar intact, in a large **polythene bag**, then seal and return it to the freezer.

FREEZER LIFE: 2 months.

THAWING: remove the polythene bag and allow cold soufflés to thaw overnight in the refrigerator before decorating. Allow hot soufflés to thaw for about ½ hour. Bake small soufflés in ramekins at 190°C/375°F/Gas 5 for approximately 30 minutes. Larger soufflés should be baked for 60–70 minutes until they have risen and turn golden. Serve immediately.

soup A liquid food made from a variety of ingredients, such as meat, fish and vegetables, that are boiled or simmered. Most soups freeze well, but it is preferable to omit the **cream** or **milk** until after **thawing**.

FREEZING: make the soup according to the recipe. Allow to cool completely, then pour into **rigid containers** leaving a 2.5 cm (1 inch) **headspace** before **sealing**.

FREEZER LIFE: 3 months.

THAWING: hold the sealed container under running hot water for a few minutes to loosen the soup. Place the block in a saucepan and reheat gently from frozen until thawed. Add milk or cream as required and season before serving.

soya milk A milky substance extracted from soya bean curds. Soya milk does not freeze satisfactorily. It separates on thawing and cannot be whisked back to its former texture.

spaghetti A type of **pasta** in the form of long strings.

spice Any of a variety of seeds, roots or stems of certain aromatic plants that are used whole or ground to add flavour to food. Dried spices store satisfactorily in a cool dry place for up to 6 months. In the freezer, they seem to change their flavour after 3–4 months either becoming peppery to taste or losing their flavour altogether. It is best not to store spiced dishes in the freezer for more than 2 months so that they retain their flavour.

spinach A leafy green **vegetable**. Spinach freezes well, but it is more convenient to cook before freezing; use fresh, young leaves.

FREEZING: strip the leaves from the stalks and place in a large saucepan. Add 1–2 tbsp of water and cook for 1–2 minutes until the leaves start to wilt, or pour boiling water over the spinach and stand for 1 minute, then drain. Squeeze out the moisture until the spinach is as dry as possible, then allow it to cool. Chop finely and pack into **polythene bags**, expelling as much air as possible before sealing.

FREEZER LIFE: 1 year.

THAWING: reheat gently from frozen until thawed and heated through.

sponge cake A light porous **cake** made without **fat**. Sponge cake freezes extremely well and can be used as a base for numerous **puddings** and **gateaux**.

FREEZING: **interleave** sponge layers with **greaseproof paper** and **overwrap** in a **polythene bag**, extracting as much air as possible before **sealing**. Filled and iced cakes should be allowed to **open**

freeze until firm, then packed into a polythene bag or **rigid container** so that they do not become damaged. Do not fill with **cream**, **jam** or **fruit** fillings before freezing because they make the sponge soggy.

FREEZER LIFE: plain sponge, 6 months; iced and filled, 2 months.

THAWING: allow the sponge to thaw for about 2 hours at room temperature. Remove the wrappings from the iced cakes before thawing so that they do not become damaged.

sponge pudding See **pudding**.

sprat A small fatty **fish** of the herring family. Sprats are best grilled or dry fried because they are very oily. They can be frozen for a short period.

FREEZING: wash, drain and pat dry. **Open freeze** on trays in the freezer until firm, then transfer into **polythene bags** and expel as much air as possible.

FREEZER LIFE: 2 months.

THAWING: allow the sprats to thaw in the refrigerator for 3–4 hours, pat dry and either grill or fry.

spring greens A variety of **cabbage** that can be blanched and frozen successfully. Choose fresh green leaves, discard any wilted or yellow leaves.

FREEZING: wash thoroughly, remove tough stalks and chop. **Blanch** in boiling water for 1–2 minutes, then plunge into cold water. Drain and allow to cool completely and pack into **polythene bags**.

FREEZER LIFE: 6 months.

THAWING: cook the greens from frozen in boiling water until tender.

spring onion A **salad vegetable** that does not freeze well due to its high water content. Spring onions become soft and mushy if frozen, losing their crisp and crunchy texture. However, over-developed spring onions, which look like button onions, may be frozen successfully.

FREEZING: chop the long stalks from the spring onions, peel the bulb and **blanch** for 3 minutes. Allow to cool, drain and then pack into **polythene bags**, extracting as much air as possible before **sealing**. Overwrap in a second polythene bag or with **foil** to prevent **cross-flavouring**.

FREEZER LIFE: 6 months.

THAWING: use in cooked dishes from frozen.

squash The large fruit of a marrow-like plant with a hard rind and a pulpy flesh. There are a variety of squashes, such as acorn squash, spaghetti squash and butternut squash, all of which have a slightly different texture and flavour. Freeze firm, unbruised sqaushes with no softening around the edges.

FREEZING: peel, remove any seeds and cut into chunks. **Blanch** in boiling water for 1–2 minutes, plunge into cold water, drain and cool. Pack into **polythene bags** and expel as much air as possible before **sealing**. Alternatively, the squash may be fully cooked and puréed before freezing in **rigid containers**, leaving a little **headspace** under the lid.

FREEZER LIFE: 1 year.

THAWING: blanched squash may be cooked from frozen in boiling water. The purée should be allowed to thaw at room temperature for 3–4 hours before using.

squid A smooth, white-fleshed mollusc. Squid must be absolutely fresh if it is to be frozen at home. Check that it has not been frozen beforehand.

FREEZING: pull the head from the body cavity of the squid and discard everything except the tentacles and the body sac. Wash thoroughly and remove the thin skin covering the body sac. Cut the sac into rings and either leave the tentacles whole or slice if desired. Drain and pat dry, then **open freeze** until firm and pack into **polythene bags**, expelling as much air as possible before **sealing**.

FREEZER LIFE: 3 months.

THAWING: squid may be cooked from frozen or, alternatively, allowed to thaw for 3–4 hours in a cool place before cooking.

star fruit (also called **carambola** or **star apple**) This **fruit** is now widely available and can be successfully frozen in syrup. It discolours rapidly, so care must be taken to ensure that it is covered in **lemon juice**.

FREEZING: trim the edges off the fruit and slice into star-shaped pieces. Remove any seeds and brush with lemon juice to prevent **discoloration**.

Pack the slices into a sugar syrup made with 500 g (1lb) of sugar to every 1 litre (2 pints) of water, adding the juice of 1 lemon. Pack into **rigid containers**, leaving a 2.5 cm (1 inch) **headspace**.

FREEZER LIFE: 9–12 months.

THAWING: allow the star fruit to thaw in its unopened container for 3–4 hours at room temperature.

star symbol A symbol that all freezers bear, which means that they can freeze fresh food at a temperature of –28°C (–18°F) or below. The white star on a black background shows that the appliance is indeed a freezer rather than just a **conservator** or refrigerator. The black star refers to the freezing compartments within refrigerators, showing the length of time that food may be stored in them. One black star represents one month; two stars, two months; three stars, three months.

steak A cut of lean meat (beef, lamb or pork) usually from the rump or loin of an animal. Steaks that are ready prepared to grill or fry can be successfully frozen. The packages must be sealed securely to prevent any air from entering and drying out the meat.

FREEZING: **open freeze** the steaks until firm, then wrap and **interleave** each one in **freezer wrap**. Pack several together in a **polythene bag**. Seal securely, label clearly – because frozen meat quickly becomes difficult to recognise – and freeze as quickly as possible.

FREEZER LIFE: 3 months.

THAWING: allow the steaks to thaw in the refrigerator in their wrappings for 5–6 hours, or cook from frozen. Frozen steaks should be cooked slowly on a gentle heat, raising the heat towards the end of the cooking time.

stew A dish usually of **meat** or **fish** that is cooked by stewing. Stews can be successfully frozen and made in bulk as a convenient way of preparing a quick meal. Cook the stew for a little less time than usual, because the cooking is completed during **reheating**. Ensure that there is plenty of liquid in the **gravy** because meat tends to dry out in the freezer.

FREEZING: make the stew as usual but do not cook completely. Cool completely and remove any **fat** that comes to the surface. Turn into **foil** freezer containers or **rigid containers** and seal securely.

Alternatively, pack the stew into a foil-lined dish and freeze until firm. Remove the frozen stew from the container and wrap securely in foil. This method allows the container to be used again and the stew to be packed neatly in the freezer.

FREEZER LIFE: 6 weeks, if there is **bacon**, **ham** or **pork** in the stew; 2 months for other meat.

THAWING: allow the stew to reheat gently from frozen.

stock A broth in which, meat, fish, bones or vegetables have been simmered for a long time. A good quality stock is very useful to keep in the freezer as a basis for **sauces** or **gravies**.

FREEZING: make the stock in the usual way and strain. Allow the stock to become completely cold and remove any of the **fat** that has risen to the surface. Reduce the stock by boiling it hard, then freeze the concentrated stock in small **rigid containers** or ice cube trays. When firm, transfer stock cubes to **polythene bags** and seal securely.

FREEZER LIFE: 6 months.

THAWING: allow the stock to thaw very gently, by heating slowly from frozen.

stock control It is important that the stocks of food in the freezer are used up sensibly and regularly so that they are all consumed within their recommended storage limits. Stock should be turned around two or three times per year, but the freezer should be kept three quarters full to maximize the benefits and keep the costs of running the machine as low as possible.

storage life The length of time that that a particular food remains fresh, retaining its colour, texture, flavour and nutritional value. Most foods can be stored indefinitely in the freezer and remain safe to eat, but the quality of every food alters after a certain time. Most foods are given a specific **freezer life**, and it is best to consume foods within the recommended storage times.

strawberry The sweet, fleshy red **fruit** of the strawberry plant. Whole strawberries may be frozen, but they do become very mushy on thawing and alter their texture and flavour. Strawberry purée freezes extremely well and is an excellent base for many **sauces** and **puddings**.

FREEZING: whole fruit should be hulled, dusted clean, but not washed, and placed on trays to **open freeze**, before packing in **polythene bags** or **rigid containers**. Strawberry purée should be sieved into rigid containers with sugar to taste and sealed securely.

FREEZER LIFE: 1 year.

THAWING: allow the whole fruit to thaw in its containers at room temperature for about 3 hours. It is best served when still frosty. Thaw purée at room temperature for about 3 hours, then use as required.

stuffing Meat and poultry must never been stuffed before freezing. There is a possibility that the centre of the stuffing may not be sufficiently thawed or cooked, which may cause **food poisoning**. Most home-made and commercially prepared stuffings can be successfully frozen separately.

FREEZING: make the stuffing according to the recipe used and then pack into **polythene bags**. Alternatively, pack into **foil** containers, which can also be used to cook the stuffing in. Dry stuffing mix should be frozen in polythene bags.

FREEZER LIFE: home-made stuffing, 1 month; dry stuffing, 6 months; sausage meat stuffing, 2 months.

THAWING: allow the stuffing to thaw in the refrigerator overnight before using. Dry stuffing may be mixed from frozen.

suet A tough, dry waxy deposit of fat found around certain organs of animals. Suet is usually manufactured semi-dried and shredded, and both fresh and packet suet can be frozen successfully.
FREEZING: pack small portions of suet into **polythene bags**, expelling as much air as possible before **sealing**.
FREEZER LIFE: 5 months.
THAWING: allow to thaw in the refrigerator overnight before using.

suet pudding A hot sweet or savoury **pudding**, which can be satisfactorily frozen after cooking.
FREEZING: prepare the pudding as usual and cook in **foil** or freezer-proof basins. Allow the pudding to cool completely. Then remove the wrappings and cover with foil, secure well and overwrap with a **polythene bag**.
FREEZER LIFE: 3 months.
THAWING: suet pudding may be either boiled or steamed from frozen, but cook it for up to 2 hours to heat through completely.

sugar pack See **dry sugar pack**.

sultana A dried white grape. See **dried fruit**.

super-freeze See **fast freezing**.

swede A bulbous root **vegetable** with pulpy, orange flesh. Swede can be frozen successfully cut into chunks or as a purée.

FREEZING: either (a), trim, peel and chop up the swede, then **blanch** in boiling water for 2 minutes. Allow to cool before draining and packing into **polythene bags**; or (b), cook the swede in simmering water, drain and allow to cool. Blend in a liquidizer or food processor until smooth, then pack into **rigid containers** leaving a 1 cm ($\frac{1}{2}$ inch) **headspace**.

FREEZER LIFE: 1 year.

THAWING: cook diced swede from frozen in boiling water until tender. The purée should be gently heated from frozen.

sweetbread The pancreas or thymus gland of an animal. Lamb sweetbreads are often purchased and cooked as **offal**, and they may be successfully frozen raw or cooked.

FREEZING: wash thoroughly and leave to soak in cold water for 4–5 hours. Trim the sweetbreads, removing any tubes. Rinse again and pat dry. Pack individual sweetbreads in **freezer wrap**, or several in a **polythene bag** or **rigid container**.

FREEZER LIFE: 3 months.

THAWING: allow the sweetbreads to thaw in the refrigerator for 4–5 hours before cooking.

sweetcorn The tender, sweet-tasting, yellow kernels of unripe maize. Sweetcorn can be either frozen whole or as **corn on the cob** or in kernels.

Choose fresh young cobs with creamy yellow, plump kernels and fine silky threads.

FREEZING: remove any leaves or silk threads. Trim off the stems and **blanch** whole cobs in boiling water for 4 minutes (small), 6 minutes (medium) and 8 minutes (large). Plunge into cold water, drain, cool and pat dry with kitchen paper. Pack whole cobs into **polythene bags**, extracting as much air as possible before **sealing**.

Alternatively, blanch as before and allow to cool. Strip off all the kernels with a knife and **open freeze** on trays in the freezer. When firm transfer into polythene bags and extract as much air as possible.

FREEZER LIFE: 1 year.

THAWING: whole cobs may be cooked from frozen in boiling water, or thawed at room temperature for about 1 hour. Cook sweetcorn kernels from frozen in boiling water for approximately 5 minutes.

sweet potato The large edible root of a tropical twining plant with sweet, yellow flesh. Sweet potatoes may be frozen after being parboiled, completely cooked or made into a purée.

FREEZING: wash, peel and cut into slices or chunks. The slices should be parboiled and allowed to cool, then packed tightly into **rigid containers**.

FREEZER LIFE: 6 months.

THAWING: partly and fully cooked sweet potatoes may be heated from frozen. Allow the purée to thaw for 2–3 hours at room temperature before gently heating through.

sweets Home-made candies and sweetmeats freeze very successfully.

FREEZING: prepare the sweets according to the recipe used, then place them in paper sweet cases or gift boxes. Alternatively, place on **foil** trays and cover with **clingfilm** or **freezer wrap**.

FREEZER LIFE: 6 months.

THAWING: due to their high sugar content, sweets defrost very quickly and should be allowed to thaw at room temperature for about 1 hour before using.

swordfish An extremely solid, firm-fleshed game **fish**, which is popular in Mediterranean countries and America. It is becoming increasingly available in the rest of Europe. Swordfish is sold in steaks and can be frozen successfully. The flesh can sometimes be a little dry, so after freezing it is best to cook it in a sauce or marinate it before grilling or barbecuing.

FREEZING: wrap each swordfish steak in **clingfilm** and **overwrap** several together in a **polythene bag**, extracting as much air as possible before **sealing**.

FREEZER LIFE: 2 months.

THAWING: allow the swordfish steaks to thaw in the refrigerator overnight before cooking. Either marinate and grill or barbecue or bake in a **sauce**.

syllabub A cold **dessert**, based on a mixture of **wine**, **cream** and sugar. Syllabubs will not freeze satisfactorily because the cream separates out from the wine.

syrup pack A method of packaging **fruit** in **rigid containers** and covering it with a cold syrup made by dissolving sugar in water. Sugar pack is the best method of freezing **fruit** that has little juice and discolours easily during preparation. The strength of the cold syrup depends on the sourness of the fruit and on individual taste. Most fruits freeze well in a syrup made by dissolving 250 g (8 oz) of sugar in 600 ml (1 pint) of water. The syrup must always be cold and it is possible to make it in advance and keep it in the refrigerator for several days.

When packaging place the fruit into a rigid container first and then cover with the syrup, leaving a 2.5 cm (1 inch) **headspace** before **sealing**. It is important that the fruit is kept under the syrup to prevent **discoloration**, and to ensure this place a small piece of crumpled **foil** on the fruit, pressing it down into the syrup before sealing securely.

tangelo See **ugli fruit**.

tangerine A small citrus **fruit**, similar to a **satsuma**, but with pips. Tangerines are a seasonal fruit, but they can be frozen for use in **fruit salads** and other desserts.

FREEZING: peel, remove the pith and divide the tangerines into segments. Then either (a), pack into **rigid containers** and cover with a cold syrup made with 250 g (8 oz) of sugar and 600 ml (1 pint) of water. Leave a 2.5 cm (1 inch) **headspace** before **sealing** with a lid; or (b), **open freeze** on a tray and then pack into polythene bags to store.

FREEZER LIFE: 1 year.

THAWING: allow the tangerines to thaw in their container for about 3 hours at room temperature before serving.

tapioca A grainy starch obtained from the cassava plant. Tapioca is commonly used to make a **milk pudding**, which can be frozen if necessary.

FREEZING: freeze leftover tapioca in a **foil** container or a plastic **rigid container** and cover with foil or a lid.

FREEZER LIFE: 3 months.

THAWING: add a little more milk and allow it to thaw slowly. Once thawed increase the heat so that the pudding is heated through thoroughly.

taramasalata A smooth, pink paste savoury **dip** made from smoked cod's **roe**, olive oil and **breadcrumbs**. Home-made and commercially prepared taramasalata can be satisfactorily frozen for up to 3 months.

FREEZING: make taramasalata as usual and pack into small **rigid containers** or plastic cartons. Seal and label clearly before freezing.

FREEZER LIFE: home-made and bought, 3 months.

THAWING: allow the taramasalata to thaw at room temperature for about 2 hours before serving.

tarragon The small leaves of an aromatic, perennial plant, which are used as a **herb**. Tarragon is often used in **chicken** and **fish** dishes and is well worth freezing.

FREEZING: either (a), wash and chop the tarragon and freeze in small plastic containers; or (b), pack into ice cube trays with a little water and freeze. When firm, transfer the cubes into a **polythene bag** to store.

FREEZER LIFE: 6 months.

THAWING: tarragon may be used straight from the freezer, in **casseroles** or **sauces**, or allowed to thaw in the refrigerator for 1–2 hours.

tayberry A large, sweet red **fruit**, which was produced by crossing a raspberry, blackberry and loganberry. Tayberries may be frozen in the same way as **raspberries**.

tea A beverage made by infusing the shredded leaves of various tea plants in boiling water. Freshly made strong tea may be satisfactorily frozen for use in iced cold drinks, such as iced tea, **fruit** cups and punches. Herbal teas may also be frozen for this purpose.

FREEZING: make a strong tea as usual and allow to cool completely. Strain and pour into ice cube trays to freeze. When firm, remove from the trays and transfer into **polythene bags** to store.

FREEZER LIFE: 6 months.

THAWING: add tea cubes from frozen or allow to thaw in the refrigerator for several hours before using.

teabread A loaf made from a sweetened yeast **dough** with the addition of dried, mixed **fruit**. Teabreads freeze extremely well and it may be useful to keep a stock in the freezer.

FREEZING: prepare and bake the teabread in the usual way and allow to cool completely. Pack into a **polythene bag** or a large sheet of **foil** and freeze.

FREEZER LIFE: 3 months.

THAWING: allow the teabread to thaw in its wrappings at room temperature for about 2–3 hours before serving.

teacake A type of flat fruit bun, which is most often served toasted. Home-made or bought teacakes can be frozen successfully.

FREEZING: prepare and bake as usual, allow to cool and pack into **polythene bags**, excluding as much air as possible before **sealing**. **Overwrap** shop-bought teacakes in a polythene bag.

FREEZER LIFE: 3 months.

THAWING: allow the teacakes to thaw at room temperature for about 45 minutes. Alternatively, partially thaw, then split and toast the teacakes.

teal A small wild bird of the **duck** family. One teal is usually served as one individual portion. It can be frozen successfully whole and is then best served either roasted or grilled. Choose young birds that have not been hung.

FREEZING: clean the teal thoroughly, but do not stuff before freezing. Pack individually into **polythene bags** and extract as much air as possible before **sealing**.

FREEZER LIFE: 6 months.

THAWING: allow the teal to thaw in the refrigerator for 4–5 hours before roasting or grilling.

terrine See **paté**.

thawing The process of raising the temperature of frozen food, so that it can then be cooked and consumed safely. Some foods, such as **vegetables**, **pastry** cases, fillets of **fish** and certain **convenience foods** do not need to be thawed before cooking. Others, such as **poultry** and **game**, need to be thawed quickly and thoroughly before cooking to minimize the risk of **food poisoning**. Food poisoning can arise if food is left for too long at a warm temperature where bacteria thrive and then not being adequately cooked. **Fruit** should be allowed to thaw until just frosty and then served just before it has completely thawed. This is so that the fruit does not lose its shape completely and begin to fall apart.

thermostat An instrument within the freezer that controls the temperature automatically. It can easily be checked by placing a freezer thermometer inside the freezer and regularly observing it. The temperature of the home freezer should be set to –18°C (0°F) and the thermostat is normally set to this during manufacture.

thyme The leaves of a temperate shrub with a strong mint-like odour. Thyme is a **herb** that can be used in many **meat** or **vegetable** dishes. It can be frozen or dried successfully.

FREEZING: either (a), freeze whole sprigs of thyme in small **polythene bags**; or (b), strip off the tiny leaves from the stalks and pack in small parcels of **clingfilm** or in small cartons or polythene bags.

FREEZER LIFE: 6 months.

THAWING: frozen thyme may be added to most dishes straight from the freezer.

tofu A smooth, bland curd made from the yellow soya bean, usually sold in blocks. Most manufacturers of blocks of tofu advise against freezing, although it is possible to buy tofu bars that are a type of **ice cream**. Always follow the manufacturers' advice with regard to freezing and refrigeration. Tofu will keep satisfactorily in the refrigerator for several weeks.

tomato The fleshy, red **fruit** of the tomato plant. Tomatoes contain a great amount of water and do not freeze satisfactorily – if they are to be eaten raw. They collapse completely when frozen and thawed. However, they can be stored successfully for use in cooking, in dishes such as **stews**, **soups** and **casseroles**.

FREEZING: either (a), freeze whole tomatoes by placing them into boiling water for a few seconds, then peeling away the skin. Allow them to cool, then pack in **rigid containers** or tightly in **polythene bags**; or (b), cut the tomatoes into halves, open freeze until frozen then transfer into **polythene bags**.

Alternatively, freeze the tomatoes as a purée. Cover with boiling water to loosen the skins, then peel and remove the pips and hard core. Simmer gently without any extra water for 5 minutes until soft. Rub through a sieve or purée in a blender or food processor until smooth. Cool and pack into small containers.

FREEZER LIFE: whole tomatoes, 10–12 months; purée, 6–8 months.

THAWING: whole tomatoes may be used straight from the freezer, in soups and casseroles. Allow tomato purée to thaw in its container for 2–3 hours at room temperature before using.

tomato juice The juice of the **tomato**. Tomato juice is quick and easy to make and stores well in the freezer.

FREEZING: chop up the tomatoes, then liquidize them until as smooth as possible. Strain, then season with salt and sugar if desired. Add water if desired and pack into **rigid containers** leaving a 2.5 cm (1 inch) **headspace** before **sealing**.

FREEZER LIFE: 1 year.

THAWING: allow to thaw overnight in the refrigerator. Thin down and season if necessary before serving.

tongue The tongue of calf, lamb and ox. Tongue may be frozen either raw or cooked and it may also be frozen when cooked with a **sauce**.

FREEZING: trim off the excess fat and gristle, and wash and dry thoroughly. Then either (a), pack raw tongues into **polythene bags**, extracting as much air as possible before **sealing**. Small tongues should be wrapped individually in **freezer wrap** before being packed together in a polythene bag; or (b), cook tongue as usual, shape and weight it down and cool completely. Wrap in **foil** and **overwrap** in a polythene bag extracting as much air as possible before freezing. Alternatively, slice the cooked tongue and pack into polythene bags, expelling as much air as possible before sealing.

FREEZER LIFE: uncooked, 3 months; cooked, 1 month.

THAWING: allow uncooked tongue to thaw in the refrigerator overnight before cooking as usual. Cooked tongue should be left to thaw in the refrigerator allowing about 6 hours per 500 g (1lb). Reheat tongues that have been frozen with a sauce gently from frozen.

Torbay sole See **witch**.

trifle A cold **pudding** made with sponge cake, fruit or jam, sherry or brandy, coated with custard and cream. Trifle does not freeze very well because the **custard** separates out and thc **jelly** becomes granular and cloudy. However, there are some commercially produced trifles that do freeze successfully.

tripe The stomach lining of sheep or ox which is eaten as **offal**. Tripe can be frozen successfully either cooked or uncooked.

FREEZING: wash raw tripe thoroughly in cold water. Dry and pack into **polythene bags**, extracting as much air as posssible before **sealing**. Alternatively, cook the tripe as usual, allow it to cool and pack into **rigid containers** leaving a 2.5 cm (1 inch) **headspace** before sealing.

FREEZER LIFE: uncooked, 3 months; cooked tripe, 1 month.

THAWING: allow the tripe to thaw overnight in the refrigerator before either cooking or **reheating**.

trout Any of several varieties (brown or river, rainbow and sea trout) of fatty, freshwater or salt-water **fish** of the salmon family. Trout must be absolutely fresh if it is to be frozen at home.

FREEZING: wash the fish, remove scales and gut (remove the head and tail if desired). Wrap each fish tightly in a **polythene bag** and freeze. Large rainbow trout should be allowed to **open freeze** and then **ice glazed**. Then transfer the fish into a large polythene bag to store.

FREEZER LIFE: 2 months.

THAWING: small trout may be cooked from frozen. Allow large rainbow trout to thaw for up to 24 hours in a cool place, then use as soon as possible.

trout, smoked See **smoked fish**.

tuna Any of various large, marine, fatty **fish**. Tuna is commonly sold in cans, but it is becoming more widely available fresh. Fresh tuna is normally sold in steaks, which must be really fresh if they are to be frozen. Refreezing them is not recommended.

FREEZING: wipe and dry the tuna steaks and **interleave** them with small sheets of **freezer wrap** before packing several together in **foil** or a **polythene bag**.

FREEZER LIFE: 2 months.

THAWING: tuna steaks may be cooked from frozen or allowed to thaw in the refrigerator ovenight before using.

turbot A large, European flatfish, which is sold either whole or as fillets or steaks. Turbot may be frozen provided that it is absolutely fresh.

FREEZING: for a whole fish, remove the head, tail, fins and gut and then **ice glaze**. Then transfer it into a **polythene bag**, extracting as much air as possible before **sealing**. **Interleave** steaks and fillets with **freezer wrap** and wrap several together in a polythene bag.

FREEZER LIFE: 2 months.

THAWING: allow whole fish to thaw in a cool place for up to 24 hours, then use as soon as possible. Fillets and steaks may be cooked from frozen.

turkey A domestic fowl of North American origin and its meat. Turkeys take up a lot of room in the freezer and it is unwise to store them for too long, although they do freeze very well. Only freeze very fresh turkeys. Ready frozen turkeys should be put in the freezer as soon as possible after purchase and not allowed to partially thaw.

FREEZING: clean and prepare in the usual way, remove **giblets** and freeze them separately if required. Do not stuff the bird before freezing. Cover any protruding bones with **foil** or **greaseproof paper**, then pack the turkey in a large **polythene bag** or **polythene sheeting**.

Turkey joints may be frozen individually wrapped in polythene bags. Leftover roast turkey can be sliced and frozen. **Interleave** the slices with greaseproof paper and pack into **rigid containers** or tightly in a polythene bag to prevent it from drying out. Cooked turkey in a **sauce** may be frozen in rigid containers, allowing 2.5 cm (1 inch) **headspace** before **sealing**.

FREEZER LIFE: uncooked bird, 6 months; cooked meat, 1 month; giblets 3 months.

THAWING: allow a whole, raw turkey to thaw in a cool room in its wrappings. A 6.8 g (15lb) bird takes approximately 48 hours. Cook as soon as possible, once thawed completely. Allow cooked turkey to thaw in the refrigerator overnight before using.

turnip A white or yellowish root **vegetable**, which can be successfully frozen. Choose small, young, tender turnips.

FREEZING: trim and peel the turnips. Leave small turnips whole, but dice large turnips. **Blanch** whole turnips in boiling water for 4 minutes, diced turnip for 2 minutes. Allow them to cool, drain and pack into **polythene bags**, extracting as much air as possible before **sealing**. Turnips may also be frozen in purée form. Trim, peel and dice and cook until tender. Drain, mash and allow to cool. Pack into **rigid containers**, leaving a 2.5 cm (1 inch) **headspace** before sealing.

FREEZER LIFE: whole, 9–12 months; purée, 8–10 months.

THAWING: cook blanched turnips from frozen in boiling water. Cooked turnips may be reheated gently from frozen.

ugli fruit (also called **tangelo**) A large citrus **fruit** with loose, wrinkled greenish yellow skin, and flesh similar to a **grapefruit**. Ugli fruit may be frozen in a **dry sugar pack** or **syrup pack**.

FREEZING: peel the fruit, removing all the pith, and divide into segments. Either pack into **rigid containers**, mixing 125–175 g (4–6 oz) of sugar to every 500 g (1lb) of fruit, or pack in a sugar syrup made with 500 g (1lb) of sugar to every 600 ml (1 pint) of water. Leave a 2.5 cm (1 inch) **headspace** before **sealing**.

FREEZER LIFE: 1 year.

THAWING: allow the fruit to thaw overnight in the refrigerator.

upright freezer A front-opening type of freezer. Upright freezers are often thought to be more convenient because they are smaller than **chest freezers**, and have drawers which make it easier to get at the food items. They fit more easily into most kitchens or utility rooms, but care must be taken to ensure that there is sufficient **ventilation**

around them. Due to the way the door is opened they use more electricity than chest freezers. They also need to be defrosted more frequently – about 3 or 4 times per year. Make sure that the door is not left open for any longer than necessary.

vanilla The pod or bean of certain varieties of tropical climbing orchid, which is used as a flavouring. Vanilla is available as pods or as an essence. It can be used satisfactorily to flavour foods, such as **ice creams**, **custards**, **cakes** and **puddings**, that are to be frozen. Do not use synthetic vanilla flavouring in frozen foods because the flavour will deteriorate over time in the freezer.

veal The flesh of a calf fed exclusively on milk or other foods low in iron. Veal freezes well, but only good quality, fresh veal should be used. Breast and shoulder can be frozen to roast, pie veal to make into **casseroles** and **pies**, and fillets cut into escalopes.

FREEZING: **interleave** escalopes of veal with **freezer wrap** and **overwrap** several together in **polythene bags**. Veal breast, shoulder and pie veal should be packed tightly into polythene bags to freeze.

FREEZER LIFE: 6 months.

THAWING: allow the veal to thaw overnight in the refrigerator before cooking as usual.

vegetables The edible leaves, fruit, roots, flowers or stalks of plants. Most vegetables can be frozen raw very successfully. **Salad vegetables** and those with a high water content, such as **lettuce** and **tomato**, do not freeze well in their raw state and must be cooked before freezing. Most vegetables will freeze better if blanched first. They may then be cooked from frozen.

See **asparagus**; **aubergine**; **beansprout**; **beetroot**; **broad bean**; **broccoli**; **Brussels sprout**; **cabbage**; **calabrese**; **carrot**; **cauliflower**; **celeriac**; **celery**; **chicory**; **chinese leaf**; **corn on the cob**; **courgette**; **cucumber**; **fennel**; **globe artichoke**; **haricot bean**; **Jerusalem artichoke**; **kale**; **kohlrabi**; **leek**; **lettuce**; **mangetout**; **marrow**; **mushroom**; **mushy peas**; **onion**; **parsnip**; **peppers**; **potato**; **pumpkin**; **radish**; **red cabbage**; **scorzonera**; **seakale**; **shallot**; **spring green**; **sweetcorn**; **sweet potato**; **turnip**.

venison The flesh of deer, which should be well hung before freezing. Venison may either be frozen completely raw or allowed to marinate overnight before freezing.

FREEZING: clean the venison and cut into joints or cut into cubes for use in dishes, such as **casseroles**. Pack the joints into **polythene bags**, padding any bones with **foil**, first. Pack cubed meat into polythene bags and extract as much air as possible before **sealing**.

FREEZER LIFE: 8–12 months.

THAWING: allow the venison to thaw in the refrigerator, allowing 5 hours per 500 g (1lb). Venison should preferably be placed in a marinade while thawing as it can begin to dry out.

ventilation A current of air should be able to circulate around a freezer to prevent condensation. When positioning a freezer it should have 5–10 cm (2–4 inches) of clear space around it, particularly where there is a grill.

vine leaves Edible, young vine leaves, which may be used to encase small birds, such as **quail** and snipe, or savoury **stuffings**. Vine leaves may be frozen, but they should be **blanched** first. Choose young, green leaves.

FREEZING: strip the leaves from the stalks and place in a large saucepan. Cover with boiling water and blanch for 1 minute. Plunge into cold water and drain. When cool, pack flat in **freezer wrap** and freeze.

FREEZER LIFE: 6 months.

THAWING: allow to thaw at room temperature for 2–3 hours and use immediately.

vol-au-vent Puff **pastry** cases that freeze extremely well. It is preferable to freeze them prepared but unbaked as they are not so fragile. They can then be cooked and filled with sweet or savoury fillings.

FREEZING: commercially prepared vol-au-vent cases are very good and can be purchased already frozen. Follow the manufacturer's instructions when freezing fresh pastry cases. Home-made vol au vents should be open frozen on trays, and when hard interleaved with small pieces of **greaseproof paper** and packed into **polythene bags** or **rigid con-**

tainers. Baked cases should be packed carefully into rigid containers and marked fragile. Ideally they should be stored at the top of the freezer so that they do not become damaged.

FREEZER LIFE: unbaked, 3 months; baked, 6 months.

THAWING: bake home-made or commercially prepared cases in a hot oven from frozen. Allow baked cases to thaw at room temperature for about 1 hour and then reheat if desired before using.

waffle A crisp, golden-brown pancake made from **batter** cooked in special waffle irons, which give it its characteristic indentations. Waffles can be frozen baked and stored satisfactorily for several weeks.

FREEZING: prepare and cook the waffles as usual, but do not overbrown them. Allow them to cool completely, then pack into **polythene bags** or stack them into **rigid containers**.

FREEZER LIFE: 2 months.

THAWING: reheat the waffles from frozen either under the grill or in the oven for about 10 mintues until well browned.

walnut The **nut** of a deciduous tree with a hard, wrinkled shell and a two-lobed kernel. Walnuts keep fresh and moist for up to a year in the freezer. They can be frozen either shelled and halved or chopped, but do not freeze salted nuts because they become **rancid**.

FREEZING: pack shelled walnuts into small cartons or pieces of **foil** and freeze.

FREEZER LIFE: 1 year.

THAWING: allow the walnuts to thaw at room temperature for about 3 hours.

warning light On most modern freezers, there is a warning light that switches itself on automatically if the door is open for longer than a few minutes. It may occur due to too much **frost** building up, causing the door to be held slightly open, in which case it must be defrosted. Alternatively, the **thermostat** may need checking to ensure that it is maintaining the correct temperature inside the freezer. Essentially, it is a safety device, so that the freezer owner will recognise when the frozen food is not cold enough to be completely safe.

water chestnut The succulent corm of a Chinese plant, traditionally used in Chinese cookery. Water chestnuts are normally sold in tins, but if there are some leftover they may be frozen for up to 3 months.

FREEZING: remove from the tin and pack into small plastic cartons. Cover them with the liquid they were purchased in, then seal with a lid and freeze.

FREEZER LIFE: 3 months.

THAWING: allow to thaw at room temperature for 1–2 hours before using.

watercress A leafy green **vegetable**, which does not freeze successfully raw because it has a high water content. Watercress can, however, be used in watercress **soup**, sauces or in herb **butter** and frozen this way.

water ice An ice cream made from a frozen sugar syrup and flavoured with fruit juice or purée. Water ices can be stored in the freezer for a short time, but as they are quite quick to make it is better to freeze surplus fruit as a purée, and then make water ices from that as required.

FREEZING: prepare the water ices as usual and pack into **rigid containers** and place in the freezer. When beginning to freeze, remove from the freezer, and beat thoroughly. Return to the rigid container and freeze.

FREEZER LIFE: 2 months.

THAWING: remove the water ice from the freezer about 15 minutes before serving to allow it to soften a little. See **sorbet**.

watermelon The fruit of an African melon plant with sweet, reddish flesh. Watermelon is difficult to prepare for the freezer due to the amount of seeds inside it. It is easier to make any extra watermelon into **fruit juice** and freeze it that way.

FREEZING: remove the skin and sieve the flesh, discarding all the seeds. Purée until smooth and sweeten as desired. Pack into **rigid containers** and freeze upright until firm.

FREEZER LIFE: 9 months.

THAWING: allow the melon juice to thaw in the refrigerator for several hours before using.

waxed cartons A type of container commonly used for commercially prepared **orange juice** and **milk**. Waxed cartons can also be purchased for home-use for liquids and fruit, but are no better than plastic, **rigid containers**.

whitebait The tiny, silver fry of **sprats** or **herrings** that are eaten whole. Whitebait must be very fresh if they are to be frozen at home. Check that thcy have not already been frozen.

FREEZING: rinse thoroughly in cold water, drain and pat dry. **Open freeze** on trays until firm, then pack tightly into **polythene bags** and return to the freezer.

FREEZER LIFE: 2 months.

THAWING: allow the whitebait to thaw in a cool place for 2–3 hours before using, then dry and deep fry as usual. They may also be fried from frozen if necessary.

white currant The small, round, white berries of a temperate shrub similar to a **redcurrant**, but much sweeter. White currants may be frozen in a **dry pack** or a **dry sugar pack**.

FREEZING: strip the **fruit** from the stalks and wash and dry. **Open freeze** on trays until firm, then pack into **polythene bags**, extracting as much air as possible before **sealing**. Alternatively, mix 125 g (4 oz) of sugar with every 500 g (1lb) of fruit before packing into bags.

FREEZER LIFE: 1 year.

THAWING: allow the fruit to thaw at room temperature for about 3 hours or cook from frozen.

white sauce See **sauce**.

whiting A small, white **fish**, related to cod, with flaky white flesh, which is normally sold whole or in fillets. Whiting must be absolutely fresh if it is to be frozen.

FREEZING: wash thoroughly, remove the scales, gut, and remove the head and tail if desired. Wrap each fish individually in a **polythene bag**, extracting as much air as possible before **sealing**. Fillets should be **interleaved** with small pieces of **greaseproof paper** or **freezer wrap** and overwrapped in **foil** or a polythene bag.

FREEZER LIFE: 3 months.

THAWING: whole fish and fillets may be cooked successfully from frozen, or allow them to thaw in the refrigerator overnight.

whortleberry See **blueberry**.

wild mushroom See **mushroom**.

wild rice Freeze as for **rice**.

wine An alcoholic drink usually made by fermenting grapes, although it may also be made by fermenting many kinds of fruit or flowers. It is possible to freeze leftover wine if desired, but it should then only be used for cooking, e.g. to flavour **casseroles**.

FREEZING: remove the leftover wine from the bottle and pour into small cartons, seal and freeze. Or pour into ice cube trays.

FREEZER LIFE: 2 months.

THAWING: wine may be added to dishes, such as casseroles, from frozen.

winkle A small mollusc, which may be frozen only if absolutely fresh.

FREEZING: wash thoroughly, then cook in boiling water for 20 minutes. Drain and allow to cool. Remove from their shells and pack into **rigid containers** to freeze.

FREEZER LIFE: 1 month.

THAWING: allow the winkles to thaw in their unopened container for 2 hours in the refrigerator before serving cold. See also **shellfish**.

winter squashes A type of winter **vegetable** from the **pumpkin** family, which is now widely available in Europe during the winter months. Winter squashes may be either served boiled and mashed as a purée or baked whole. They can be frozen successfully either raw and **blanched** or fully cooked, so that they may be enjoyed the whole year round.

FREEZING: wash and peel the squash and remove the seeds. Cut into small chunks and either blanch for 2 minutes or steam or boil until tender. Plunge blanched squashes into cold water, drain, dry and pack into **polythene bags**, extracting as much air as possible before **sealing**. Alternatively, mash cooked squash with **butter** and allow to cool completely. Then pack into **rigid containers**, leaving a 2.5 cm (1 inch) **headspace** before **sealing**.

FREEZER LIFE: 1 year.
THAWING: allow the squash to thaw in the refrigerator for 3–4 hours before using either as an accompanying **vegetable** or in **pies** and **soups**.

witch (also called **Torbay sole**) A North Atlantic flatfish, similar to a **Dover sole**, but with less flavour. Witch can be frozen successfully either whole or in fillets.
FREEZING: wash the whole fish, remove the scales, gut and then **ice glaze**. Wrap it in **clingfilm** and **overwrap** in a **polythene bag**. Separate fillets with clingfilm or **freezer wrap** and overwrap in **foil** before freezing.
FREEZER LIFE: whole fish and fillets, 3 months.
THAWING: allow a whole fish to thaw in a cool place for up to 24 hours, then use as soon as possible. Fillets may be cooked from frozen or allowed to thaw in the refrigerator for 1–2 hours before using.

woodcock A small **game** bird that should be plucked, the intestines removed and the gizzard and crop cleaned, but replaced inside. It may be frozen for up to 6 months.
FREEZING: pack whole birds into **polythene bags** and remove as much air as possible before **sealing**.
FREEZER LIFE: 6 months.
THAWING: allow to thaw overnight in the refrigerator in its wrappings for 5 hours per 500 g (1lb).

wrapping It is important when freezing food to ensure that it is carefully packed and wrapped.

This is so that the air cannot enter the package and cause the food to dry out. Unless food is properly wrapped, it may suffer from **freezer burn** and loss of texture and flavour. Moisture escaping from frozen food due to poor wrapping will build up as **frost** inside the freezer, necessitating frequent **defrosting**. Every item in the freezer should be wrapped in moisture- and vapour-proof material. **Greaseproof paper** is not sufficient as a wrapping material. Strong materials such as heavy gauge polythene and rigid plastic should be used. See also **clingfilm**; **cross-flavouring**; **foil**; **freezer wrap**; **packaging**; **polythene bags**.

yam The starchy tuber of any of various tropical, twining plants. Choose undamaged and firm yams for freezing.

FREEZING: wash the yams, then peel and dice. Cook in boiling water with a little **lemon juice**, to prevent **discoloration**, until just undercooked. Allow to cool and pack into **polythene bags**, extracting as much air as possible before **sealing**.

FREEZER LIFE: 3 months.

THAWING: allow to thaw for 2–3 hours in the refrigerator before **reheating**.

yeast Any of various single-celled fungi of the genus *Saccharomyces*. Fresh yeast is not always readily available so it is useful to freeze it.

FREEZING: place 15 or 30 g ($\frac{1}{2}$ or 1 ounce) cubes individually in a piece of **foil**, then **overwrap** several together in a **polythene bag**. Extract as much air as possible before **sealing**.

FREEZER LIFE: 6 weeks.

THAWING: allow each cube to thaw at room temperature for 30 minutes before activating in warm water as usual.

yoghurt A thick, custard-like dairy product made by curdling milk with certain strains of bacteria. Most fruit-flavoured yoghurts store quite well in the freezer although they may separate on **thawing**. Yoghurt with honey freezes very well.

FREEZING: the yoghurt may **expand** and burst through its lid, so place the pot in a **polythene bag** before freezing.

FREEZER LIFE: 1 month.

THAWING: allow the yoghurt to thaw overnight in the refrigerator, then beat thoroughly to regain its former smooth texture before serving.

Yorkshire pudding A light, puffy, baked pudding made from a batter consisting of eggs, flour and milk. Cooked Yorkshire puddings can be frozen successfully. Although they do not puff up quite as well as fresh Yorkshire puddings when reheated.

FREEZING: bake the Yorkshire pudding as usual and when crisp and golden allow them to cool completely. **Open freeze** until firm, then pack into **polythene bags** and return them to the freezer.

FREEZER LIFE: 2 months.

THAWING: place frozen Yorkshire puddings on a baking sheet and reheat for about 10 minutes.

Youngberry A cross between a **loganberry** and a **blackberry**, which may be frozen on its own or with sugar if desired.

FREEZING: wash and dry and place on trays in the freezer to **open freeze**. When firm, transfer the **fruit** into **polythene bags**, adding 125 g (4oz) of sugar to every 500 g (1lb) of fruit if desired. Extract as much air as possible before **sealing** and replacing in the freezer.

FREEZER LIFE: 1 year.

THAWING: allow the fruit to thaw overnight in the refrigerator or for 3 hours at room temperature, or cook slowly from frozen.

zucchini See **courgette**.

Appendix I

Buying, using and maintaining a freezer

What to look for when buying a freezer

When buying a freezer, a determining factor is the amount of space available in the kitchen, or any other utility room where the freezer is to be kept; as well as the amount of money that is being considered for the purchase. There are several types of freezer: chest freezers, upright freezers and refrigerator freezers (see below).

Chest freezers take up a great deal of floor space and are more suitable for those who have a large kitchen or garage. Upright freezers occupy far less space and are easy to load and unload. Refrigerator freezers, which have both a refrigeration and a freezing compartment, are very popular and convenient for those with a limited amount of space. The size of the freezer you need is also dependent on how often you plan to bulk buy, how many there are in the household, and whether you plan to freeze home-grown produce. It is usually suggested that you should allow about 56 litre (2 cubic feet) per person and an extra 56 litre (2 cubic feet).

Another determining factor for the model that you choose, is what kind of food is going to be frozen. If, for example, the freezer is going to be used mainly for meat and poultry, such as whole lambs and large joints of beef, then it would be best to buy a large chest freezer. If though, the purchaser was proposing to only freeze ready meals and commercially frozen food for convenience, then it would make more sense to buy an upright freezer or a combination refrigerator and freezer.

When buying a freezer it is most important to check that the freezer carries a star symbol with a large star in front of three smaller stars, which indicates that it can freeze fresh food. An appliance that only carries one, two or three stars can only be used to store ready frozen food. This type of appliance is known as a conservator.

Most modern freezers now have a warning light that operates if the freezer is not working correctly or if the door is open. Some freezers also have a section within them that is designed specifically for fast-freezing fresh foods. This can be very helpful for successful freezing, or alternatively they may have a fast-freeze switch for this purpose. If you are planning to freeze a lot of home produce or, for example, large quantities of meat, check the recommended maximum amount that can be frozen in 24 hours. Some freezers also have a drain in the base, which enables the freezer to be defrosted quickly and efficiently. The drain saves having to wipe out the last bits of melted ice at the base. If you have small children it is best to buy a chest freezer that can be locked, so that no one can become trapped inside.

Finally, when buying a freezer check that it is easy and convenient to use. That it has all the shelves and freezer baskets required, and that it is the right height to allow you to reach all the food easily. Also buy a model with an interior light (although most models do now have one), which is extremely helpful in identifying packages of frozen food, especially in large chest freezers.

Chest freezers

Chest freezers are generally large capacity freezers with a top-closing lid that hinges from the top. Most are long, deep and narrow and take up a great deal more space than the upright types. Sizes range from about 112 litre (4 cubic feet) to about 706 litre (25 cubic feet). When situating a chest freezer remember to have sufficient space overhead, so that the lid can be opened wide enough to be able look inside and reach for the contents easily. Due to their size, chest freezers are often located out of sight in garages, outhouse or on landings. They should therefore be checked frequently to see that they are working properly (for example, check for warning lights) and should always be kept locked.

They are less expensive to buy than upright models and cheaper to run, because they do not lose so much cold air when the freezer is opened. However, they are more difficult to manage because it is necessary to lean in and search for the food you require, which can be quite a task if the freezer is full and the food you are looking for is at the bottom. The top of the freezer can be useful as a temporary work surface, although it cannot be used to store things permanently because the lid will need to be opened.

Chest freezers normally have a separate fast-freezing compartment or a fast-freeze switch so that fresh food may be frozen quickly and efficiently. Overall, because they are spacious and can accommodate large, bulky food packages, they are best-suited for long-term storage and not for food that will be required everyday.

Upright freezers

These are freezers that stand upright and have the door hinging either on the right or the left. They are the same shape and size as a normal refrigerator, ranging in size from about 57 litre (2 cubic feet) to 570 litre (25 cubic feet) capacity. Upright freezers occupy a minimal amount of floor space and are easy to load and unload. They are more convenient to use than chest freezers because the food is always easily accessible in drawers or baskets. The top may also be used as a work surface or shelves may be built above it. They are, however, more expensive to run because opening the door allows a a stream of cold air to escape and the motor has to then work harder to remove the warm air that is now inside. They also need to be defrosted more regularly than chest freezers. Opening the door causes a constant interchange of hot and cold air, which causes frost and ice to build up more quickly. However, it is easier to defrost an upright model. As with any new appliance it is advisable to check that it is easy to operate, that it is the right height and that it has a strong seal on the door to prevent warm air from entering more than necessary.

Refrigerator/freezers

These combine a freezer unit with a standard refrigerator. They are extremely useful if space is very limited, although they are not cheap to buy. It is possible to freeze fresh food in them, but only in small amounts. Refrigerator/freezers have all the advantages of a self-contained upright freezer, but need only the same amount of floor space as an ordinary refrigerator. The freezer capacity is normally about 170 litre (6 cubic feet)

Conservator

This is a cold-storage cabinet designed only to store food that is already frozen. It cannot freeze fresh foods and is therefore not particularly useful as a household item. They are most often used for storing commercial ice creams and convenience foods, for example in supermarkets, and only maintain a temperature of −18°C (0°F).

Buying a second-hand or reconditioned freezer

Second-hand freezers can be very good value for money provided that they are not over 5 years old. This is often the age when mechanical parts may start to deteriorate and the appliances will not work as efficiently. Also, it may become increasingly difficult to obtain spare parts for very old models. It is important to check a second-hand freezer thoroughly before purchasing it. Try to see the freezer in action, because it is important to ensure that the motor is not labouring and that it appears to be operating efficiently at -18° (0°F). Make sure that fresh food can be frozen down properly and that it is not merely a conservator for storing previously frozen food (they look very similar). A true deep freeze must display a four star symbol, which means that it is designed to freeze fresh foods as well as to store frozen foods. Check that all the controls work and the door shuts securely. The door seal is often one of the first parts to go wrong.

A reconditioned freezer is often a good buy, because some shops will take in old freezers and recondition the motors, then sell them at relatively low prices. They also generally come with a short guarantee.

Freezer management

Where to put the freezer

The most convenient place to situate a freezer is obviously in the kitchen or a utility room nearby, but if there is no space available a freezer may be located anywhere on the ground floor, or in an outhouse or garage. If siting it upstairs, care should be taken to ensure that it is placed across the joists as freezers, especially large chest types, will become extremely heavy when full. Freezers also tend to make a certain amount of engine noise, so it is advisable not to place them in, for example, a bedroom or dining room.

The cost of running a freezer does depend largely upon where it is located and the ideal spot should be constantly cool and dry. If the freezer is always warm the engine will have to work harder to maintain the temperature within it down to –18°C (0°F). This will use up more electricity and there will be greater wear and tear on the motor. A freezer should not be located where there are constant or frequent changes in the surrounding temperature (hot or cold), such as near large windows or radiators. If it becomes very damp it will become rusty very quickly and the freezer will not operate effectively.

Finally, if the freezer is placed outside the house or where it is fairly unobtrusive, it should be fitted with an alarm so that it can warn you if there is any power failure or if a fuse has blown.

Installing a freezer

Wherever the freezer is going to be sited, it is vitally important that the cabinet is completely level so that the lid or door closes securely. If it is not sealed properly the freezer will not work effectively. The constant struggle to maintain a low temperature will use a lot of electricity and it will therefore become very expensive to run. It is also very important to allow a current of air to circulate around the freezer to prevent condensation. It is best to allow about 5–10 cm (2–4 inches), especially at the back and the sides. Those models with fan-assisted condensers will need space around the grill outlet, which is normally situated on the side and at the base. When it has been placed correctly it is advisable to allow the freezer to settle for about an hour before switching on the power. This is so that any oil that has been displaced during moving can return to the compressor. It will need a 13 or 15 amp plug and socket, and once the machine has been turned on it is a good idea to tape over the switch with a strip of insulation tape so that it does not inadvertently get switched off. If it is possible it is a good idea to fit an alarm system so that major disasters, such as having to throw away the whole of the contents in the freezer due to power failure, can be avoided.

While it is switched off, it is a good idea to clean it thoroughly with a solution of ½ tablespoon of bicarbonate of soda to 500 ml (1 pint) of warm water. Dry it well before switching on, so that ice does not immediately begin to form. Check that all the lights and switches are working and then allow it to reach the normal running temperature of 0°C (–18°F) over a period of 24 hours before placing any food inside it. Check that the temperature is correct with a freezer thermometer and then previously frozen food may be stored in it.

If you plan to freeze fresh food straight away, remember to switch on the super-freeze switch for

2–3 hours before freezing, so that it can be frozen as quickly and efficiently as possible.

Loading the freezer

The most efficient way of loading a freezer would be to stack square boxes on top of each other. This is obviously not always possible, but there are certain ways that you can ensure that the freezer is loaded sensibly.

Large chest freezers can sometimes be difficult to organise efficiently, although with a little forethought it is possible to devise a straightforward system. It is easiest to divide up the chest freezer into compartments by means of either wire baskets or different coloured or labelled bags or boxes. Each compartment should stock one category of food, such as meat or cakes and bakery products, and be labelled with specific coloured labels or coloured ties. Then each category should be recorded in a record book, kept by the freezer, where you should list everything that goes into the freezer and the date, and make a list of every item that is taken out. This means that there will always be a good rotation of stock in the freezer and as little food as possible will either be wasted or be stored for longer than the recommended storage life.

The bottom section of a chest freezer should be used for long-term storage items and bulky parcels, such as large joints of meat. Above this should be compartments for fruit and vegetables, bread and cakes, meat, cooked dishes and any other group of foods that is likely to be consumed within 1–2 months. The top layer should contain items that are going to be used up fairly rapidly, such as soups, sauces, ice creams and puddings, and the small, light more delicate items, such as pots of chopped herbs and breadcrumbs. If there is a specific section for fast-freezing fresh foods, this should be kept as free as possible, so that it is always available for freezing. In this way, what could seem an enormous chest that is constantly dived into and always untidy can become an efficient type of store cupboard.

An upright freezer is simpler to load as it is already divided into small compartments. It is still a good idea to mark each compartment for each category of items and have a record of all the items that are inside. As with a chest freezer it is best to load long-term storage items in the lower part of the freezer and put the smaller items and those with a short storage life, such as butter, patés and leftovers, in the smaller, upper compartments with doors.

Using freezer space efficiently

Whatever the size and type of the freezer, it is always important to stock it neatly and efficiently to make maximum use of the space available. Careful and secure packaging is essential so that the food remains as good as it was when placed inside the freezer. Badly wrapped food will lead to the food drying out and freezer burn, which will make the food lose its quality and flavour. The storage capacity of the freezer will depend on the packing methods used, because if all the food is packed in identical containers you will make the maximum use of the freezer space. Obviously this is not always practical, but it is advisable to be as neat as you can and not waste space.

All packages of food should be labelled clearly using either a permanent ink felt-tip pen or a Chinagraph pencil. It is very easy to forget what food has been placed in the freezer and certain foods, especially meat, become quickly obscured by frost once frozen, making it impossible to determine what they are. It is also important to write the date that the food was frozen on each label as every food has a different storage life. Thus it is helpful to compile a freezer record with a list of the food that has been frozen, the date it was frozen and the storage life so that the food can be thawed and consumed regularly and safely.

Freezer maintenance

The cost of maintaining a freezer

The cost of running a freezer is determined by a number of factors: the size and type of freezer, the frequency with which the door is going to be opened, efficient and regular defrosting, careful chilling of food prior to freezing and local electricity charges. Very roughly, a freezer of 6 cubic feet will consume approximately 0.3 kW per cubic foot; a freezer of 18 cubic feet will consume approximately 0.2 kW per cubic foot over a 24 hour period.

It is possible to keep the costs as low as possible in the following ways. First, it is important to keep the freezer away from central heating, boilers, hot ovens and direct sunlight. The cooler the freezer is the easier it is for the motor to maintain a constant low temperature.

Second, if the freezer door or lid is opened as little as possible it means that again the engine does not have to work so hard to maintain a constant low temperature.

Last, it is vital that only cold or chilled foods are placed in the freezer for the same reasons. Warm food could lead to other foods becoming partly thawed, which could be dangerous.

Running repairs

Freezers are generally fairly reliable, as long as they are looked after properly and defrosted regularly. From time to time, however, there may be problems that can often be solved without having to call in an engineer. A power failure might be caused by a local power cut, a blown fuse in the plug or the plug accidentally being turned off. If the compressor has actually broken this can be checked by turning on the fast-freeze switch. If there is no noise it is not working and it will be necessary to call an engineer. If the freezer motor suddenly appears to be very noisy it may well be that it has been accidentally pushed too close to the wall.

One of the most common repairs necessary to maintain the freezer is that of a faulty or perished door or lid seal. These seals can usually be obtained easily direct from the freezer manufacturer and are simple to replace.

Servicing the freezer

Once a new freezer has been installed and is working correctly it is unlikely to cause many problems for several years. It is unlikely to break down and does not really need to be serviced in its first few years of life. Most models now come with a guarantee, which is between one and five years, and this should cover any new parts and the labour time involved that might be needed during that period. The most expensive part in a freezer to replace is the compressor and if this is faulty it should show up within the first year.

After the warranty period it is possible to take out a further service guarantee, which may well include a form of food insurance and possibly a stand-by freezer while yours is out of action. Alternatively, it is possible to take out separate insurance to cover breakdown repair costs. When the freezer reaches about 10 years old, it becomes less reliable and consequently it becomes more difficult to obtain insurance unless the machine is regularly serviced.

Power cuts

If you have advanced warning of a power cut it is possible to take certain precautions that will allow the food to remain undamaged for 48 hours. If it is very sudden, the food will still be undamaged for at least 24 hours, providing that the freezer is not opened during the power failure. If there is advanced warning of at least 6 hours, pad out any gaps in the freezer with crumpled newspapers or towels, ensuring that it is packed as full as possible. Turn on the fast-freeze switch to make it as cold as possible. Then cover the freezer with a blanket for additional insulation, but leave the back of the freezer open to the air. When the power is restored, leave the fast-freeze switch on for 2–3 hours, before returning it to normal temperature.

Defrosting the freezer

It is important to defrost the freezer regularly to ensure that it works efficiently. Frost may form around the lid or the door of older machines and this can be removed with a plastic spatula or scraper. Frost on the walls of the freezer does not affect the machine's efficiency as much as frost around the door or lid, but it should be removed as soon as it reaches a thickness of 0.5 cm ($\frac{1}{4}$ inch). It is easiest to defrost the freezer when stocks are low because the food can then be easily transferred to a cool place, wrapped in newspaper until the freezer is clean.

To defrost a freezer, switch off the power and tap as much ice off as possible with a plastic spatula. Bowls of hot water may be placed in the freezer to speed up the melting process. Never use sharp or metal tools and always follow the manufacturer's instructions on the method of defrosting most effectively. Then wipe out the freezer with a solution of 15 ml (1 tbsp) of bicarbonate of soda to every litre (2 pints) of warm water to freshen it and remove any odours. Then wipe the freezer completely dry with a cloth before switching it on again. Allow the freezer to run for about 30 minutes before replacing all the food.

The outside of the machine may be cleaned with a solution of washing up liquid and warm water. Dry thoroughly and (if sited outside the house) apply a thin coat of silicon polish to prevent damp.

Moving a freezer

If the freezer has to be moved, for example if moving house, it is vital that it is kept as upright as possible. Tipping it by more than 30° could cause an airlock in the cooling system. Before moving it, remove the food and defrost it and clean it thoroughly. When it is then installed in its new location switch it on to check that it is working correctly, then switch it off for several hours to allow it to settle before using it.

Appendix II

Freezing, packaging and thawing

Freezing techniques

Freezing works by basically converting the water within foods to ice crystals. Quick freezing results in tiny ice crystals forming, which leave the structure of the food undamaged after thawing. Slow freezing will result in large ice crystals forming, which leads to the cell structure within the food becoming damaged, causing loss in taste, texture, colour and flavour. In order to prevent this damage from occurring it is important that slow freezing is prevented. This can be ensured by never freezing more than one-tenth of the freezer's capacity at one time, over a period of 24 hours. By adding unfrozen food to the freezer, the temperature within it is raised, thus affecting the ice crystal formation that could be so damaging to the food. Warm food should never be introduced into the freezer because of this, and food should preferably be chilled before freezing.

The fast-freeze switch

Most modern freezers now have a fast-freeze or super-freeze switch, which enables you to freeze food quickly by reducing the temperature from –18°C (0°F) to below –28°C (–18°F). By overriding the freezer thermostat, fresh food can be frozen quickly without affecting any other food in the freezer. As a general rule the fast-freeze switch should be turned on about 2 hours before new food is going to be added to the freezer, and then left on for about 4 hours after it is added. If large amounts of fresh food are to be frozen it would be advisable to turn on the switch about 6 hours beforehand and leave it on for about 24 hours or so.

If there is no fast-freeze switch on the freezer, it is advisable to adjust the thermostat to its coldest setting before adding any new fresh foods to the freezer.

Stocking the freezer

Because some foods are better to freeze than others, before stocking the freezer it is a good idea to plan the best items to store in this way. Obviously, if there are some items that are easily available in the shops all year round it is a waste of space to freeze a lot of these items. It is also important to only freeze foods in quantities that you can consume easily, because food that is thawed and not consumed should not be refrozen unless it is cooked properly first.

What can you freeze?

a) All types of raw meat, offal, poultry, game and fish.
b) Most vegetables, except salad vegetables and those with a high water content, freeze successfully. Most vegetables store better if they are blanched first.

c) All fruit freezes well except for melon, which tends to become tough and leathery. However, soft fruits, such as raspberries and strawberries, will soften with freezing

d) Most types of bakery produce, both raw and cooked, freeze well: dough, bread, pastry, cakes and sponges (either iced or plain), buns and teacakes.

e) Some dairy products do not freeze very well. Eggs should not be frozen whole or hard boiled, but they may be frozen as separate egg whites and yolks or beaten together. Full-fat milk will not freeze well, but skimmed, semi-skimmed and homogenized milk may be frozen. Cream with over 40% butterfat, butter and hard cheese will freeze, but blue cheese tends to become very crumbly and cream cheese will separate out.

f) Many cooked foods and made up dishes may be frozen, such as soups, meat and fish dishes, puddings and sauces. It is important to remember, however, that garlic and herbs should be omitted prior to freezing because they both tend to develop rather unpleasant flavours during storage in the freezer.

Freezing meat

Meat needs very little preparation before freezing except for trimming off any excess fat, because this will turn rancid over time. If possible, remove bones from the meat as they take up space in the freezer, and they can be frozen separately for use in stocks. It may be best to ask the butcher to cut up large joints into smaller pieces, such as chops, for separate, easy packing. When freezing meat ensure that it is packaged correctly, because if any air comes into contact with frozen meat it can cause freezer burn, which turns the meat an unpleasant grey colour and it loses flavour and texture. It is also important to label meat clearly as frost build up quickly obscures the meat and makes it difficult to identify.

Freezing poultry

Only freeze young, plump tender birds. If possible turn the freezer down to its lowest setting or turn on the fast-freeze switch at least 24 hours beforehand. Once the poultry is frozen return the temperature to its normal setting. Poultry should be wrapped carefully and securely because it is prone to freezer burn – patches of dry grey skin, where the air has reached the meat, making it lack in flavour and taste.

Freezing fish

All fish and shellfish must be really fresh if it is to be frozen, preferably it should be frozen on the day it is caught. All fish should be thoroughly washed, gutted and the scales removed. Whole fish freeze best if they are covered in a covering of ice – a method known as ice glazing. To ice glaze a whole fish, place it in the freezer, unwrapped until firm. Then remove it from the freezer and dip into cold water until there is a thin film of ice over the fish. Return it to the freezer until firm once more. Repeat this process at half-hourly intervals until there is an ice covering of about 0.5 cm ($\frac{1}{4}$ inch) thick over the fish. Then wrap the fish in freezer wrap and overwrap in a polythene bag. Larger fish should be supported by a board before storing in the freezer. Fish steaks and fillets should be interleaved with freezer wrap or clingfilm before wrapping in polythene bags.

Freezing vegetables

Most vegetables freeze successfully except for those with a very high water content, such as lettuce and cucumbers. Most vegetables are best blanched before freezing, which involves dipping them briefly in either boiling water or steam to destroy the enzymes within them that make the food deteriorate. Blanching also helps to preserve colour, flavour and texture and retain nutritional value. After blanching vegetables should be cooled quickly in cold water and frozen in polythene bags, extracting as much air as possible before sealing.

Freezing fruit

Fruit should be just ripe if it is to be frozen. Fruit that is overripe can be frozen as purée. There are four methods of freezing fruit: dry pack, dry sugar pack, syrup pack and purée.

DRY PACK – fruits that do not discolour easily, such as blackcurrants and raspberries, can be frozen whole without the addition of any sugar or syrup. Spread the fruit on trays and place in the freezer unwrapped until firm. Then tip into polythene bags and seal securely. The fruit will remain free flowing and separate, and can consequently be used in small amounts as desired.

DRY SUGAR PACK – Fruits that can be frozen in dry packs, i.e. those that do not discolour easily, may be sprinkled with sugar prior to freezing. Mix the fruit thoroughly with 50 g (2 oz) of sugar to every 500 g (1lb) of fruit and pack into polythene bags. On thawing the sugar melts with the liquid from the fruit and provides a delicious fruit syrup.

SYRUP PACK – Fruits that tend to discolour easily and firm fruits, such as peaches and pears, are best frozen in a sugar syrup. Make a syrup by dissolving dissolving 250 g (8 oz) of sugar in 600 ml (1 pint) of water. The syrup must always be cold and it is possible to make it in advance and keep it in the refrigerator for several days. Allow approximately 300 ml (½ pint) of syrup to every 500 g (1lb) of fruit. Dip the fruit into lemon juice, then pack into rigid containers and cover the fruit with the syrup, submerging it by placing a piece of crumpled greaseproof paper or aluminium foil on top. Make sure that there is a headspace of about 2 cm (1 inch) before sealing to allow for expansion.

PURÉE – Cook the fruit with sugar or use overripe fruit then blend until smooth. Sieve to remove any pips if desired and pack into rigid containers, allowing a 2 cm (1 inch) headspace for expansion before sealing.

Freezing liquids

Due to the fact that water expands by one tenth during the freezing process, it is advisable to leave at least a 2 cm (1 inch) headspace in the top of containers before sealing. If there is no headspace liquids may well expand and push off the lids of their containers.

Packaging techniques

The correct and thorough packaging of food that is to be frozen is essential in order to protect the quality of the food. If the food is not sealed in securely and air is allowed to come into contact with the food, it will become dehydrated and fruit will lose its colour. There are many types of packaging manufactured specifically for use in the freezer, although there are also many cheaper alternatives that can be just as effective. All containers should be thoroughly cleaned and checked to ensure that they are airtight and moisture proof.

Clingfilm/freezer wrap

This is a useful packaging material for the freezer because it clings to itself, to plastic and to metal. Freezer wrap, which is thicker than ordinary clingfilm, can be used alone to wrap up frozen food, but it is preferable to overwrap each package with a polythene bag to keep out as much air as possible. Clingfilm is also very useful for wrapping items separately, which can then be packed all together in a polythene bag, such as fillets of fish or chops. Freezer wrap can also be used to wrap foods such as sandwiches and rolls, and to cover dishes and containers that do not have lids.

Never thaw foods in a microwave wrapped in ordinary clingfilm, only specially designed microwave-safe clingfilm can be used.

Foil

Aluminium foil is a useful packaging material because it is moisture- and vapour-proof. It is also very useful for packaging awkwardly shaped foods. However, it has its drawbacks because it can be torn and damaged, which then allows air to come into contact with the food. It is possible to purchase special freezer foil that is very thick, but ordinary kitchen foil may be used successfully if it is doubled in thickness. Do not use foil with acidic fruits because they may react with the aluminium and become discoloured. The acid in the fruit will also cause pitting in the foil.

Foil can also be used to line casserole dishes when preparing food for the freezer. The food can be frozen in the dish and then removed and wrapped up in the foil, allowing you to use the dish again.

It is possible to buy aluminium foil dishes, which are very useful if you are cooking a lot of prepared or individual meals for the freezer. They come in many different shapes and sizes and are often manufactured with their own close-fitting lids. They are strong enough to be washed and used more than once, as long as you are careful to keep their shape and not to bend or crush them. They can also be used to cook, freeze and reheat, although they are not suitable for use in the microwave.

Glass

Glass should never be used in the freezer because it shatters, scattering tiny splinters of glass around the freezer, which could be extremely dangerous. Never freeze liquids in bottles, because they expand by one-tenth when frozen and will cause the bottle to shatter.

Special toughened glass containers can be purchased from specialist freezer manufacturers, but make sure they are suitable for use at temperatures as low as –18°C (–28°F). Before using always read the manufacturer's instructions carefully.

Polythene bags

Polythene bags are invaluable for use in the freezer. They are relatively cheap, can usually be used more than once and come in a variety of sizes. Heavy duty polythene is best to use in the freezer because the thinner type may be porous and therefore not suitable. Cooked dishes, such as stews and casseroles, may be frozen in a polythene bag placed inside a container. When firm, they may be removed from the containers and stored in convenient shapes.

Polythene sheeting is useful for packing meat and for overwrapping foil and strong-flavoured or odorous foods.

Rigid containers
These are containers made of rigid plastic designed specifically for use in the freezer. They are invaluable in the freezer because they come in various sizes and are in convenient shapes for stacking and storing. They can be used many times and therefore are worth the extra cost. Rigid containers are normally sold with their own well-fitting lids, which are essential to keep the air out. If necessary, seal the lids tightly with freezer tape.

Other packaging
Containers, such as yoghurt pots, large family-size margarine and ice cream tubs, can be particularly efficient, cheap items to use as containers for freezing food. Although they will not last for very long they are ideal for short-term use, providing they are thoroughly cleaned and dried before use. Seal the lids if necessary with freezer tape.

Packaging to avoid
Before buying any containers or packaging materials that are to be used specifically for the freezer, it is important to check that they are moisture- and vapour-proof. That they will withstand up to 12 months' storage at –18°C (0°F) and also that they will not taint the food by being odorous themselves.

Avoid the following materials:

1) Any material that is not guaranteed as moisture- and vapour-proof, or will not withstand up to 12 month's storage in the freezer.

2) Any material that will leak, such as a thin polythene bag.

3) Any material that will rust, such as metal containers made of tin.

4) Any material that might break or become brittle with storage at low temperatures, such as glass and hard plastic, which is not designed for the freezer.

Methods of wrapping food for the freezer

Efficient wrapping of foods to be frozen is essential because if air is allowed to reach the food through an ineffective seal, the food may well dry out, lose its colour, texture and flavour. The technique of good wrapping is to eliminate air as much as possible and keep it out by sealing securely.

WRAPPING IN SHEET MATERIALS – Place the food in the centre of the sheet (such as freezer wrap or polythene) and draw two sides of the sheet together. Fold them over and downwards towards the food, to make a tight wrap. Fold the ends like a parcel, making sure to get them as close to the food as possible. All foods should then be sealed with a special freezer tape. It is advisable to overwrap parcels of food with a polythene bag if possible.

WRAPPING IN BAGS – Pack the food as neatly as possible into the bags and press out as much air as possible from all corners. Seal securely and tightly with wire ties or freezer tape.

HEADSPACE – Liquid and semi-liquid food expands to up to one tenth of its original size during freezing, so room must be allowed for this between the food and the seal of the package. If this is not done the contents will expand and the containers may split. Generally, approximately 1.25 cm (0.5 inches) should be allowed between most foods and the seals of their containers, although 2.5 cm (1 inch) should be left with liquids and very liquid foods.

SEALING AND LABELLING – Successful sealing is essential to keep air out of packages for the freezer. A simple, cheap seal for polythene bags is a wire fastener or the plastic tags used on packs of sliced bread. Most bags are now provided with plastic or wire ties and these should be used to secure the bags tightly.

Packages in freezer wrap and polythene sheeting should be secured with special adhesive freezer tape. Rigid containers should have well fitting lids, but if there is any doubt about the effectiveness of these lids, secure them with a strip of freezer tape.

All packets of frozen food should be labelled clearly with either a Chinagraph pencil or a permanent ink felt-tip pen that will not smudge. State the type of food, the date it was placed in the freezer and the weight or quantity. Frost builds up over time, making some foods difficult to identify, and it is easy to forget what item was frozen and when.

Thawing

When thawing food it is essential that it is done gently and evenly. When food is thawed, the small ice crystals that have developed inside the food melt first, and the thawing process is only completed when all the ice crystals have completely dissolved. Thawing times may be reduced by immersing frozen packages in cold water, but this draws out the flavour as well as the ice crystals and is not recommended. Food can be thawed in the microwave in far less time than with most conventional methods, but again it should be thawed gently and evenly, and turned regularly. If thawing is too rapid in the microwave the food will start to cook on the outside before the centre has defrosted. Always thaw food on the low or defrost setting, and allow the food to stand for up to 20 minutes after thawing and before cooking.

Most foods should be thawed before cooking, although frozen vegetables retain a better texture if cooked from frozen. Cooked meals may also be reheated from frozen as long as they are heated thoroughly. Fish fillets and steaks may also be cooked from frozen, although they will have less flavour than those that are thawed first.

Thawing poultry and game

All poultry and game must always be completely thawed before cooking. Once thawed it should be cooked and consumed as soon as possible. Poultry and game are a fruitful source of salmonella bacteria, which is not killed off by the freezing process, but merely lies dormant. Consequently, as thawing begins the birds should be defrosted at a temperature that discourages these bacteria to multiply. New research has shown that it is safer to thaw poultry at a cool temperature of 16°C (65°F) or in the refrigerator. Salmonella bacteria thrive and rapidly multiply in warm temperatures (such as room temperature). These bacteria are killed off, however, by correct, thorough and adequate cooking, which means that the birds are cooked right through to the inside cavity where most bacteria live. Uncooked meats should never be refrozen, especially if they are then to be served cold.

Thawing fish

Fish may be satisfactorily cooked from frozen, although it may lose flavour and texture. If possible, it should be allowed to thaw in the refrigerator overnight before cooking, then eaten as soon as possible.

Thawing meat

Raw meat should be completely thawed before cooking. It has been suggested that meat may be cooked from frozen, but it is difficult to ensure that the meat is thoroughly cooked right through to the insides at a temperature that destroys any bacteria that may have developed. Cooking times are difficult to calculate to ensure that the insides are cooked thoroughly without the outside being overcooked first. A meat thermometer inserted into the meat shortly before the estimated cooking time is complete should read at least 70°C (160°F) to be absolutely safe from the possibility of food poisoning.

Cooked meat dishes, such as casseroles and pies, may be reheated from frozen as long as they are adequately heated through. It is easier to thaw them at room temperature first to break up the pieces and then reheat them thoroughly to avoid any opportunity for bacteria to multiply and cause food poisoning.

Cooked, frozen and thawed meats must never be refrozen.

Partly thawed food

Never refreeze food that has been thawed and kept at room temperature for more than a few hours, for example, when returning from the supermarket. If it has only just softened on the outside it can be refrozen, but it will suffer some loss of colour, texture flavour and nutritional value.

Uncooked frozen food may be safely thawed, cooked, cooled and refrozen again.

Thawing in the microwave

Compared to more traditional thawing methods, frozen food can be thawed and reheated in a microwave far more quickly. Consequently the freezer and microwave are both excellent modern aids for today's more hectic and busy lifestyles. Generally, cooked and frozen food that is then reheated in the microwave does not tend to change in texture, and frozen meals can be served quickly and successfully. Likewise, large joints of meat and poultry can be thawed, ready for conventional or microwave cooking in a matter of minutes.

However, it is important that when thawing frozen food that it thaws gently and evenly so that the food does not begin to cook on the outside before it has thawed completely. Most modern microwave models have a defrost setting, but if the microwave only has high, medium or low temperature settings, it is important to thaw food on the low setting, turning the cooker off every 30 seconds and allowing the food to stand for 1–2 minutes before turning it on again. This procedure should be repeated, until the food has thawed completely, when it may then be cooked properly. During resting periods, the food should be stirred or turned so that the thawing process can be as efficient and swift as possible. Dense foods, such as large joints of meat, whole birds, should be left to stand for at least 30 minutes before cooking. This is because the thawing or microwave cooking continues during standing time and consequently the food may be overcooked and dried out if it is not allowed to stand for a sufficient length of time.

Defrost setting

This automatic control on most modern microwaves ensures the gentle and even thawing of food in the microwave. When this control is used in connection with the timer it automatically turns the microwave energy on and off in short bursts, so that the food is thawed at an even rate. This will prevent the food from cooking before it has been allowed to thaw out properly.

Thawing meat in the microwave

Joints of meat should be placed in the microwave still in their wrappings (pierced in two or three places) and the defrost setting switched on. After a little while, remove the wrapping and continue to thaw on a roasting rack so that the meat does not stand in the thawing liquid. Continue to remove as much of the liquid that is exuded during the thawing process, and turn the meat at regular intervals so that it thaws evenly. If it appears to be beginning to cook, turn off the machine and allow the meat to rest for 30–60 minutes. Meat is thawed when the thickest part can be easily skewered. See below, MICROWAVE THAWING TIMES; TABLE I.

Thawing poultry in the microwave

Poultry should be placed in the microwave in its wrappings, which should be pierced in several places. Remove any thawing liquid that collects and turn the birds over during thawing. Allow the birds to rest for 30 minutes after thawing in the microwave and if possible, finish off the thawing process in a bowl of cold water until completely defrosted through to the insides. This helps to prevent the outside surface of the meat from drying out. See below, MICROWAVE THAWING TIMES; TABLE 2.

Thawing fish and shellfish in the microwave

Place fish and shellfish on a plate in the microwave and cover with a sheet of absorbent kitchen paper to absorb any thawing liquid which is exuded. As with poultry, it is advisable to complete the thawing process in cold water so that the fish does not dry out. See below, MICROWAVE THAWING TIMES; TABLE 3.

Microwave Thawing Times

(Based on a 650 W microwave)

Table 1: Meat

FOOD	THAWING TIME (approx.)	STANDING TIME
Beef joint (on the bone)	10–12 min/500 g (1lb)	1 hour
Beef joint (boneless)	8–10 min/500 g (1lb)	1 hour
Beef, cubed	6–8 min/500 g (1lb)	10 minutes
Beef, minced	8–10 min/500 g (1lb)	10 minutes
Beef steak	8–10 min/500 g (1lb)	10 minutes

FOOD	THAWING TIME (approx.)	STANDING TIME
Kidney	6–9 min/500 g (1lb)	5 minutes
Lamb chops	8–10 min/500 g (1lb)	10 minutes
Lamb joint (on the bone)	5–6 min/500 g (1lb)	1 hour
Lamb joint (boneless)	5–6 min/500 g (1lb)	1 hour
Lamb, minced	8–10 min/500 g (1lb)	10 minutes
Liver	8–10 min/500 g (1lb)	5 minutes
Pork chops	8–10 min/500 g (1lb)	10 minutes
Pork joint (on the bone)	7–8 min/500 g (1lb)	1 hour

FOOD	THAWING TIME (approx.)	STANDING TIME
Pork joint (boneless)	7–8 min/500 g (1lb)	1 hour
Pork, tenderloin	8–10 min/500 g (1lb)	10 minutes
Sausages	5–6 min/500 g (1lb)	5 minutes
Veal, cubes	6–8 min/500 g (1lb)	10 minutes
Veal joint (on the bone)	5–6 min/500 g (1lb)	1 hour
Veal joint (boneless)	5–6 min/500 g (1lb)	1 hour
Veal, minced	8–10 min/500 g (1lb)	10 minutes

Microwave Thawing Times

(Based on a 650 W microwave)

Table 2: Poultry & Game

FOOD	THAWING TIME (approx.)	STANDING TIME
Chicken, duck & game birds	6–8 min/500 g (1lb)	30 minutes in cold water
Chicken portions	5–7 min/500 g (1lb)	10 minutes
Turkey	10–18 min/500 g (1lb)	2–3 hours in cold water

Microwave Thawing Times

(Based on a 650 W microwave)

Table 3: Fish & Shellfish

FOOD	THAWING TIME (approx.)	STANDING TIME
Lobster tails, crab claws	3–4 min/250 g (8 oz)	5 minutes after each 2 minutes of thawing
Oily fish (e.g. trout or mackerel)	2–3 min/250 g (8 oz) plus 3–4 mins	5 minutes after each 2 minutes of thawing
Prawns & shrimps	2–3 min/125 g (4 oz)	2 minutes
White fish fillets, (e.g. plaice)	3–4 min/500 g (1lb)	5 minutes after each 2 minutes of thawing

Storage life of food in the freezer

Frozen food will in fact store indefinitely in the freezer, but over time it will begin to deteriorate in flavour, colour and texture. However, due to the fact that bacteria that cause food poisoning are dormant at freezing temperatures, food that goes beyond its recommended storage life will still be safe to eat (providing that it is thawed and cooked correctly and thoroughly). Different foods have different storage lives due to their composition. Refer to the individual entries in the A to Z section for specific details.

Appendix III

The preparation of food for the freezer

Blanching
This is a method of pre-cooking food by placing it into boiling water or steam for a very short time. Most vegetables that can be frozen satisfactorily should be blanched before freezing, because the action of the enzymes within them, which cause discoloration and deterioration, can be inhibited.

Blanching is achieved by placing prepared vegetables in boiling water or steam for several minutes. It is important to refer to individual items for the exact times as they all differ (see the blanching table at the end of this appendix). Too little blanching will not destroy or inhibit the action of the enzymes. Too much will spoil the flavour, colour and crisp texture of the vegetables, because they will have been partly cooked. After blanching, the vegetables must be cooled quickly and thoroughly, which is most easily achieved by plunging them into a large bowl of ice-cold water or rinsing them under a running cold tap. If they are not cooled sufficiently they will continue to cook on the inside and end up being very soft. They should then be left to drain in a collander and dried before freezing.

Blanched frozen vegetables are successfully cooked from frozen, retaining their original colour and texture extremely well. Blanching also helps to retain the vitamin C content within the vegetables, which can so easily leach out.

Light fruits that discolour easily may also be blanched or cooked before freezing. Apples, peaches and pears all freeze very successfully if blanched first.

Cooking for the freezer

There is no doubt that a supply of ready cooked meals in the freezer can be an enormous help in many situations, such as unexpected guests, school holidays and large family gatherings (e.g. Christmas). The cooking for all of these events can be undertaken well in advance so that last minute cooking times are reduced to the minimum. This will save a great deal of time and effort.

Equally for everyday requirements the freezer can be a great boon. Freezing allows busy families to have ready meals to hand for several weeks ahead. Although it must be remembered that pre-cooked food has a relatively short storage life. Pre-cooked food should be stored for as little time as possible, because the fat within foods, such as casseroles and soups, turns rancid over time, and cooked food may gradually lose its flavour and texture. However, with a little planning and organisation the freezer stock can be used and replaced within storage limits.

Generally, most cooked foods may be frozen, apart from those unfreezable items listed in the A to Z section, but it is advisable to follow certain rules before freezing cooked foods:

1) Always use good quality raw foods and do not add any foods that are unsuitable for freezing.

2) Make sure that all food and equipment is spotlessly clean, during preparation.

3) Do not overcook the food before freezing as it will cook a little more during reheating.

4) Cool cooked food thoroughly and quickly.

5) Pack carefully, seal securely and label clearly before freezing.

Some important points to remember when freezing cooked food

1) Starchy foods, such as potatoes and rice within casseroles, are inclined to become very soft when thawed and reheated, so it is best to add them after freezing.

2) Hard boiled eggs become hard and leathery if frozen.

3) Mayonnaise will curdle if frozen.
4) Dishes containing milk or cheese tend to separate or curdle on thawing, but they can usually be beaten back into an emulsion again. Also dishes containing gelatin do not freeze successfully.

5) Fried foods tend to turn rancid very quickly.

6) It is important to skim off as much fat as possible from casseroles, gravies and sauces because fat will separate during freezing.

7) Thickened sauces and gravies will become thicker in the freezer so it is best to not make them too thick beforehand. Alternatively, they may be thinned down with a little extra stock or water during reheating.

8) Do not over season food that is to be frozen because the flavour tends to increase in strength during storage. More seasoning may be added during reheating.

9) Remember to always use pre-cooked frozen foods within the recommended storage time.

Freezing soup

Most clear soups can be frozen satisfactorily. Soups containing milk or cream may curdle on thawing, but they can usually be beaten until smooth. Starchy foods, such as potatoes, should not be added to the soup until after thawing because they will become very soft and mushy. Remember to allow a 2.5 cm (1 inch) headspace between the soup and the lid of the container to allow for expansion in the freezer. Do not store soups for longer than 2 months.

Freezing cooked meat and poultry

The best way of freezing cooked meat and poultry is in a sauce, because dry cooked meat tends to dry out in the freezer and lose flavour. Do not overcook as reheating will continue to cook the food a little. Meat dishes, such as casseroles and stews, should be cooled quickly after cooking. This type of food is most susceptible to the growth of food poisoning bacteria, such as salmonella. When cool, pack the food into rigid containers and leave a 2.5 cm (1 inch) headspace before sealing securely. Always thaw cooked meat and poultry thoroughly in the refrigerator before reheating. Reheat until piping hot to ensure that any bacteria that might possibly have developed are killed.

Freezing leftovers

Any leftovers should be frozen as soon as possible after cooking. Never refreeze leftovers that have already been frozen. Do not store leftovers in the freezer for longer than 2 weeks.

Freezing sauces

Most sauces can be satisfactorily frozen, although they may need to be thoroughly beaten after thawing and thinned down to the correct consistency.

Freezing composite dishes

Composite dishes, such as lasagne and macaroni cheese, can be successfully frozen providing that all the ingredients are suitable for storage in the freezer (check the individual foods in the A to Z section). It is important to omit any ingredient that stores badly as otherwise it will affect the end result of the dish. Cooked dishes are particularly susceptible to bacterial growth, especially if they contain meat or poultry, so they must be cooled and frozen as rapidly as possible after cooking. It is important to thaw them in the refrigerator and reheat thoroughly before serving to avoid any risk of food poisoning.

Freezing bread, cakes and pastry

Bread, cakes and pastry can all be cooked completely, cooled and frozen satisfactorily. Providing that bakery items are frozen on the day they are baked and are absolutely fresh, they will retain all their texture and flavour after thawing. Cooked pies containing either savoury or sweet fillings freeze very well, but pies containing meat and poultry must always be thawed completely before reheating thoroughly to avoid any possible risk of bacterial activity which could lead to food poisoning.

Freezing baby food

To save the cost of buying ready prepared baby foods, it is relatively simple to prepare home-made baby food and store it satisfactorily in the freezer. A small quantity of the family meal, such as casserole, potatoes and vegetables, may be puréed in a blender and packed into small, sterilized pots, which can be stored in the freezer. It must always be remembered though that a very high standard of hygiene and cleanliness is essential during the preparation of baby food, so make sure that all the food is fresh and all the utensils used are as clean as possible. The preparation should be completed quickly so the cooked food should be cooled rapidly, the freezing accomplished quickly and the eventual thawing and reheating done thoroughly and speedily.

Cooking from frozen

Most commercially prepared foods, such as fish fingers, pastry and vegetables, are best cooked from frozen. Most home-frozen vegetables are also best if cooked when frozen. Ready cooked meals and composite dishes may be reheated from frozen, but care must be taken to ensure that they are heated right through and thoroughly.

Raw poultry and game, however, must be thoroughly thawed before cooking. With such foods there is a possibility that bacteria might have developed inside the meat. If it is then cooked before it has thawed completely, there is the likelihood that the intense heat will not penetrate right through to the inside before the outside is overcooked or burnt. Consequently, the bacteria that may be lurking inside will not be destroyed and could lead to food poisoning.

Other meats, however, may be cooked from frozen, although it is definitely preferable to thaw them overnight first. As with poultry and game they may not be fully cooked in the middle before the outside is dry and overcooked. A meat thermometer is essential to check that the temperature reaches 70°C (160°F) in the centre of the meat, which will ensure that the bacteria are destroyed and the meat will be perfectly safe to eat.

The cooking time for frozen meat should be calculated according to the way the meat is required, obviously medium-rare beef does not take as long as well-done beef. It is also important that the correct temperature is reached in the centre of the meat for the best result to be achieved. Never serve meat that has not reached 71°C (160°F) during cooking, if it has been cooked from frozen.

Blanching Times for Vegetables

VEGETABLE	PREPARATION	TIME
Asparagus	cut into short lengths	2 min (small) 3 min (medium) 4 min (large)
Aubergine	peel and slice	4 min
Beansprout	wash thoroughly	1 min
Broad bean	remove from shells	3 min
Broccoli	trim stalks & separate into spears	3 min
Brussels sprout	remove outer leaves & wash thoroughly	3 min
Cabbage	wash thoroughly & separate the leaves	1–2 min

VEGETABLE	PREPARATION	TIME
Carrots	wash, remove tops & peel sliced carrots	3 min 2 min
Cauliflower	wash & divide into small florets	3 min with juice of 1 lemon
Celeriac	peel & cut into chunks	4 min
Celery	trim & cut into small lengths	2 min
Chicory	remove outer leaves & wash thoroughly	2 min
Chilli	trim off stalks, remove seeds & pith	2 min
Chinese leaf	wash & shred or cut into chunks	1 min
Corn on the cob	remove husks and trim ends	4 min (small) 8 min (large)

VEGETABLE	PREPARATION	TIME
Courgette	wash & cut in 1 cm ($\frac{1}{2}$ inch) slices	1 min
Fennel	trim & slice bulbs into small pieces	2 min
Globe artichoke	remove outer leaves, trim base	7 min
Kale	wash thoroughly	2 min
Kohlrabi	trim bases, leaves & stalks & wash thoroughly	3 min
Leek	wash & slice thick leeks young & small whole leeks	2 min 3–4 min
Mangetout	trim ends & remove strings	2 min
Marrow	peel & cut into 2.5 cm (1 inch) slices	3 min
Okra	remove stems & wash well	3–4 min

VEGETABLE	PREPARATION	TIME
Onions (whole)	peel and wipe clean	3 min
Parsnip	wash, trim & peel; cut into small strips	2 min
Peas	remove from shells	1–2 min
Peppers	wash, remove stems, seeds and pith; cut into halves, slices or rings	3 min (halves) 2 min (slices)
Red cabbage	wash & slice	$1\frac{1}{2}$ min
Runner bean	trim, remove strings, slice thickly	2 min
Salsify	scrub, but do not peel	2 min
Seakale beet	remove stalks and wash leaves & stalks separately cut stalks into short lengths	2 min (leaves) 3 min (stalks)

VEGETABLE	PREPARATION	TIME
Shallot	peel and wipe clean or peel and chop finely	2 min (whole) 1 min (chopped)
Spring green	wash, remove tough stalks & shred	1–2 min
Squash	peel, remove seeds and cut into chunks	1–2 min
Swede	trim, peel and chop	2 min
Turnip	trim, peel and leave whole or chop into small chunks	4 min (whole) 3 min (chunks)